2017 INTERNATIONAL COMPARISON
PROGRAM FOR ASIA AND THE PACIFIC

PURCHASING POWER PARITIES AND REAL EXPENDITURES

A Summary Report

MAY 2020

ICP International Comparison Program
for Asia and the Pacific **2017**

ADB

© 2020 Asian Development Bank
6 ADB Avenue, Mandaluyong City, 1550 Metro Manila, Philippines
Tel +63 2 8632 4444; Fax +63 2 8636 2444
www.adb.org

Some rights reserved. Published in 2020.

ISBN 978-92-9262-199-5 (print); 978-92-9262-200-8 (electronic); 978-92-9262-201-5 (ebook)
Publication Stock No. TCS200013-2
DOI: http://dx.doi.org/10.22617/TCS200013-2

The views expressed in this publication are those of the authors and do not necessarily reflect the views and policies of the Asian Development Bank (ADB) or its Board of Governors or the governments they represent.

ADB does not guarantee the accuracy of the data included in this publication and accepts no responsibility for any consequence of their use. The mention of specific companies or products of manufacturers does not imply that they are endorsed or recommended by ADB in preference to others of a similar nature that are not mentioned.

By making any designation of or reference to a particular territory or geographic area, or by using the term "country" in this document, ADB does not intend to make any judgments as to the legal or other status of any territory or area.

Please contact pubsmarketing@adb.org if you have questions or comments with respect to content, or if you wish to obtain copyright permission for your intended use that does not fall within these terms, or for permission to use the ADB logo.

Corrigenda to ADB publications may be found at http://www.adb.org/publications/corrigenda.

Notes:
In this publication, "$" refers to United States dollars, unless otherwise stated.

Cover design by Rhommell Rico.

Cover photos:
Top, left to right
Construction workers working with metal bars to create pillars for a building in Calamba, Laguna, Philippines (photo by Al Benavente, ADB). Dil Maya Magar shows off some of her bumper crop from her farm in Thade, Nepal. The Decentralized Rural Infrastructure and Livelihood Project was designed to reduce rural poverty and to increase access to economic opportunities and social services (photo by Kiran Panday, ADB). The goods from the PRAN factory are loaded unto to trucks for distribution. PRAN (Programme for Rural Advancement Nationally) founded in 1980, is the largest food and nutrition company in Bangladesh (photo by Abir Abdullah, ADB).

Middle, left to right
Produce and meat stalls do brisk business at the Kalibo Town Market. Traditional open markets remain part of everyday life throughout the Philippines (photo by Lester V. Ledesma, ADB). Worker plucking chillies, from the fields at Gabbur, district Raichur, Karnataka, India (photo by Rakesh Sahai, ADB).

Bottom, left to right
Yanur Begum is a worker at the Wool Tex Sweaters Limited in Shewrapara, Dhaka, Bangladesh. The Skills Development Project helped improve the skills of millions of workers in the ready-made garments and textiles, light engineering, and construction industries – the three main employers in the country (photo by Abir Abdullah, ADB). Street vendors sell bags in Kolkata, West Bengal, India (photo by Amit Verma, ADB). Daily operations at the 15-megawatt (MW) Sermsang Khushig Khundii Solar plant in Khushig valley, Tuv aimag, which is located 40 kilometers (km) from Mongolia"s capital, Ulaanbaatar, and 17 km from the new international airport. The private sector project involves the operation and maintenance of the solar plant. In addition it will also include the construction of a 110/10kV substation, a 14-km long 110kV double circuit overhead electricity transmission line, as well as the extension of the 110/10kV Khushig substation owned by the National Power Transmission Grid SOJSC (photo by Ariel Javellana, ADB).

Contents

Appendixes

Tables, Figures, and Boxes

Foreword

The International Comparison Program (ICP), under the auspices of the United Nations Statistical Commission (UNSC), is the largest global statistical initiative aimed at estimating purchasing power parities (PPPs) to compare the real size and price levels of economies around the world. In the 2017 cycle, 176 economies participated from Africa, Asia and the Pacific, the Commonwealth of Independent States, Latin America and the Caribbean, Western Asia, and the regular PPP program managed by the Organisation for Economic Co-operation and Development (OECD) and the Statistical Office of the European Communities (Eurostat), with the World Bank coordinating the global program. The Asian Development Bank (ADB) continues as the regional implementing agency (RIA) for the ICP in Asia and the Pacific. The 2017 ICP cycle marks ADB's successful completion of the third benchmark under its stewardship, after the 2005 and 2011 benchmarks.

During its 47th session in March 2016, the UNSC considered the evaluation report of the 2011 ICP by the Friends of the Chair group and accepted its recommendation to establish the ICP as a permanent element of the global statistical work program, to be conducted more frequently, which led to the decision to implement the ICP every three years, beginning with 2017. It also recommended keeping the general methodology from 2011 stable for the 2017 cycle, except for fine-tuning some methods.

Asia and the Pacific is a unique, diverse region that includes the world's most populous economies and very small island states; the richest economies in per capita gross domestic product (GDP) and economies near the bottom of the ladder; and economies with widely divergent capacity in their statistical systems. The 22 participating economies in the 2017 ICP in the region are Bangladesh; Bhutan; Brunei Darussalam; Cambodia; Fiji; Hong Kong, China; India; Indonesia; the Lao People's Democratic Republic; Malaysia; Maldives; Mongolia; Myanmar; Nepal; Pakistan; the People's Republic of China; the Philippines; Singapore; Sri Lanka; Taipei,China; Thailand; and Viet Nam.

This publication presents the estimates of 2017 regional PPPs and summary results of real GDP and its major components for the 22 participating economies. A final report with a detailed description of ICP methods, results for 2017, and revised 2011 results will be released around middle of 2020. In line with the global consensus to keep the general methodology from the 2011 ICP, ADB only adopted certain refinements introduced at the global level to improve the robustness of the methods. ADB also applied these refinements to the 2011 revisions to ensure consistency and comparability between the 2011 revised PPPs and the 2017 benchmark PPPs.

ADB's ICP team rigorously validated the data submitted by the economies, using enhanced data validation tools in close collaboration with the implementing agencies from participating economies to ensure high quality of the data used to calculate the PPPs and other results. As part of ongoing research to improve the methodology for comparing dwelling services, ADB developed a new methodology, which the ICP Technical Advisory Group recommended for introduction in the 2020 ICP. While using standard PPP computation tools formulated by the World Bank for calculating the results, ADB also developed a program in Stata software to replicate and validate these results.

With more than half the world's population living in the 22 participating economies, the PPPs and results from the region are critical inputs to the global PPPs estimated by the World Bank. These PPPs enable real comparisons of GDP and its components across economies in terms of volumes of final goods and services by accounting for price level differences. Increasingly, the PPPs produced from the ICP are appearing in other applications. One major use of PPPs is the estimation of poverty incidence to monitor Sustainable Development Goal (SDG) 1 to eliminate poverty from the world. In addition, other PPP-based indicators in the SDG framework help monitor income inequality, energy intensity, labor productivity, and carbon dioxide emissions per unit of GDP.

I trust that the regional results will also be useful for researchers for comparative analysis and policy making. I am also pleased to see that the ICP continues to be a platform for statistical capacity building in price statistics and national accounts, which is evident as economies increasingly apply good practices from ICP to price statistics and national accounts statistics. As in 2005 and 2011, the guiding principles in implementing the 2017 ICP have been transparency, ownership, and a bottom-up approach, which have proven fundamental to the success of the ICP in Asia and the Pacific.

I wish to expresses my sincere appreciation to all who have made this project a success: the ICP Regional Advisory Board for Asia and the Pacific for its overall guidance; the ICP's group of experts for their technical and methodological advice; the World Bank ICP Global Office for its continued technical guidance to the regional program; the dedicated ICP team of the Statistics and Data Innovation Unit, ADB; and most of all, the implementing agencies in the participating economies for their hard work and cooperation, without whom the program cannot be successful.

Yasuyuki Sawada
Chief Economist and Director General
Economic Research and Regional Cooperation Department
Asian Development Bank

Acknowledgments

The 2017 International Comparison Program (ICP) for Asia and the Pacific was implemented by the Statistics and Data Innovation Unit of the Economic Research and Regional Cooperation Department of the Asian Development Bank (ADB) through regional—research and development technical assistance financed by ADB.

The successful completion of the 2017 ICP for Asia and the Pacific was made possible with the contributions and support of many governments, organizations, and individuals. We thank the implementing agencies in the 22 participating economies, whose invaluable support and cooperation at every stage of the project is fundamental to its successful completion. ADB therefore expresses its sincere appreciation and thanks to the heads of the following implementing agencies: Bangladesh Bureau of Statistics, Bangladesh; National Statistics Bureau, Bhutan; Department of Economic Planning and Statistics, Brunei Darussalam; National Institute of Statistics, Cambodia; Fiji Bureau of Statistics, Fiji; Census and Statistics Department, Hong Kong, China; Ministry of Statistics and Programme Implementation, India; Badan Pusat Statistik, Indonesia; Lao Statistics Bureau, Lao People's Democratic Republic; Department of Statistics, Malaysia; National Bureau of Statistics, Maldives; National Statistics Office of Mongolia, Mongolia; Central Statistical Organization, Myanmar; Central Bureau of Statistics, Nepal; Pakistan Bureau of Statistics, Pakistan; National Bureau of Statistics of China, People's Republic of China; Philippine Statistics Authority, Philippines; Department of Statistics, Singapore; Department of Census and Statistics, Sri Lanka; Directorate-General of Budget, Accounting, and Statistics, Taipei,China; Trade Policy and Strategy Office, Thailand; and General Statistics Office, Viet Nam.

The 2017 ICP project is indebted to the following ICP team coordinators and their teams in the above implementing agencies for their dedication and commitment through active and timely participation in collecting, editing, validating, and submitting price and other data: Abul Kalam Azad and Md. Nazmul Hoque, Bangladesh; Penjor Gyeltshen and Bikash Gurung, Bhutan; Norsalina Mat Salleh, Brunei Darussalam; Sim Ly, Cambodia; Peni Waqawai, Fiji; Karen Ka-lin Chan, Leo Chun-keung Yu, and Kwok-shun Lau, Hong Kong, China; M. V. S. Ranganadham, Pravin Srivastava, G. S. Lakshmi, and Dilip Kumar Sinha, India; Yunita Rusanti and Nurul Hasanudin, Indonesia; Kor Yang Pamah and Salika Chanthalavong, Lao People's Democratic Republic; Tn Hj Ibrahim bin Jantan and Fuziah Md. Amin, Malaysia; Aishath Hassan, Sajida Ahmed, Maldives; Erdenesan Eldev-Ochir, Mongolia; Wah Wah Maung and Cho Cho Myint, Myanmar; Ganesh Prasad Acharya and Gyanendra Bajracharya, Nepal; Attiq-ur-Rehman, Pakistan; Wang Jinping, People's Republic of China; Lisa Grace Bersales, Divina Gracia del Prado, and Elena Varona, Philippines; Chau Wun, Singapore; A. M. U. K. Alahakoon and M. D. S. Senanayake, Sri Lanka; Ya-Mei Chen, Jia-Yuan Mei, Chien-Chung Hsu, and Shwu-Chwen Chiou, Taipei,China; Chanikarn Dispadung, Nat Tharnpanich, and Wasinee Yaisawang, Thailand; and Do Thi Ngoc, Viet Nam. We truly appreciate the wonderful job they accomplished in implementing rigorous ICP activities in their economies.

ADB gratefully acknowledges the advice and guidance of members of the 2017 ICP Asia and the Pacific Regional Advisory Board, including members from participating economies and institutions as well as ex-officio members. Members from participating economies include the commissioner, Census and Statistics Department, Hong Kong, China; chief statistician of India and secretary, Ministry of Statistics and Programme Implementation; chief statistician, Badan Pusat Statistik, Indonesia; head, Lao Statistics Bureau, Lao People's Democratic Republic; director general, International Statistical Information Center, National Bureau of Statistics of China, People's Republic of China; director general, Department of Census and Statistics, Sri Lanka; director general, General Statistics Office, Viet Nam. Institutional members include the chief economist and director general, ADB; general manager, Macroeconomic Statistics Division, Australian Bureau of Statistics; director, Statistics Division, United Nations Economic and Social Commission for Asia and the Pacific; and director, United Nations Statistical Institute for Asia and the Pacific. Ex-officio members include the advisor, Office of the Chief Economist and Director General, and head, Statistics and Data Innovation Unit, Economic Research and Regional Cooperation Department, ADB; and director, Development Data Group, World Bank. The regional coordinator of the ICP Asia Pacific, ADB, member-secretary, provided invaluable support for the smooth conduct of the Regional Advisory Board meetings.

The regional program significantly benefited from the technical contributions of the international experts—Eric Bruggeman; Aloke Kar; Ramesh Kolli; Arturo Pacificador, Jr.; Prasada Rao; Sergey Sergeev; Peter Tabor; and Aaron Wright at different stages of project implementation. The ICP Global Office, led by Nada Hamadeh at the World Bank, provided extensive technical advice from Yuri Dikhanov, Marko Oliver Rissanen, Inyoung Song, and Mizuki Yamanaka.

Yasuyuki Sawada, chief economist and director general, Economic Research and Regional Cooperation Department, provided motivation to the project at all stages. Kaushal Joshi, principal statistician, Statistics and Data Innovation Unit of the Economic Research and Regional Cooperation Department, served as the regional coordinator of the 2017 ICP for Asia and the Pacific. He provided leadership to ADB's ICP project team with assistance of Eileen Capilit; Arturo Martinez, Jr.; and Stefan Schipper during the early stages of the project implementation and with Criselda de Dios, economics and statistics analyst, providing technical and coordination support throughout the project implementation. ADB's ICP project team comprised national consultants Mel Lorenzo Accad, Paolo Kris Adriano, Rhea-Ann Bautista, Juan Miguel dela Cruz, Virginia Ganac, Mario Ilagan II, Lea Ortega, and Eleanore Ramos. The team provided invaluable support in project implementation, extensive data validation ensuring high data quality, data analysis for calculation of regional results, and preparation of this report, in addition to providing technical and administrative support to the ICP teams of participating economies. Maria Roselia Babalo, Oth Marulou Gagni, and Aileen Gatson provided administrative support. Kaushal Joshi and Prasada Rao led the analysis of the results and preparation of this report. Rana Hasan provided useful comments on the draft report. Narisara Murray edited the report manuscript. Rhommell Rico created the cover design and typeset the report with support of Joseph Manglicmot. The publishing team in ADB's Department of Communications provided guidance on production issues, performed overall compliance checks, and assisted in web dissemination. The Logistics Management Unit of the Office of Administrative Services facilitated the timely printing of the publication.

Elaine S. Tan
Advisor, Office of the Chief Economist and Director General
and Head, Statistics and Data Innovation Unit

Abbreviations

ADB	Asian Development Bank
AICH	actual individual consumption by households
CPD	country-product-dummy
CPI	consumer price index
Eurostat	Statistical Office of the European Communities
GDP	gross domestic product
GEKS	Gini-Èltetö-Köves-Szulc
GFCE	government final consumption expenditure
GFCF	gross fixed capital formation
ICEG	individual consumption expenditure by government
ICEH	individual consumption expenditure by households
ICP	International Comparison Program
NPISH	nonprofit institutions serving households
OECD	Organisation for Economic Co-operation and Development
PLI	price level index
PPP	purchasing power parity
RIA	regional implementing agency
SDG	Sustainable Development Goal
SPD	structured product description
UNSC	United Nations Statistical Commission

1. Introduction

What Is the International Comparison Program?

The International Comparison Program (ICP) is the world's largest global statistical initiative. It aims to produce globally comparable measures of gross domestic product (GDP) and its components—such as household consumption expenditure, government consumption expenditure, gross fixed capital formation, and net exports—based on purchasing power parities (PPPs) for economies across the world. In different economies, statistical offices publish macroeconomic aggregates of national accounts statistics in their local currency units and, therefore, these aggregates are strictly not comparable across economies. Exchange rates are readily available for converting these aggregates into a common currency unit such as the United States (US) dollar. However, exchange rates have severe limitations when used to compare real income or expenditures across economies. Exchange rates—determined by the demand for and the supply of respective local currencies—do not reflect relative price level differentials across economies. Exchange rates are also volatile, reflecting a range of factors that affect currency markets. Using exchange rates to compare GDP and household consumption is meaningful only when the *absolute purchasing power parity theory*, which predicts that price levels will be the same across countries, holds. However, in the presence of a large proportion of non-tradeable goods and services in GDP, high and differential transport costs, and imperfect international markets with different tax and tariff regimes, the purchasing power parity theory does not hold, so exchange rates are not meaningful in comparing real incomes across economies.

A Brief History of the International Comparison Program

The need for a meaningful alternative to exchange rates led Irving Kravis, Alan Heston, Robert Summers, and Zoltan Kenessey to establish the ICP at the University of Pennsylvania. The seminal studies of Milton Gilbert and Kravis (1954) and Gilbert and Associates (1958) demonstrated that a considerable gap can exist between exchange rates and the PPPs that adequately reflect relative price differences across economies. Their research and findings finally led to the establishment of the ICP.

The ICP aims to provide statistically and economically sound measures of price level differences, in the form of PPPs of currencies, and to compile and disseminate internationally comparable measures of real GDP and its components. Kravis et al. (1975 and 1978) were instrumental in establishing the procedures and guidelines for undertaking international comparisons.

In 2018, the ICP reached a milestone that marked 50 years since beginning work on international comparisons of national accounts aggregates. The ICP started in 1968 as a small-scale research project at the University of Pennsylvania, led by professors Kravis, Heston, and Summers. Since then, jointly undertaken with the United Nations Statistics Division, the project has grown steadily over 5 decades, finally achieving the status of a global statistical initiative. The ICP is currently conducted under the charter and auspices of the United Nations Statistical Commission (UNSC), which oversees its implementation to ensure timeliness, quality, and reliability of international comparisons of GDP and its main aggregates.

In 1970, the first phase of the ICP covered only 10 economies, steadily increasing to 16 in 1973 and 34 in 1975, 60 in 1980, and 64 in 1985, and 115 economies in 1993. The ICP covered 146 economies in the 2005 cycle, when the ICP adopted a new global governance, with national statistical offices responsible for price and national accounts data, regional agencies coordinating regional activities, and the World Bank coordinating the global program. The 2011 ICP round was the largest ever conducted. It included 177 economies participating at the full economy level, covering all components of GDP, and an additional 22 economies covering only the household consumption aggregate. With 176 participating economies, the current 2017 ICP cycle covers more than 99% of the world population and the world's economic activity and is thus justifiably recognized as a global statistical program.

Evaluation of 2011 International Comparison Program

In 2014, at its 45th session, the UNSC established the Friends of the Chair group to evaluate the 2011 ICP

THE PRINCIPAL OBJECTIVE OF THE INTERNATIONAL COMPARISON PROGRAM

The **principal objective** of the International Comparison Program (ICP) is to provide statistically and economically sound measures of price level differences, in the form of purchasing power parities (PPPs) of currencies, and to compile and disseminate internationally comparable measures of real gross domestic product (GDP) and its components.

cycle. The group presented its preliminary report in 2015 at the 46th Session of the UNSC and its final report at its 47th Session in 2016. The UNSC endorsed the group's finding and made three important recommendations that have largely guided the 2017 ICP cycle: (i) instituting the ICP as a permanent element of the global statistical work program, to be conducted at more frequent intervals; (ii) keeping the general methodology from 2011 stable for the 2017 comparison cycle; and (iii) implementing a short-term research agenda limited to fine-tuning methods in areas such as implementing a rolling benchmark approach and building a PPP time series, integrating ICP and consumer price index (CPI) survey activities, streamlining the use of productivity adjustments for government services, global linking procedures, and quality assurance of the resulting 2017 PPPs. Implementing the first recommendation, the World Bank, which has been acting as the Global Office for the ICP, has now established the ICP in the work program of the Development Data Group. The second recommendation, to keep the general methodology stable during the 2017 ICP cycle, has been strictly adhered to by the ICP Global Office at the World Bank as well as the regional implementing agencies, except for minor refinements. Finally, for the third recommendation, task forces established under the ICP undertook research in fine-tuning methods and procedures.

Structure of the Report

This summary report gives an overview of the main results from the 2017 ICP cycle in Asia and the Pacific for readers who are familiar with the ICP and for uninitiated readers who are interested in information on relative sizes of the participating economies.

Chapter 2 introduces the ICP's global governance, history, structure, and implementation in Asia and the Pacific. Chapter 3 explains the key concepts of PPPs, price levels, and the notion of nominal and real expenditures, in order to help the readers who may not be familiar with these terms better understand ICP results. Chapter 4 presents the main results from the 2017 ICP in Asia and the Pacific: PPPs, price levels, real expenditures, rankings of economies by GDP; individual consumption expenditure by households (ICEH) and nonprofit institutions serving households (NPISH); actual individual consumption by households (AICH); government final consumption expenditure (GFCE); and gross fixed capital formation (GFCF). The definitions of these terms and concepts are provided in the Glossary at the end of this report. Chapter 5 is devoted to a comparative analysis and appraisal of the consistency between results from the 2017 ICP cycle and extrapolations from the revised results of 2011 ICP in Asia and the Pacific. Chapter 6

summarizes key results and conclusions with notes on the lessons learned from implementing the 2017 ICP cycle and thoughts on future ICP activities in Asia and the Pacific. The report includes additional details on ICP methodology (Appendix 1); the membership of the Regional Advisory Board (Appendix 2); implementing agencies in the participating economies (Appendix 3); detailed statistical tables for the 2017 ICP results (Appendix 4); detailed statistical tables for the revised 2011 ICP results (Appendix 5); the structure of GDP and changes in the ICP classification (Appendix 6); reference basic headings in calculating other basic headings (Appendix 7); and the scope and coverage of main GDP aggregates in 2011 and 2017 (Appendix 8).

2. The International Comparison Program in Asia and the Pacific, 2017

Global Governance

Following the recommendations of the United Nations Statistical Commission (UNSC), the World Bank established the following governance structure to implement the 2017 cycle of the International Comparison Program (ICP) (World Bank 2016a).

- **ICP Governing Board**. This strategic body sets policies that govern the compilation of purchasing power parities (PPPs), approves methodological improvements, and conducts outreach and fundraising.
- **ICP Global Office at the World Bank.** The ICP Global Office acts as the global implementing agency which (i) coordinates and implements the global aspects of the ICP, and (ii) calculates and disseminates the global ICP results.
- **Inter-Agency Coordination Group.** Chaired by the World Bank, this group includes regional implementing agencies (RIAs) and the International Monetary Fund, who jointly determine activities for data collection, validation, calculation and dissemination work plans, and capacity building.
- **Technical Advisory Group and task force(s).** This pool of experts in the fields of index numbers, PPPs, price statistics, and national accounts ensures methodological soundness and overall quality in the PPP estimates and is responsible for setting and steering the ICP research agenda.
- **Regional implementing agencies**. These agencies coordinate regional comparisons and calculate regional ICP results. These include the Asian Development Bank (ADB) for Asia and the Pacific, the African Development Bank (for Africa), the Interstate Statistical Committee of the Commonwealth of Independent States (for

the Commonwealth of Independent States), the United Nations Economic Commission for Latin America and the Caribbean (for Latin America and the Caribbean), and United Nations Economic and Social Commission for Western Asia (for Western Asia). Reflecting existing arrangements, Statistical Office of the European Union (Eurostat) for European countries and the Organisation for Economic Co-operation and Development (OECD) for non-European OECD countries are responsible for Eurostat-OECD PPP Program.

The 2017 Cycle in Asia and the Pacific

The ICP's nature and operation has changed significantly over time. From its inception in 1968 until 1985, the ICP's price and real gross domestic product (GDP) expenditure comparisons were global in their item selection, the survey framework for collecting prices, and the subsequent methodology for aggregating price and national accounts data. Since the 1980 cycle, the ICP has gradually moved toward a regional approach that undertakes price comparisons first at the regional level, considering differences in types of goods and services available in different regions, and subsequently derives global comparisons using specially designed linking procedures.

Rigorous implementation of a regionalized ICP, outside the European Union and the OECD group of economies, began in earnest from the 2005 ICP cycle. The ICP set appropriate governing structures and methods for regional comparisons and subsequent linking and global comparisons (Rao 2013). RIAs assumed responsibilities for their regions while the ICP Global Office at the World Bank coordinated activities across regions and compiled and published results at the global level. The national statistical offices undertook the roles of implementing agencies for carrying out ICP price surveys for their economies and submission of required data to their RIA. ADB took the lead and responsibility as the RIA for implementing the ICP in 2005 in Asia and the Pacific and continued its stewardship for the 2011 and 2017 ICP cycles in the region.

In implementing the ICP in Asia and the Pacific, ADB established the principles of ownership, transparency, and a commitment to the quality and integrity of the data that underpins the compilation of PPPs and real expenditures. ADB has striven to foster mutual cooperation and strong commitment among the participating economies. Throughout the implementation of the 2017 ICP, all the participating economies adhered to the general guidelines developed for the ICP at the global and regional levels.

After the establishment of the new ICP global governance structure in 2016, ADB established a revamped regional governing structure to smoothly and efficiently implement the 2017 ICP. Participating economies entered into formal "no objection" agreements with ADB for participation under ADB's technical assistance and financial arrangements. A specially conducted inception workshop with the heads of national implementing agencies from each economy clearly explained these arrangements along with an informal framework of partnership defining roles and responsibilities of ADB and the national implementing agencies. ADB, as the RIA, was responsible for implementing the ICP in Asia and the Pacific, and it received advice and guidance from a specially constituted Regional Advisory Board. The RIA at ADB engaged closely with the ICP teams formed by national implementing agencies, which includes the heads of national statistical agencies and ICP national coordinators of the participating economies. The RIA ensured active participation and close cooperation

among these economies through regular workshops on product specification, ICP methodologies and, more importantly, on validation of price and national accounts data that the participating economies compiled and submitted.

Participating Economies

The following 22 economies of the region participated in the 2017 ICP cycle for the Asia and Pacific region, with ADB as the RIA: Bangladesh; Bhutan; Brunei Darussalam; Cambodia; Fiji; Hong Kong, China; India; Indonesia; the Lao People's Democratic Republic; Malaysia; Maldives; Mongolia; Myanmar; Nepal; Pakistan; the People's Republic of China; the Philippines; Singapore; Sri Lanka; Taipei,China; Thailand; and Viet Nam.

HOW BIG IS THE INTERNATIONAL COMPARISON PROGRAM FOR ASIA AND THE PACIFIC?

The International Comparison Program (ICP) for the Asia and Pacific region covers a major share of the world's population within the 22 participating economies: 3.785 billion people out of the world population of 7.511 billion in 2017. According to projections of the size of the real economy from 2011 to 2017, the People's Republic of China is the world's largest economy, with India and Indonesia among the top ten economies by size.

Sources: The regional population is based on population mid-year estimates supplied to ADB by the participating economies for the 2017 ICP; the world population is from the World Development Indicators database. World Bank. World Development Indicators. https://databank.worldbank.org/source/world-development-indicators (accessed 18 March 2020).

The participating economies were classified into four subregional groups in order to determine product lists for price surveys, data validation, and comparative analysis of regions. Three of the four groups are geographically determined; the fourth is the *high-income group,* determined by level of development.

- **High-income economies.** Brunei Darussalam; Hong Kong, China; Singapore; and Taipei,China.
- **Mekong.** Cambodia; the Lao People's Democratic Republic; Myanmar; Thailand; and Viet Nam.
- **South Asia.** Bangladesh; Bhutan; India; Maldives; Nepal; Pakistan; and Sri Lanka.
- **Southeast Asia and Others.** Fiji; Indonesia; Malaysia; Mongolia; the People's Republic of China; and the Philippines.

The results in this report are based on the comparison of prices for more than a thousand well-defined and comparable products and services that represent (i) consumption expenditure of households and the government, and (ii) investments in gross fixed capital formation (GFCF) in these 22 economies.

Innovations

In implementing the 2017 ICP cycle, the ICP Global Office and the RIAs strictly adhered to the UNSC recommendation to keep the general methodology stable. This recommendation aims in part to ensure that results from the 2017 ICP cycle are comparable with extrapolated results from the 2011 ICP cycle. Working within the general parameters set by the UNSC, ADB introduced innovative methods and tools designed to improve the quality and comparability of basic data used in compiling price and real expenditure comparisons which are discussed in this section.

- **Improvements in basic data and methodology for comparing housing expenditure.** Comparisons of prices and real expenditures for housing proved problematic in the 2005 and 2011 ICP cycles. The two recommended approaches for housing comparisons—the rental approach and the quantity indicator approach—attempted in the 2005 and 2011 ICP cycles failed to yield plausible relative price and real expenditure comparisons. This problem was largely attributed to gaps in quantity data, incomplete measures of quality indicators, and less reliable rental price data. In the 2017 ICP cycle, the RIA at ADB devoted considerable resources to improving the quality of data for dwelling comparisons.
  - First, in addition to collecting data on the three standard quantity indicators (number of dwellings, number of rooms per 100 people, and the number of square meters per person) and the three quality indicators (availability of electricity, inside running water, and private toilets), the RIA enhanced the range of quality indicators by using data collected as a part of the water supply, sanitation, and hygiene indicators that track Sustainable Development Goal (SDG) 6, which focuses on water and sanitation.[1]
  - Second, the RIA structured and streamlined the collection of rental data during the 2017 ICP cycle. To improve comparability of rental data, the RIA improved the specification of rental dwellings and the scope and coverage of the rental price surveys. Notwithstanding these significant improvements in the quality of data for housing comparisons, the recommended quantity and rental approaches failed to provide plausible price and real expenditure comparisons.
  - Finally, the RIA developed a mixed quality-adjusted rental and quantity approach, which was found to be a significant improvement over the existing approaches. However, the Regional Advisory Board for the ICP in Asia and the

---

[1]   The World Health Organization and United Nations Children's Fund Joint Monitoring Programme is the custodian of global data on water supply, sanitation, and hygiene (WASH).

Pacific and the Technical Advisory Group of the ICP at the World Bank recommended deferring implementation of this approach until the 2020 ICP cycle. Accordingly, the RIA at ADB decided to maintain the status quo and make use of the reference volume approach, used in 2005 and 2011, for the 2017 ICP cycle in Asia and the Pacific.

- **Enhanced in-house capacity for computation of results**. During the 2017 ICP cycle, ADB enhanced in-house computational capacity by developing codes in the statistical software package Stata to replicate results obtained using the tools from the World Bank. Developing independent codes leads to an enhanced understanding of the methods and processes involved in the computation of ICP results, independently checks the results, and ensures that results are replicable. In the coming years, ADB may be able to implement ICP procedures using software tools and/or codes developed completely in-house.
- **Enhanced one-on-one communications with national implementing agencies.** ADB also introduced new processes during ICP 2017 to communicate with the national implementing agencies. In addition to conducting workshops to interact with implementing agencies to discuss item list preparation, survey framework, and the subsequent data validation, ADB increased the frequency and intensity of one-on-one communications with participating economies. These communications, initially in emails and data file sharing, expanded to include web-based videoconferences to train staff and discuss and resolve outstanding data-related issues. Increased use of videoconference facility achieved the twin goals of increased efficiency and reduced travel and administrative costs. ADB envisages increased use of videoconferencing facilities for workshops, facilitating remote participation during the ICP 2020 cycle.

- **An enhanced tool to validate inter-temporal household prices**. To validate price data collected by the participating economies, the RIA introduced an enhanced tool that measured the discrepancy between ICP inflation—computed using prices for ICP items priced in both 2011 and 2017 benchmark years—and the basic heading level consumer price index (CPI) inflation over the same period. ADB flagged large observed differences in these two alternative measures of inflation to the concerned implementing agencies for checking the outliers (if any) in ICP product prices for ensuring high data quality of the ICP. The differences would then be indicative of reasons such as suitability of CPIs used and differences in the quality of the ICP products priced in 2017 compared with same products in 2011. The tool further strengthened the standard data validation process, which is based on usual measures of intra-economy and inter-economy variability in prices: the minimum–maximum range for price quotations, coefficient of variation, comparisons of average prices of individual products for an economy with regional and subregional average prices, and the Dikhanov tables.[2]
- **Productivity adjustments to government compensation data**. In 2005, because of the high disparities observed in the wages and salaries of government employees across economies, the RIA at ADB was the first to recognize the need to introduce productivity adjustments to compare the data on government compensation paid to the employees. ADB pioneered efforts in this direction and implemented a method for productivity adjustment that other regions subsequently adapted and used. In the 2011 ICP cycle, ADB fine-tuned the methodology and introduced transitive productivity adjustments that were simpler to implement. Intermediate estimates of labor and capital stock as well as the capital share were estimated at the regional level. The ICP Global

---

[2] Dikhanov tables compare average prices of the same item across different economies in order to screen average national prices for possible errors (for further detals, see Appendix 1).

Office made productivity adjustments in the process of global linking, leading to improved price and real expenditure comparisons for government compensation in 2011.

In the 2017 ICP cycle, ADB implemented a refined methodology for adjusting productivity of government employees. ADB recognized that the labor shares used in 2011 were in broad classes and further fine-tuning was necessary to find more reliable estimates of the labor and capital shares. To address these concerns, ADB decided to implement a refined method first described by Robert Inklaar and Marcel Timmer (2013a); because Inklaar played a major role in the development and implementation of the methodology for estimating productivity adjustment factors for government compensation for the 2017 ICP cycle, this

report refers to it as the Inklaar method (Inklaar 2019). The ICP Technical Advisory Group discussed and endorsed this method for the 2017 ICP cycle. Further details of the productivity adjustment methodology are presented in Appendix 1.

The innovations introduced in the 2017 ICP cycle in Asia and the Pacific have resulted in improved and more reliable price and national accounts data thereby enhancing the quality of PPP estimates and real expenditures. Fine-tuning the productivity methodology and the use of more realistic labor and capital shares had a profound effect on the estimates of PPPs and real expenditures for government compensation. These and the flow-on effects on estimates of real government expenditure and real GDP are fully documented in Chapter 5 of this report.

3. Purchasing Power Parities and Other Concepts and Measures

Purchasing Power Parities

The concept of purchasing power parity (PPP) of a currency is critical to all the real expenditure measures compiled by ICP and presented in this report (see Box 3.1).

> **Box 3.1: Purchasing Power Parity Defined**
>
> A working definition of a PPP is that it represents the number of currency units required to purchase the amounts of goods and services equivalent to what can be bought with one unit of the currency unit of the base or reference or numeraire country (World Bank 2013).

The following example illustrates the meaning of PPP and how it gets measured. Imagine a person from the United States plans to travel to India as a tourist, believing that India is a low-cost tourist destination. Currently, one US dollar ($), when exchanged in a bank, fetches around 72 Indian rupees (₹). Suppose further that what one can buy with $1 in the United States can be purchased with ₹25 in India, at least for the main items that interest a tourist—food, accommodation, transport, and shopping. This means a tourist with ₹72 (exchanged in a bank for $1) can buy nearly three times as much in India as can be purchased in the United States for $1. Thus, prices in India are roughly one-third of those in the United States. While the exchange rate of ₹72 per US dollar can be easily looked up online, it is not always clear how much one needs to spend in India to buy what one dollar buys in the United States. The rate of ₹25 per US dollar is the *purchasing power parity* or PPP between the US dollar and the Indian rupee: this key figure is provided by the ICP.[3]

Each PPP includes three critical elements. First and foremost, what is the reference (or base) economy and currency? In the example above, the base economy is the United States and the reference currency is the US dollar. Second, what is the currency of the economy for which the PPP is measured? In our example, the Indian rupee is the currency for which PPP is considered. Third, what is the basket of goods? In the example, the basket of goods and services are those that are typically relevant for tourists.

This report refers to economies in Asia and the Pacific, so the reference or base economy also belongs to the region, which has been Hong Kong, China since the 2005 ICP cycle and with Hong Kong dollar as the reference currency. The selection of the base economy and the reference currency is important only for the purpose of presentation but the relative price levels and real and nominal expenditures between any two economies would be the same even if currency of another economy were chosen as the reference currency. The main reasons for the choice of Hong Kong, China as the base economy are: (i) well-functioning market structure without price distortions; (ii) well-developed and broadly-based economy where a large variety of goods and services are available which ensures good overlap of price data with other participating economies; (iii) a strong statistical system for price and national accounts statistics; and, finally, (iv) Hong Kong dollar is a stable currency in the Asia and Pacific region. Throughout the

---

3   The PPP applies to India as a whole; in specific locations within India, price levels may be much higher or lower than the national price levels that the ICP measures.

rest of this document, the base or reference economy is Hong Kong, China and the reference currency is the Hong Kong dollar (HK$).[4]

Box 3.2 shows PPPs for the Malaysian ringgit (RM) to the Hong Kong dollar for two different baskets of goods and services. The basket for the first PPP contains only one item, the Big Mac, available in many economies. (The Big Mac Index, which contains PPPs based on the price of the Big Mac in different economies, regularly appears in *The Economist*.) The second PPP is for monthly household expenditures, a typical basket of goods and services drawn from 2017 ICP data.

The PPP based on the Big Mac is RM0.46 per Hong Kong dollar (HK$1 = RM0.46), while the PPP for monthly household expenditures is HK$1 = RM0.28, illustrating that different PPPs are necessary for different items or baskets of items. The Big Mac Index is of limited applicability for comparing the cost of living because it relies on a single item which may not be representative of household consumption.

Box 3.2: Purchasing Power Parities for the Big Mac and Household Expenditure
(Malaysian ringgit per Hong Kong dollar)

Big Mac Prices

Hong Kong, China: HK$20.50
Malaysia: RM9.50

PPP for Malaysian ringgit
RM9.50/HK$20.50 = RM0.46
per Hong Kong dollar

Monthly Household Expenditure

Hong Kong, China: HK$20,130
Malaysia: RM5,636

PPP for Malaysian ringgit =
RM5,636/HK$20,130 = RM0.28
per Hong Kong dollar

HK$ = Hong Kong dollar, PPP = purchasing power parity, RM = Malaysian ringgit.
Sources: *The Economist*. 2020. Burgernomics – The Big Mac Index. https://www.economist.com/news/2020/01/15/the-big-mac-index (accessed 4 March 2020) and Asian Development Bank estimates (Big Mac prices as of 14 January 2020).

Uses of Purchasing Power Parities and Real Expenditures

The most important use and main purpose of PPPs is to convert national accounts aggregates into a common currency unit after accounting for price level differences, thus allowing for comparisons of real expenditure levels of gross domestic product (GDP) and its component expenditures across economies. These national accounts aggregates include GDP and its main components—individual consumption expenditure by households (ICEH), actual individual consumption by households (AICH), government final consumption expenditure (GFCE), and gross fixed capital formation (GFCF). Different PPPs are needed to convert each of these aggregates.

Per capita levels of real GDP and its various components are useful in several analytical contexts, especially for comparing living standards between economies (definitions of GDP and nominal and real expenditures are provided in the succeeding sections). Measures such as per capita AICH are more appropriate than GDP for comparing living standards or as inputs to poverty measurements. International organizations and national policy makers use PPPs for a variety of purposes. One of the earliest and most important uses of PPPs was to determine an international poverty line to measure global and regional poverty. In 1990, the World Bank used PPPs to construct the $1/day and $2/day international poverty lines, which led to the formulation of the first of the Millennium Development Goals, set in 2000, aimed at halving extreme poverty by 2015. In 2015, the member states of the United Nations adopted the 17 Sustainable Development Goals (SDGs); eliminating extreme poverty continues to be high on that agenda. Apart from the use of the PPPs to monitor poverty, other PPP-based indicators in the SDG framework help monitor income inequality, education and health expenditure, energy intensity, labor productivity, and carbon dioxide emissions per unit of GDP. ADB's policy paper *ADB Corporate Results Framework, 2019–2024*

---

4   The methods employed are such that price comparisons between different economies are not affected by the choice of the base economy.

(2019) is aligned with the SDG agenda and includes SDG indicators whose measurement depends on PPPs to track development progress in Asia and the Pacific.

Over the last three decades, the United Nations Development Programme has used and continues to use per capita GDP or income in PPP terms to construct the Human Development Index, the Inequality-Adjusted Human Development Index, and the Gender Development Index. The International Monetary Fund uses PPP-converted GDP weights to estimate global growth and allocate quotas for member states. The European Commission uses PPP-converted GDP to allocate structural funds intended to decrease economic disparities across its member states.

PPP-converted aggregates are useful for analysis and policy formulation at the economy level. These converted aggregates include real ICEH, real expenditure by government on behalf of individuals (known as individual consumption expenditure by government or ICEG), real collective government consumption, and real investment (GFCF). These aggregates allow us to comparatively analyze price levels and relative levels of investment, competitiveness, and catch-up and convergence within Asia and the Pacific as a region and across economies in different subregions, yielding valuable inputs that can help identify areas for policy intervention.[5]

Reliability and Limitations of Purchasing Power Parities and Real Expenditures

Users of PPPs must be aware that PPPs are essentially estimates of the purchasing power of currencies based on data collected from price surveys for a comparable basket of large number of goods and services. Therefore, PPPs calculated at the basic heading level are subject to sampling and non-sampling errors and measures of reliability.[6] National accounts expenditures in local currency units at the basic heading level are used as weights in calculating PPPs; these expenditures are also subject to similar errors. The reliability of real measures of expenditures also depends upon the relative shares of expenditure aggregates and how reliably they are estimated in national accounts. For example, PPPs and PPP-based expenditures for the aggregate "food" would generally be more reliable than the PPPs and PPP-based expenditures on "bread and cereals", which in turn are expected to be more reliable than for the aggregate "bread" or "rice." Caution therefore must be used in ranking economies based on PPP-converted real GDP and its per capita measures when the differences between economies are small. While it is largely expected that all economies compile their national accounts estimates following the System of National Accounts 2008 (United Nations 2009), the underlying input data may vary in quality and may not adequately capture the unobserved economy such as the informal sector.

PURCHASING POWER PARITIES AND THE SUSTAINABLE DEVELOPMENT GOALS

While the major use of purchasing power parities (PPPs) is to compare economic variables such as gross domestic product (GDP), they also have an important role, direct as well as indirect, in monitoring progress toward the attainment of several Sustainable Development Goals (SDGs). One major use of PPPs in SDGs is the estimation of poverty incidence based on international poverty line of $1.90-a-day.

---

5   For a comprehensive review of the uses of PPPs at the national and international level the reader may consult Ward (2009), Silver (2013), Inklaar and Timmer (2013b) and Hamadeh and Abu Shanab (2016).

6   Basic headings are the lowest level of aggregation of items in the GDP breakdown for which expenditure data are to be compiled. For example, prices will be collected for 20 varieties of rice, and the expenditures across all rice varieties will be aggregated under the basic heading "rice."

Because PPPs are essentially measures of price level differences across different economies covering both traded and non-traded goods and services, these PPPs should not be used for the purpose of determining whether exchange rates of currencies are overvalued or undervalued.

Exchange Rates

Exchange rates are used to convert the currency of one economy into currencies of other economies and are also known as market exchange rates. An exchange rate for a given currency is the number of local (domestic) currency units per one unit of the reference or foreign currency. Exchange rates depend on a range of factors that affect the demand for and supply of different currencies; therefore, they fluctuate, or could be regulated or managed in some economies.[7] Individuals use exchange rates for transactions across borders; multinational organizations use them for accounting and transfer of funds. All official monetary transactions, including foreign aid and transfers, use exchange rates. However, exchange rates do not indicate differences in price levels across different economies and, therefore, do not reflect the relative purchasing power of different currencies. Thus, use of exchange rates to compare real income or real expenditure can be misleading.

The Price Level Index

How do we decide if the price level in one economy is higher or lower compared to another economy? Answering this question means comparing PPPs and exchange rates. Recall that the PPP of a currency shows how many units of that currency are needed to purchase something that can be purchased in a reference economy. For example, the PPP for household consumption in Malaysia is HK\$1 = RM0.28 (see Box 3.2). What does this imply about price level in Malaysia? This question can be answered only by comparing the PPP of the Malaysian ringgit with the exchange rate, which is HK\$1 = RM0.55. This means that HK\$100 can be exchanged for RM55 at a bank. However, what can be purchased in Hong Kong, China for HK\$100 can be purchased in Malaysia with just RM28, implying that price level in Malaysia is lower than that in Hong Kong, China. Formally, the *price level index* (PLI) for a given economy is defined as the ratio of its PPP to the exchange rate and is expressed as an index with a base of 100. Thus, the PLI is defined as:

$$PLI_j = \frac{PPP_j}{XR_j} \quad \text{where } j \text{ refers to an economy}$$

and the PLI for Malaysia, according to the example, is:

$$PLI_{Malaysia} = \frac{0.28}{0.55} \times 100 = 50.91$$

This means that the price level for household consumption in Malaysia is lower and roughly half of the price level in Hong Kong, China. By definition, the PLI for the reference economy is always 100 because its PPP and the exchange rate are both equal to 1.

Price Level Index and Real Exchange Rate

The *real exchange rate* (RER) is a concept used by economists in the context of foreign trade. The real exchange rate is defined for a domestic currency, Malaysian ringgit in this example, relative to a foreign currency, Hong Kong dollar here. The real exchange rate is derived by adjusting exchange rate, showing the number of foreign currency units (HK\$) per one unit of domestic currency (RM), with the ratio of domestic prices to foreign prices. The ratio of prices in Malaysia to prices in Hong Kong, China is exactly the PPP discussed before, and it is equal to 0.28. The exchange rate, number of HK\$ per one RM is 1.81. This is the

---

[7] A related concept of interest is the real exchange rate which is closely aligned with the notion of price level index (PLI) discussed in this chapter.

reciprocal of the exchange rate of RM0.55 per HK dollar. Exchange rates can be defined symmetrically as number of RM per HK$ or number of HK$ per RM. In the definition of RER, number of HK$ per RM is used. The real exchange rate, RER, is then given by the following equation:

$$RER_{RM, HK\$} = XR_{RM, HK\$} \times PPP_{HK\$, RM}$$

$$= 1.81 \times 0.28 = 0.5091 = PLI_{Malaysia} = \frac{PPP_{HK\$, RM}}{XR_{HK\$, RM}}$$

This discussion and the numerical example shows that the concept of *real exchange rate* for the domestic currency, RM, against the foreign currency, HK$, used by economists is the same as the price level index for Malaysia expressed relative to Hong Kong, China equal to 1.

The Price Level Index of Asia and the Pacific

The PLIs of different economies in Asia and the Pacific can also be expressed relative to the region as a whole, with the PLI of Asia and the Pacific at 100, using a normalization process that guarantees that the real values (converted using PPPs with Asia and the Pacific as the base) and nominal values (converted using exchange rates) of a given aggregate (such as GDP) are the same for the whole region. The PLIs for household consumption reported in Table 4.2 in Chapter 4 shows that with the PLI for Asia and the Pacific at 100, the PLI for Hong Kong, China is 173 and the PLI for Malaysia is 87. This means that prices for household consumption aggregate in Hong Kong, China are well above the regional average but prices in Malaysia are below the regional average. It may be noted that whether the base is Hong Kong, China or the region as a whole, the price level index for household consumption in Malaysia is half of the price level in Hong Kong, China.

Gross Domestic Product

The ICP aims to provide internationally comparable measures of economic activity in the participating economies. The standards set in the System of National Accounts 2008 (United Nations 2009) guide these measures of economic activity: most of the economies in Asia and the Pacific have adopted the System of National Accounts 2008 and are at various stages of its implementation. GDP is a measure of total economic activity: the market value of all final goods and services produced within an economy in a given period. There are three approaches to measuring GDP: the production approach, the income approach, and the expenditure approach, all yielding same results. For the purposes of the ICP, the expenditure approach is preferred because the collection of prices and GDP expenditure components is more feasible. Also, the expenditure side provides more direct measures of the standards of living of people residing in the participating economies. The accounting period for this ICP report is the calendar year of 2017.

WHAT IS A PRICE LEVEL INDEX?

A price level index (PLI) for an expenditure aggregate is the ratio of its PPP to the exchange rate and is expressed as an index with a base of 100. For example, a PLI of 110 for an economy indicates that prices in that economy are on average 10% higher than the prices in the reference economy, whereas a PLI of 90 indicates that the prices are lower by 10% on average.

The expenditure side of GDP equals the sum of all the following:

- ICEH (or individual consumption expenditure by households);
- NPISH (or individual consumption expenditure by nonprofit institutions serving households);
- ICEG (or individual consumption expenditure by government);
- CCEG (or collective consumption expenditure by government);
- GFCF (or gross fixed capital formation);
- changes in inventories and net acquisition of valuables; and
- exports less imports.

In the next section, ICP results focus on the following aggregates:

- GDP;
- ICEH and NPISH;

REAL GROSS DOMESTIC PRODUCT IN PURCHASING POWER PARITY TERMS

In the International Comparison Program (ICP), real gross domestic product (GDP) or volume of goods and services produced in economies are estimated indirectly by using direct measures of relative prices—the purchasing power parities (PPPs)—that eliminate the differences in the price levels across economies. Thus, the real GDP of an economy is obtained by dividing its GDP in local currency unit by its PPP for GDP.

- AICH (or actual individual consumption by households, which equals ICEH plus NPISH plus ICEG);
- GFCE (or government final consumption expenditure, which equals ICEG plus CCEG; and
- GFCF.

Nominal versus Real

For each of the aggregates listed above, the ICP provides measures of nominal and real expenditure aggregates. In different economies, statistical offices produce these aggregates and express them in respective local currency units; therefore, we cannot compare these aggregates across economies. *Nominal GDP* in local currency units of an economy can be converted into a common currency unit using exchange rates:

$$\text{Nominal GDP} = \frac{\text{GDP in local currency units}}{\text{Exchange rate}}$$

This aggregate is referred to as *nominal* since exchange rate simply serves as a currency conversion factor; as such, it does not reflect the price level in the economy.

The *real GDP* expresses GDP in a common currency unit and at the same time adjusts for price level differences in different economies. The real GDP is obtained by converting GDP in local currency units using the PPP for the economy:

$$\text{Real GDP} = \frac{\text{GDP in local currency units}}{\text{Purchasing Power Parity (PPP)}}$$

Both the exchange rate and PPP depend on the reference (or base) currency. If the Hong Kong dollar is the base currency, then the exchange rate and PPP for Hong Kong, China would be equal to 1, consequently, the nominal GDP, real GDP, and GDP in local currency units are all equal for the base economy.

The same convention for nominal and real applies to all the aggregates described above. For example, we obtain the nominal ICEH by converting the ICEH aggregate in local currency units using the exchange rate; we obtain the real ICEH by converting the ICEH aggregate in local currency units using the corresponding PPPs. A word of caution: the PPP for the GDP aggregate cannot be used to convert ICEH and vice versa. PPPs are specific to the aggregate under consideration.

Nominal aggregates, converted using exchange rates, are additive: the sum of the nominal aggregates of household consumption, consumption by NPISH, government consumption, GFCF, change in inventories and net acquisition of valuables, and net exports will equal nominal GDP. This additivity property holds because all the component aggregates of GDP are converted using the same exchange rate. This property, additivity of individual aggregates to total GDP, does not hold in the case of real aggregates. Because each real aggregate is converted using a PPP specific to the aggregate, the sum of real values of components of GDP do not equal the real value of GDP. Therefore, real aggregates presented in the tables in Chapter 4 cannot be summed across components.[8]

---

8   There are aggregation methods like the Geary-Khamis method, which produce international comparisons that are additive but suffer from other deficiencies. See Diewert (2013) for a discussion of the additivity property and related issues.

4. A Summary of the Results in Asia and the Pacific

Introduction

Understanding the diversity and complex nature of the Asia and Pacific region will help the readers and users appreciate the 2017 International Comparison Program (ICP) results presented in this chapter. The Asia and Pacific region plays a major role in the world economy. The region holds a major share of the world population: in 2017, the 22 participating economies of the region accounted more than half of the world's population with 3.785 billion inhabitants in the region.[9] The region is also home to two of the world's most populous economies—India and the People's Republic of China exceeding 1.3 billion each—and also to economies with very small populations like Brunei Darussalam and Maldives with fewer than half a million people each in 2017. Between 2011 and 2017, 14 out of 22 economies grew at an average annual growth rate of more than 5% with the two largest economies, People's Republic of China and India, respectively growing at an average rate of 7.6% and 6.8% per annum.[10] Economies like Cambodia, the Lao People's Democratic Republic, and Mongolia have also posted impressive growth rates exceeding 7.0% during the same period. The region has some of the richest economies—Brunei Darussalam; Hong Kong, China; and Singapore—with very high per capita incomes and it has economies with some of the lowest per capita incomes like Bangladesh, Nepal, and Myanmar. The economies in the region exhibit considerable disparities in living standards and diversity in consumption patterns. The geographic diversity of the region is equally significant. The region has fully urbanized economies like Hong Kong, China and Singapore; economies with large land mass like India and the People's Republic of China; island economies like Fiji and Maldives; and landlocked economies like Bhutan, the Lao People's Democratic Republic, Mongolia, and Nepal.

The ICP does not include Australia, Japan, the Republic of Korea, or New Zealand in Asia and the Pacific because they are traditionally included in the Organisation for Economic Co-operation and Development (OECD) comparisons.

Key Measures

This chapter presents measures of gross domestic product (GDP) and its components expressed in Hong Kong dollars, the reference currency for comparisons in the region, converted using purchasing power parities of currencies of the 22 participating economies and compiled as a part of the 2017 ICP Cycle in the region. These results provide crucial information for assessing economic performance and for comparing standards of living across economies in the region. Estimates of real size of the economies, measured by real GDP, their shares in the region, and estimates of price levels at the GDP level and at lower levels of aggregates including price levels for different commodity groups such as food, transport, education, health and others are presented in the form of tables and charts. Results from ICP, presented in this chapter, provide valuable information for policy makers, at the national and international levels, pursuing evidence-

---

[9] The regional population is based on population mid-year estimates supplied to ADB by the participating economies for the 2017 ICP; the world population is from the World Development Indicators database. World Bank. World Development Indicators. https://databank.worldbank.org/source/world-development-indicators (accessed 18 March 2020).

[10] The economy-level growth rates presented here are simple average of annual GDP growth rates calculated from data in Key Indicators Database. Asian Development Bank. https://kidb.adb.org/kidb/ (accessed 16 March 2020) and World Development Indicators database. World Bank. World Development Indicators. https:// databank.worldbank.org/source/world-development-indicators (accessed 27 March 2020).

based policy making. A wealth of information is available to users through this Summary Report and from the Main Report which is expected to be released by the middle of 2020.

GDP—a widely used measure of economic activity recommended in the United Nations' System of National Accounts—is the principal measure in the ICP. Among the three approaches to measuring GDP (production, income, and expenditure), the ICP focuses on the expenditure side of GDP for two reasons. First and foremost, collecting price and expenditure data—necessary for compiling PPPs, real GDP, and its components—is more feasible from the expenditure side than the production side. Second, comparisons of expenditures provide more direct consumption-based measures of the material well-being of people residing in the participating economies. Comparing per capita real GDP provides valuable information about the cross-economy comparison of average living standards of the population. However, GDP per capita as a measure of cross-economy comparisons also has some known weaknesses. In particular, GDP per capita does not take into account income distribution in an economy. Caution must be exercised in interpreting it as an indicator of overall well-being. Stiglitz, Sen, and Fitoussi (2009) comprehensively discuss the advantages and limitations of GDP, and the need to look beyond it. Their report makes a compelling case for using a dashboard of indicators that reflect several dimensions of economic performance and quality of life, with a special focus on health, education, risk of unemployment, poverty, and security. Notwithstanding their recommendations, per capita GDP continues to be a summary measure which reflects and highly correlates with other dimensions of economic progress and quality of life.

Summary Results

The following sections provide summary and a brief analysis of the results of 2017 ICP in Asia and the

REFERENCE CURRENCY FOR THE REGIONAL COMPARISON

The reference currency unit used for Asia and the Pacific comparisons has been the Hong Kong dollar since the 2005 International Comparison Program (ICP) round. The purchasing power parities (PPPs) and real and nominal expenditures are therefore expressed in Hong Kong dollar. The relativities between economies are not affected by the choice of reference currency—it is simply a device for comparisons.

Pacific. These results relate to the key concepts and measures explained in Chapter 3. Box 4.1 presents some special notes that readers should keep in mind when looking at the ICP results for Asia and the Pacific. The tables in this chapter present PPPs, price level indexes (PLIs), real and nominal expenditures, real and nominal expenditures per capita, real and nominal expenditure per capita indexes, and real and nominal economy shares in Asia and the Pacific. The chapter presents and analyzes key aggregates: GDP, individual consumption expenditure by household (ICEH) and nonprofit institutions serving households (NPISH), actual individual consumption by households (AICH), government final consumption expenditure (GFCE), and gross fixed capital formation (GFCF). More detailed expenditure aggregates for the year 2017 as well as the revised tables for 2011 are available in Appendixes 4 and 5. For all tables in this chapter, Hong Kong, China is the reference economy and the Hong Kong dollar (HK$) is the reference currency, unless otherwise specified.[11]

The core results for real and nominal GDP and respective per capita measures from the 2017 ICP in Asia and the Pacific are in Table 4.1. Column 2

---

11   The methodology used in the ICP ensures that results presented are invariant to the choice of the reference currency: the relative levels of real GDP would remain the same even if other economies or currencies are used as the base or reference economy.

Box 4.1: Notes on Data and Definitions in this Report

- In the tables presented in the report, "Asia and the Pacific" refers to the 22 participating economies in the 2017 International Comparison Program (ICP) for the Asia and Pacific region; coverage of the Pacific is limited to Fiji.

- In the analysis presented in the report, "real" refers to purchasing power parity (PPP)-converted values of expenditure aggregates, while "nominal" refers to exchange rate-converted expenditure values when converted to the Hong Kong dollar.

- Price data for ICP products used in calculating PPP are estimated based on national annual average prices for 2017. Results presented in this report are produced by the ICP Asia Pacific regional implementing agency, based on data supplied by all the participating economies, and in accordance with the methodology recommended by the ICP Technical Advisory Group and approved by the Asia and the Pacific Regional Advisory Board. As such, these results are not produced by participating economies as part of the economies' official statistics. For the 2017 ICP cycle, the estimation methodologies remain the same as in 2011 ICP cycle, with some refinements.

- The gross domestic expenditures in local currency units were disaggregated into 155 basic headings by the participating economies according to the 2017 ICP classification. In many cases in the absence of published or readily available estimates at that basic heading level, higher-level aggregates were required to be split using data and indicators available from household expenditure surveys, government accounts, and other most recent available data sources. Further, in accordance with the ICP guidelines, economies were also required to allocate statistical discrepancy (if any) on the expenditure side to one or more basic headings based on their best judgment. As such the nominal expenditure estimates presented in the tables in this report are the best possible estimates, and some of the expenditure aggregates in this report may be different from the published expenditure estimates by the economies.

- Bangladesh, India, Myanmar, Nepal, and Pakistan compile their gross domestic product (GDP) according to the financial year. As the ICP requires calendar year GDP expenditures from the economies in local currency units, these estimates were converted to calendar year estimates using different approaches depending on the availability of detailed expenditure estimates in each of these economies.

- In some economies, data for household expenditures include the expenditures undertaken by the nonprofit institutions serving households (NPISH) because it is difficult to segregate NPISH data, with the exception of the People's Republic of China, where NPISH data is included with government expenditures. In some economies, only total expenditure by NPISH was provided and these were broken down into relevant NPISH components using ratios from household consumption. It may be noted that the NPISH expenditures were not allocated to household expenditures, unlike in the 2011 ICP round, according to the decision taken by the Inter-Agency Coordination Group for uniform treatment of NPISH expenditures by all regional implementing agencies.

- Net purchases abroad, although available as a separate estimate in some economies, were not distributed to household expenditure's international tourism-related basic headings, as was done in the 2011 ICP round. This was also based on the decision taken by the ICP Inter-Agency Coordination Group for uniform treatment of available data on net purchases abroad to be followed by all regions.

- PPPs and results estimated in this report are based on data finalized and submitted by the implementing agencies from each economy as of January 2020.

- The 2011 ICP results were also revised because of revisions in the estimates of GDP and population and due to the refinements in methods for 2017 ICP, such as methodology for estimating the adjustment factors for the differences in productivity of government, minor changes in ICP classification between 2017 and 2011, revisions in the reference PPPs, and treatment of expenditures by NPISH and on net purchases abroad. The 2011 revised results are produced by the ICP Asia Pacific regional implementing agency, based on data supplied by all the participating economies, and in accordance with the methodology recommended by the ICP Technical Advisory Group and approved by the Asia and the Pacific Regional Advisory Board. As such, these results are not produced by participating economies as part of the economies' official statistics.

Source: Asian Development Bank.

Table 4.1: Summary Results for Gross Domestic Product, 2017
(Hong Kong, China as base)

Economy	PPPs (HK$ = 1.00)	Exchange Rates (HK$ = 1.00)	Expenditure (HK$ billion) Based on PPPs	Expenditure (HK$ billion) Based on XRs	Expenditure per Capita (HK$) Based on PPPs	Expenditure per Capita (HK$) Based on XRs	Expenditure per Capita Indexes — Asia and the Pacific = 100 Based on PPPs	Asia and the Pacific = 100 Based on XRs	HKG = 100 Based on PPPs	HKG = 100 Based on XRs	Shares (Asia and the Pacific = 100.00) Expenditure Based on PPPs	Expenditure Based on XRs	Population	PLIs Asia and the Pacific = 100	PLIs HKG = 100	Reference Data Population (million)	Reference Data Expenditure in LCU (billion)
(1)	(2)	(3)	(4)	(5)	(6)	(7)	(8)	(9)	(10)	(11)	(12)	(13)	(14)	(15)	(16)	(17)	(18)
Bangladesh	4.95	10.32	4,272	2,047	26,401	12,654	43	32	7	4	1.84	1.38	4.27	75	48	161.80	21,131
Bhutan	3.20	8.36	52	20	70,855	27,094	115	69	20	8	0.02	0.01	0.02	60	38	0.73	165
Brunei Darussalam	0.11	0.18	156	95	362,379	220,065	590	560	101	61	0.07	0.06	0.01	95	61	0.43	17
Cambodia	237.61	519.75	378	173	23,853	10,904	39	28	7	3	0.16	0.12	0.42	71	46	15.85	89,831
China, People's Republic of	0.70	0.87	117,929	94,638	85,061	68,262	139	174	24	19	50.76	63.57	36.62	125	80	1,386.40	82,075
Fiji	0.16	0.27	71	42	80,772	47,572	132	121	22	13	0.03	0.03	0.02	92	59	0.88	11
Hong Kong, China	1.00	1.00	2,663	2,663	360,247	360,247	587	916	100	100	1.15	1.79	0.20	156	100	7.39	2,663
India	3.43	8.36	48,395	19,893	36,965	15,194	60	39	10	4	20.83	13.36	34.58	64	41	1,309.20	166,226
Indonesia	781.12	1,716.98	17,394	7,913	66,419	30,217	108	77	18	8	7.49	5.32	6.92	71	45	261.89	13,587,213
Lao People's Democratic Republic	463.97	1,071.64	303	131	43,944	19,026	72	48	12	5	0.13	0.09	0.18	68	43	6.90	140,698
Malaysia	0.28	0.55	4,916	2,453	153,532	76,589	250	195	43	21	2.12	1.65	0.85	78	50	32.02	1,353
Maldives	1.36	1.97	55	38	112,187	77,137	183	196	31	21	0.02	0.03	0.01	107	69	0.49	75
Mongolia	131.66	313.06	212	89	67,241	28,278	110	72	19	8	0.09	0.06	0.08	66	42	3.15	27,876
Myanmar	61.00	174.56	1,409	493	26,519	9,268	43	24	7	3	0.61	0.33	1.40	55	35	53.15	85,981
Nepal	5.20	13.41	503	195	17,431	6,754	28	17	5	2	0.22	0.13	0.76	60	39	28.83	2,611
Pakistan	5.59	13.53	5,954	2,459	29,905	12,349	49	31	8	3	2.56	1.65	5.26	64	41	199.11	33,270
Philippines	3.22	6.47	4,902	2,444	46,721	23,295	76	59	13	6	2.11	1.64	2.77	78	50	104.92	15,808
Singapore	0.15	0.18	3,171	2,637	564,960	469,907	921	1,195	157	130	1.36	1.77	0.15	130	83	5.61	467
Sri Lanka	8.22	19.56	1,621	681	75,587	31,748	123	81	21	9	0.70	0.46	0.57	66	42	21.44	13,317
Taipei,China	2.62	3.91	6,688	4,480	283,878	190,165	463	484	79	53	2.88	3.01	0.62	105	67	23.56	17,501
Thailand	2.14	4.36	7,232	3,548	106,892	52,444	174	133	30	15	3.11	2.38	1.79	77	49	67.65	15,452
Viet Nam	1,230.21	2,870.44	4,069	1,744	43,179	18,506	70	47	12	5	1.75	1.17	2.49	67	43	94.24	5,005,975
Asia and the Pacific	n.a.	n.a.	232,344	148,874	61,375	39,326	100	100	17	11	100.00	100.00	100.00	100	n.a.	3,785.65	n.a.

n.a. = not applicable; HK$ = Hong Kong dollar; HKG = Hong Kong, China; LCU = local currency unit; PLI = price level index; PPP = purchasing power parity; XR = exchange rate.
Sources: Asian Development Bank estimates. For exchange rates: International Monetary Fund. International Financial Statistics. http://data.imf.org/ (accessed 17 September 2019). Data for population refers to mid-year estimates supplied by the participating economies for the 2017 International Comparison Program.

shows PPPs of currencies at GDP level: the number of currency units that have the same purchasing power as one Hong Kong dollar. For example, in the case of Indonesia, the PPP indicates that 781.12 rupiah (Rp) have the same purchasing power as one Hong Kong dollar (HK$1 = Rp781.12). In contrast, the exchange rate is HK$1 = Rp1,716.98 (column 3), which indicates that the average price levels in Indonesia for goods and services in the GDP are much lower than in Hong Kong, China. This is true for each of the 21 economies (excluding Hong Kong, China); the PPPs of each of these are lower than their respective exchange rates, regardless of the size or relative level of development of the economies concerned (columns 2 and 3). This means that each of the 21 economies has price levels lower than those of Hong Kong, China (column 16; also refer to the discussion on price level index in this chapter).

In the table, the relative sizes of the economies—their real GDPs, which are obtained by dividing their respective GDPs in local currency units by their corresponding PPPs—are in column 4, while their nominal GDPs, or GDP converted using exchange rates, are in column 5. The GDP of Asia and the Pacific is HK$232.344 trillion in real (or PPP) terms, but only HK$148.874 trillion in nominal (or exchange rate) terms, a significant difference that results from the fact that PPPs (with respect to the Hong Kong dollar) for every economy are lower than the exchange rates. To

> ## COMPARISONS ARE INDEPENDENT OF THE UNITS USED
>
> Results can be expressed in a reference currency or as index numbers, but the relativities between economies do not change when different units are used for the comparison.

gain a proper perspective on the real and nominal size of the economy of Asia and the Pacific, it is necessary to compare it with other regions. The report to be prepared by the World Bank's ICP Global Office will present these comparisons.

Real and Nominal Levels of Gross Domestic Product and Rankings

Figure 4.1 shows the relative sizes of the economies in real and nominal terms and demonstrates the differences in nominal and real GDP estimates. For all economies, real GDP is larger than nominal GDP, except in the case of Hong Kong, China where, as constructed, nominal and real GDP are the same (for Hong Kong, China, PPP = exchange rate = 1).

Table 4.1 (column 4) further shows that, among the participating economies of Asia and the Pacific, the People's Republic of China is the largest economy by far, with a real GDP of HK$117.9 trillion, followed by India with HK$48.4 trillion and Indonesia with HK$17.4 trillion. In contrast, the smallest economies are Bhutan at HK$52 billion, Maldives at HK$55 billion, and Fiji HK$71 billion. This shows wide differences in the sizes of the economies of this region, where economies differ in size by a factor of about 2,300 between the largest (the People's Republic of China) and the smallest (Bhutan), according to real GDP. High-income economies such as Singapore and Hong Kong, China are essentially cities with small economies and populations.

The distribution of real and nominal GDP in the form of shares of different economies in the region are in Figure 4.2. The 12 economies shown in Figure 4.2 together account for nearly 98.0% of the real GDP and 98.7% of the nominal GDP expenditure of all participating 22 economies in Asia and the Pacific, with remaining 10 small economies accounting for only about 2.0% and 1.3% of the real and nominal GDP respectively. The shares of the top three economies in real terms are 50.76% for the People's Republic of China, 20.83% for India, and 7.49% for Indonesia. The People's Republic of China's share is nearly seven

Figure 4.1: Real and Nominal Gross Domestic Product, 2017 (HK$ billion)

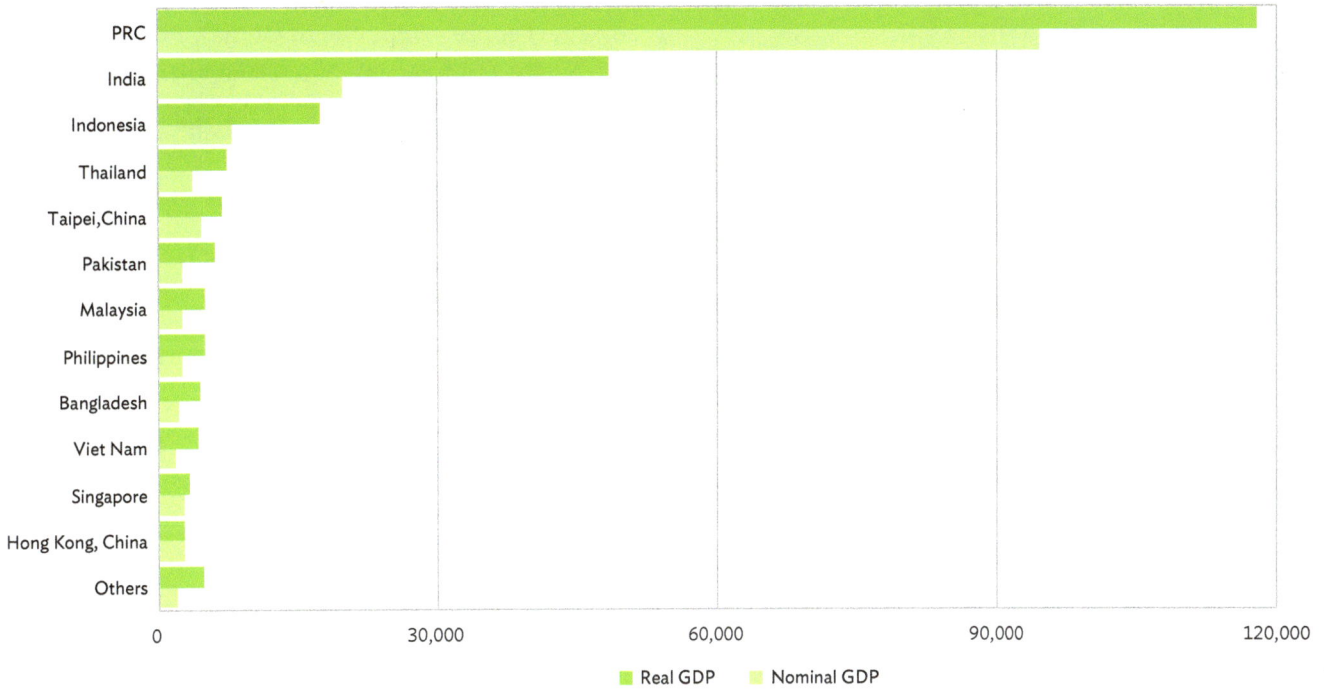

GDP = gross domestic product, HK$ = Hong Kong dollar, PRC = People's Republic of China.
Source: Table 4.1.

Figure 4.2: Economy Shares of Real and Nominal Gross Domestic Product, 2017 (%)

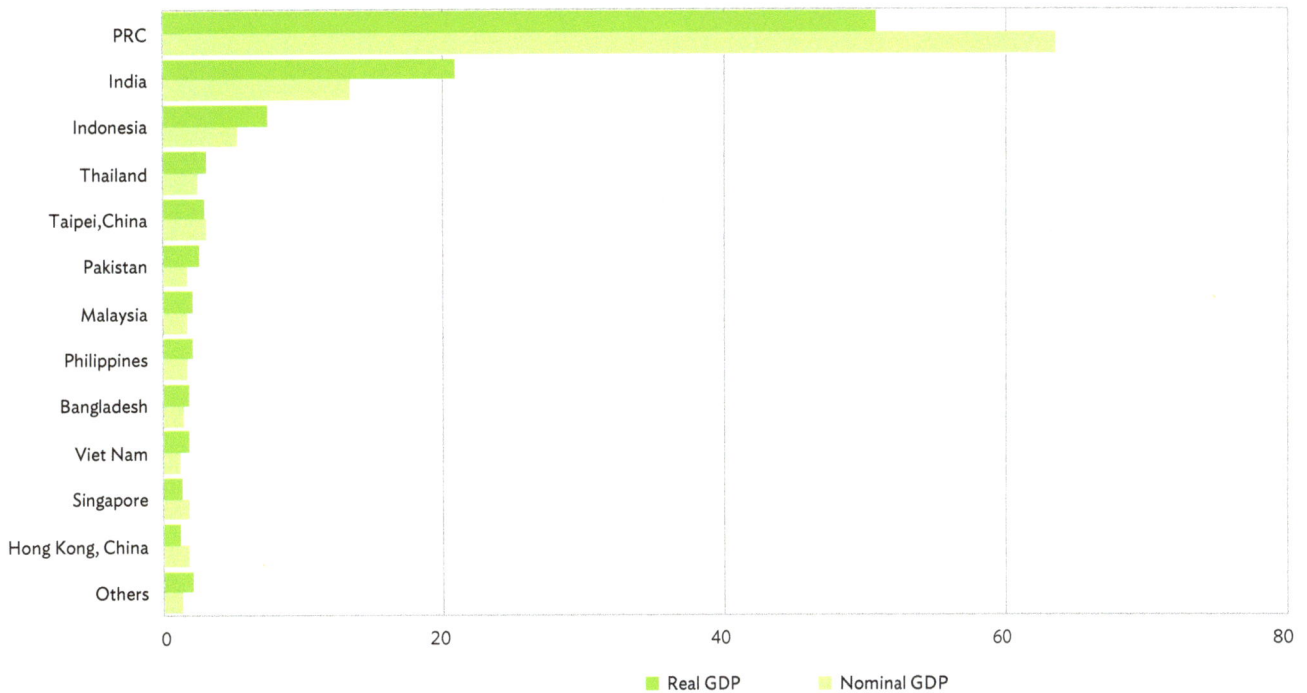

GDP = gross domestic product, PRC = People's Republic of China.
Source: Table 4.1.

GROSS DOMESTIC PRODUCT

When estimated from the expenditure side, gross domestic product (GDP) is defined as the total value of the final consumption expenditures of households, nonprofit institutions serving households, and general government plus gross capital formation plus balance of exports and imports.

Source: World Bank 2015.

times that of Indonesia. These are also the most populous economies of the region with shares of 36.62% (People's Republic of China), 34.58% (India), and 6.92% (Indonesia). Thus, the three economies together account for 79.08% of the region's GDP and 78.12% the region's population. India is ranked second in terms of total real GDP, but the real size of the Indian economy is only 41% of the People's Republic of China's economy. Because both economies have almost similar population sizes, India is ranked well below the People's Republic of China in terms of per capita real GDP.

Figure 4.3: Rankings for Real and Nominal Gross Domestic Product, 2017

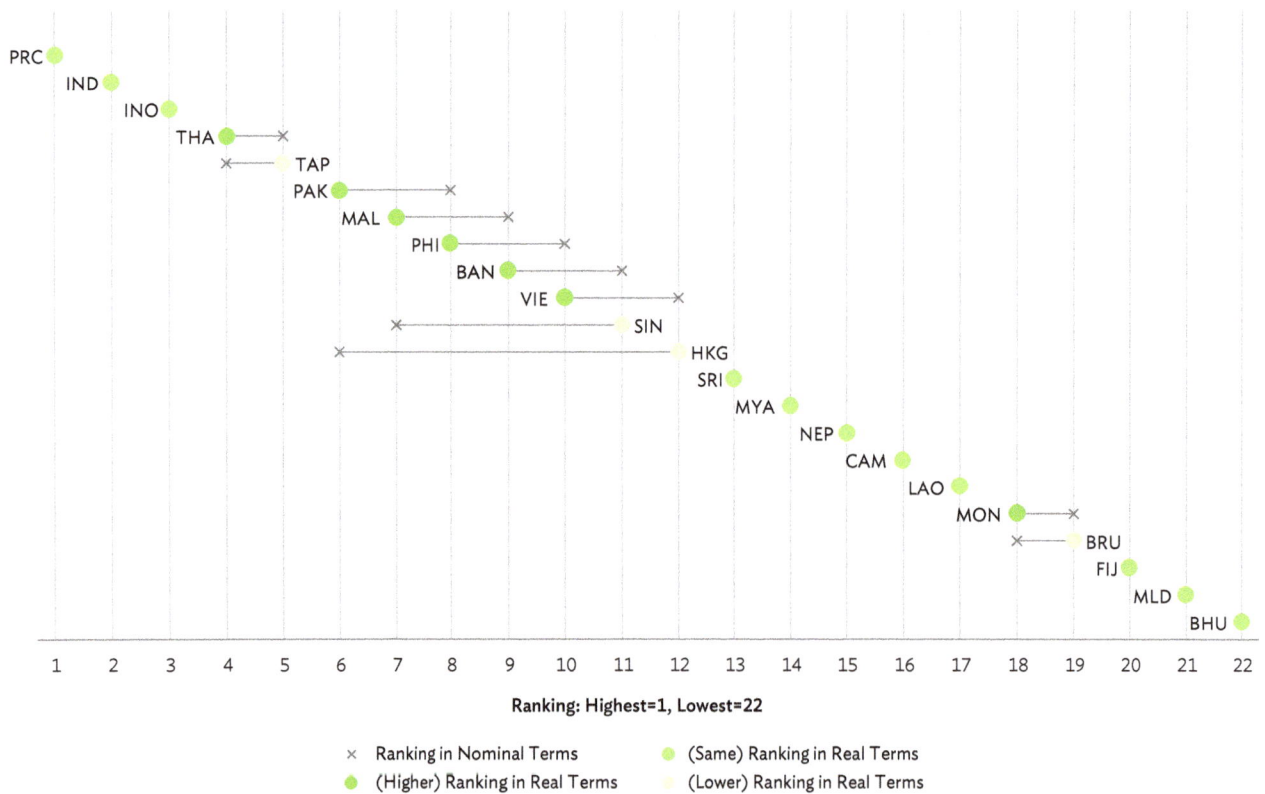

Ranking: Highest=1, Lowest=22

× Ranking in Nominal Terms
● (Higher) Ranking in Real Terms
● (Same) Ranking in Real Terms
● (Lower) Ranking in Real Terms

BAN = Bangladesh; BHU = Bhutan; BRU = Brunei Darussalam; CAM = Cambodia; FIJ = Fiji; HKG = Hong Kong, China; IND = India; INO = Indonesia; LAO = Lao People's Democratic Republic; MAL = Malaysia; MLD = Maldives; MON = Mongolia; MYA = Myanmar; NEP = Nepal; PAK = Pakistan; PHI = Philippines; PRC = People's Republic of China; SIN = Singapore; SRI = Sri Lanka; TAP = Taipei,China; THA = Thailand; VIE = Viet Nam.
Source: Asian Development Bank estimates.

When the economies are ranked by size, both real and nominal, we can see that rankings based on real and nominal GDP are identical for the three largest and three smallest economies, as shown in Figure 4.3. In contrast, the high-income economies have significantly different rankings in real and nominal terms. Singapore is ranked 7th in nominal terms but drops to 11th in real terms; and Hong Kong, China is ranked 6th in nominal terms but 12th in real terms. Other medium-sized economies have smaller shifts in rankings.

The per capita GDP—an indicator of the standard of living or affluence of people in different economies—varies by a factor of 32.4 in per capita *real* GDP and a factor of 69.6 in per capita *nominal* GDP respectively between Singapore, the richest economy in terms of per capita GDP, and Nepal, the poorest, as shown in Figure 4.4.

Table 4.1 shows that the average per capita real GDP for the region is HK$61,375 as against HK$39,326 in nominal terms. The four economies with the highest per capita real GDP are, from highest to lowest, Singapore (HK$564,960); Brunei Darussalam (HK$362,379); Hong Kong, China (HK$360,247); and Taipei,China (HK$283,878); they are also the top four in terms of per capita GDP in nominal terms. At the other end of the spectrum, Myanmar (HK$26,519), Bangladesh

Figure 4.4: Per Capita Real and Nominal Gross Domestic Product, 2017 (HK$)

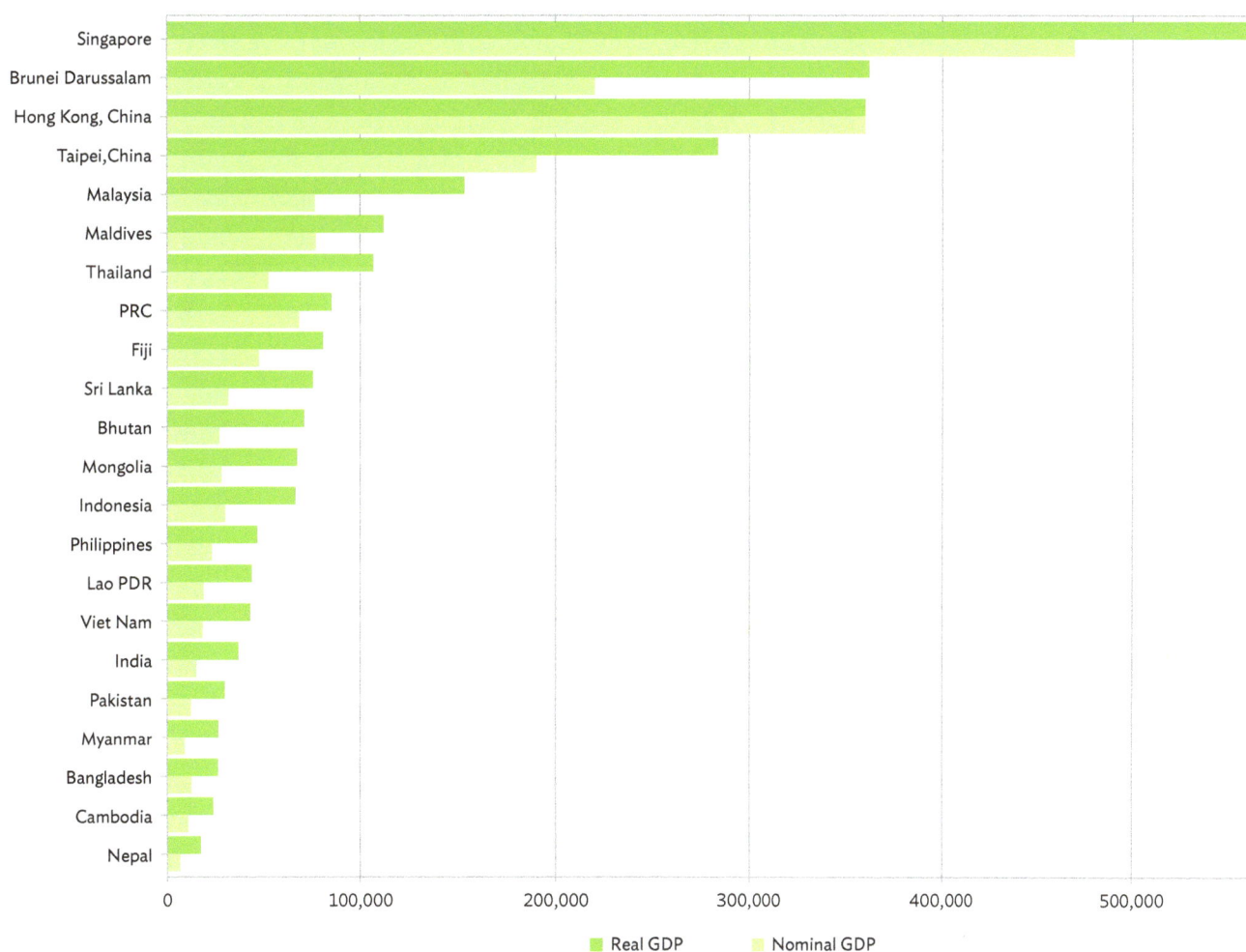

GDP = gross domestic product, HK$ = Hong Kong dollar, Lao PDR = Lao People's Democratic Republic, PRC = People's Republic of China.
Source: Table 4.1.

(HK\$26,401), Cambodia (HK\$23,853), and Nepal (HK\$17,431) are the four lowest ranked economies by per capita *real* GDP. Although the People's Republic of China and India are the two largest economies in real GDP, the People's Republic of China is ranked 8th and India is 17th in terms of per capita real GDP.

The Lorenz curve in Figure 4.5 plots the cumulative percentage shares of expenditures against the cumulative percentage shares of population of the economies in Asia and the Pacific, starting in order from the economy with lowest per capita GDP to the highest. The 45 degree line represents the line of equality; the area between the line of equality and the line representing per capita distribution represents the inequality.

The distribution of per capita GDP is more equal when real GDP is used in comparison with the nominal GDP,

as shown in Figure 4.5. This is consistent with the fact that PPPs are significantly lower than exchange rates for low-income economies. It may be noted that the Lorenz curves in Figure 4.5 only measure inequality in the distribution of income where only economy-specific per capita GDP and population size are considered and do not account for inequality within each of the 22 economies. These Lorenz curves also show that the poorest 40% of the population in the region accounts for around 22% of *real* GDP of the region whereas they account for only about 14% of the *nominal* GDP of the region.

The PLIs in Table 4.1 for GDP show that Hong Kong, China with a PLI of 156 (with Asia and the Pacific =100) has the highest price levels in the region followed by Singapore (130) and the People's Republic of China (125). The lowest price levels are in Myanmar at 55 followed by Bhutan and Nepal at 60 each. Finally, the PLIs (with Asia and the Pacific = 100) are presented against per capita real GDP (in log scale) in Figure 4.6.[12] The clear positive association between PLIs and per capita real GDP implies that price levels tend to be high in richer economies, generally referred to as the Penn effect. The fitted line shows a significant positive slope.[13] It shows the expected PLI for an economy with a given level of per capita real GDP. The figure shows that Hong Kong, China; Maldives; and the People's Republic of China exhibit price levels well above the expected PLIs implied by the fitted line. At the other end of the spectrum, a number of middle- and low-income economies, such as India, Indonesia, Myanmar, and Viet Nam, exhibit lower than expected price levels.

Figure 4.5: Lorenz Curves for Per Capita Real and Nominal Gross Domestic Product, 2017

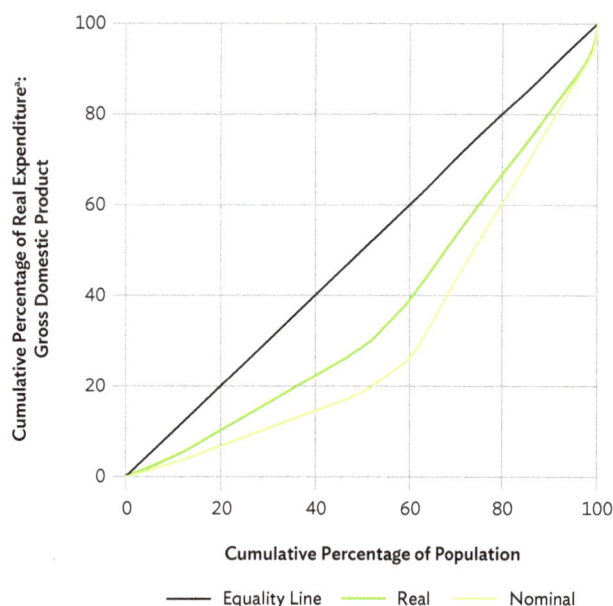

a Expenditure is represented by the economy-specific per capita gross domestic product.
Source: Asian Development Bank estimates.

Household Final Consumption

Household final consumption is a general indicator of material well-being because it represents the total volume of goods and services consumed by households. As discussed in Chapter 3, household consumption

---

12   The axis in log scale provides less clustered visualization for situations where the majority of the data points are concentrated in the lower range, while a very few data points are exponentially higher than the rest. This is achieved by making each fixed interval of the axis to represent an exponentially increasing value, e.g., 10, 100, 1,000, 10,000 100,000, 1,000,000, and so on.
13   The fitted line is based on semi-log specification, i.e., the PLI is regressed on natural log of per capita real GDP.

Figure 4.6: Price Level Index versus Per Capita Real Gross Domestic Product, 2017

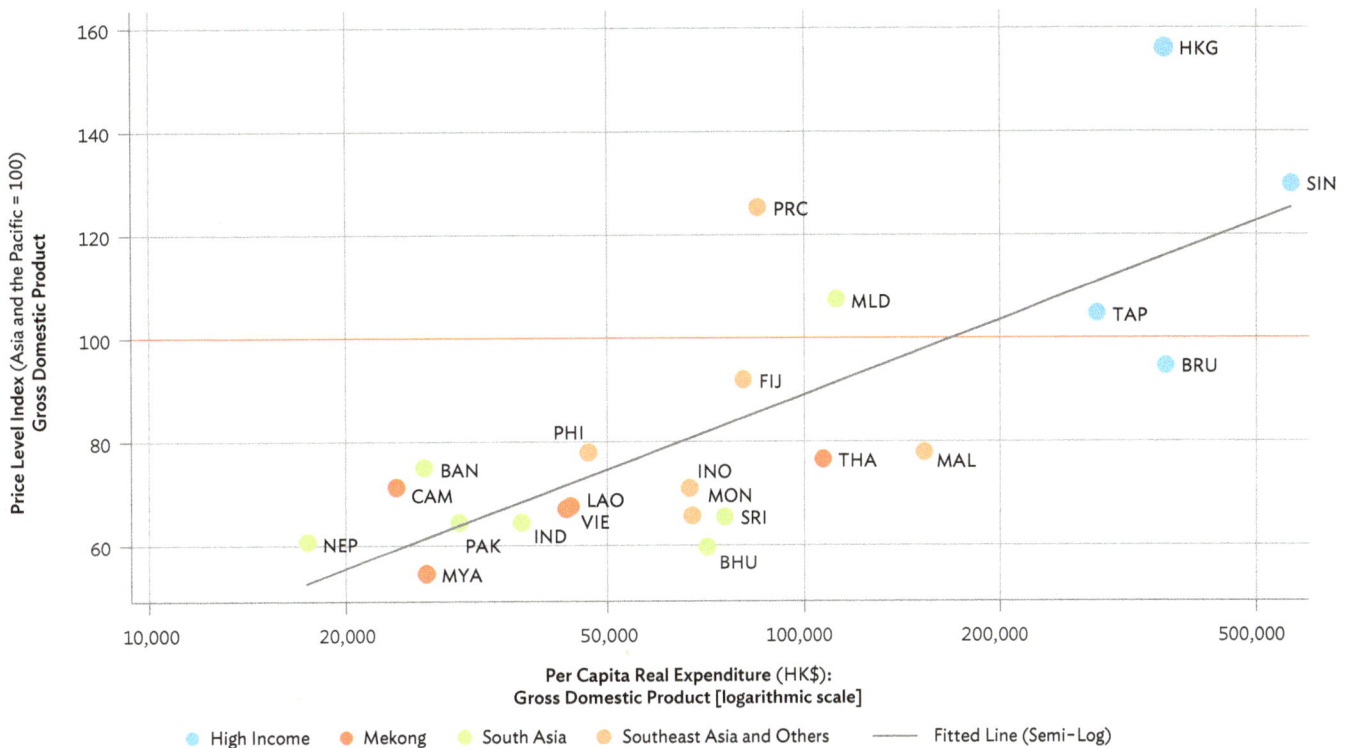

BAN = Bangladesh; BHU = Bhutan; BRU = Brunei Darussalam; CAM = Cambodia; FIJ = Fiji; HK$ = Hong Kong dollar; HKG = Hong Kong, China; IND = India; INO = Indonesia; LAO = Lao People's Democratic Republic; MAL = Malaysia; MLD = Maldives; MON = Mongolia; MYA = Myanmar; NEP = Nepal; PAK = Pakistan; PHI = Philippines; PRC = People's Republic of China; SIN = Singapore; SRI = Sri Lanka; TAP = Taipei,China; THA = Thailand; VIE = Viet Nam.

Source: Asian Development Bank estimates.

may be undertaken by households themselves, known as *individual consumption expenditure by households* (ICEH) or by *nonprofit institutions serving households* (NPISH). In addition to these, there is *individual consumption expenditure by government* (ICEG) on behalf of households, typically on housing, health, education, and recreation and cultural services. The sum of ICEH, NPISH, and ICEG is referred to as the *actual individual consumption by households* (AICH). In any economy, AICH provides a comprehensive measure of the total volume of goods and services consumed by households, regardless of who pays for it. However, the relative proportions of ICEH, NPISH, and ICEG tend to vary across economies in the region as governments in some economies tend to be proactive and provide services aimed at low-income households.

Individual Consumption Expenditure by Households

Estimates of PPPs, PLIs, real and nominal expenditures of ICEH, and per capita expenditures are in Table 4.2.

It may be noted that in the discussions that follow, ICEH is inclusive of the expenditures by NPISH.

PER CAPITA

The Latin term "per capita" is loosely translated to English as "by head." A per capita figure is calculated by dividing an economic aggregate, for example, gross domestic product (GDP), by the total population to approximate as an income-based measure of average "standard of living" of residents in an economy. Although interpreted as "per person," per capita GDP does not provide information as to how income is distributed across the population within an economy.

Table 4.2: Summary Results for Individual Consumption Expenditure by Households, 2017
(Hong Kong, China as base)

Economy	PPPs (HK$ = 1.00)	Exchange Rates (HK$ = 1.00)	Expenditure (HK$ billion)		Expenditure per Capita (HK$)		Expenditure per Capita Indexes				Shares (Asia and the Pacific = 100.00)			PLIs		Reference Data	
							Asia and the Pacific = 100		HKG = 100		Expenditure		Population	Asia and the Pacific = 100	HKG = 100	Population (million)	Expenditure in LCU (billion)
			Based on PPPs	Based on XRs	Based on PPPs	Based on XRs	Based on PPPs	Based on XRs	Based on PPPs	Based on XRs	Based on PPPs	Based on XRs					
(1)	(2)	(3)	(4)	(5)	(6)	(7)	(8)	(9)	(10)	(11)	(12)	(13)	(14)	(15)	(16)	(17)	(18)
Bangladesh	4.73	10.32	3,120	1,429	19,282	8,833	62	49	8	4	2.66	2.12	4.27	79	46	161.80	14,752
Bhutan	3.28	8.36	26	10	36,422	14,296	118	80	15	6	0.02	0.02	0.02	68	39	0.73	87
Brunei Darussalam	0.11	0.18	31	19	71,556	45,068	231	253	30	19	0.03	0.03	0.01	109	63	0.43	3
Cambodia	238.51	519.75	303	139	19,097	8,763	62	49	8	4	0.26	0.21	0.42	80	46	15.85	72,194
China, People's Republic of	0.66	0.87	46,611	35,703	33,620	25,753	109	144	14	11	39.80	52.85	36.62	133	77	1,386.40	30,964
Fiji	0.16	0.27	47	28	53,908	32,106	174	180	22	13	0.04	0.04	0.02	103	60	0.88	7
Hong Kong, China	1.00	1.00	1,785	1,785	241,555	241,555	781	1,354	100	100	1.52	2.64	0.20	173	100	7.39	1,785
India	3.12	8.36	31,360	11,706	23,954	8,941	77	50	10	4	26.78	17.33	34.58	65	37	1,309.20	97,813
Indonesia	815.39	1,716.98	9,551	4,536	36,471	17,320	118	97	15	7	8.16	6.71	6.92	82	47	261.89	7,788,168
Lao People's Democratic Republic	502.05	1,071.64	152	71	22,065	10,337	71	58	9	4	0.13	0.11	0.18	81	47	6.90	76,447
Malaysia	0.28	0.55	2,707	1,357	84,526	42,379	273	237	35	18	2.31	2.01	0.85	87	50	32.02	749
Maldives	1.57	1.97	19	15	38,688	30,743	125	172	16	13	0.02	0.02	0.01	138	79	0.49	30
Mongolia	139.95	313.06	107	48	33,862	15,137	109	85	14	6	0.09	0.07	0.08	77	45	3.15	14,922
Myanmar	62.45	174.56	784	281	14,750	5,278	48	30	6	2	0.67	0.42	1.40	62	36	53.15	48,963
Nepal	4.89	13.41	410	149	14,212	5,180	46	29	6	2	0.35	0.22	0.76	63	36	28.83	2,003
Pakistan	5.33	13.53	5,135	2,022	25,791	10,153	83	57	11	4	4.39	2.99	5.26	68	39	199.11	27,355
Philippines	3.11	6.47	3,738	1,796	35,630	17,115	115	96	15	7	3.19	2.66	2.77	83	48	104.92	11,614
Singapore	0.17	0.18	969	947	172,694	168,702	558	945	71	70	0.83	1.40	0.15	169	98	5.61	168
Sri Lanka	8.89	19.56	929	422	43,335	19,698	140	110	18	8	0.79	0.63	0.57	79	45	21.44	8,263
Taipei,China	2.66	3.91	3,484	2,372	147,894	100,673	478	564	61	42	2.98	3.51	0.62	118	68	23.56	9,265
Thailand	2.13	4.36	3,466	1,694	51,232	25,042	166	140	21	10	2.96	2.51	1.79	85	49	67.65	7,378
Viet Nam	1,250.81	2,870.44	2,364	1,030	25,088	10,932	81	61	10	5	2.02	1.52	2.49	76	44	94.24	2,957,280
Asia and the Pacific	n.a.	n.a.	117,100	67,560	30,933	17,846	100	100	13	7	100.00	100.00	100.00	100	n.a.	3,785.65	n.a.

n.a. = not applicable; HK$ = Hong Kong dollar; HKG = Hong Kong, China; LCU = local currency unit; PLI = price level index; PPP = purchasing power parity; XR = exchange rate.

Note: In this table, individual consumption expenditure by household (ICEH) includes expenditures by household (ICEH) includes expenditures by nonprofit institutions serving households (NPISH).

Sources: Asian Development Bank estimates. For exchange rates: International Monetary Fund. International Financial Statistics. http://data.imf.org/ (accessed 17 September 2019). Data for population refers to mid-year estimates supplied by the participating economies for the 2017 International Comparison Program.

The PPPs (column 2) for ICEH are generally well below the exchange rates (column 3). For example, for India, PPP for ICEH is 3.12 Indian rupees (₹) for one Hong Kong dollar, or HK$1 = ₹3.12, compared to the exchange rate of HK$1 = ₹8.36. The PLIs (with Hong Kong, China = 100), are below 100 for all the economies. Moreover, 15 out of 22 economies have PLIs less than or equal to 50 (column 16). The PLI (with the PLI for Asia and the Pacific = 100) for Hong Kong, China is 173 and six more economies have price levels above the regional level of 100 (column 15). The PLI for the People's Republic of China is 33% higher than the regional average. The PLIs of Maldives (138)

and Fiji (103) show that the price level in the two island economies is higher than the regional average of 100 by 38% for Maldives and 3% for Fiji; price levels in the rich economies of Brunei Darussalam; Hong Kong, China; Singapore; and Taipei,China are also higher than the regional average.

In Table 4.2 (column 4), the total size of real ICEH (in PPP terms) for the region is HK$117.10 trillion, with the highest ICEH in the People's Republic of China at HK$46.61 trillion and India at HK$31.36 trillion. The following figure shows the economies' rankings in nominal and real ICEH.

Figure 4.7: Rankings for Real and Nominal Individual Consumption Expenditure by Households, 2017

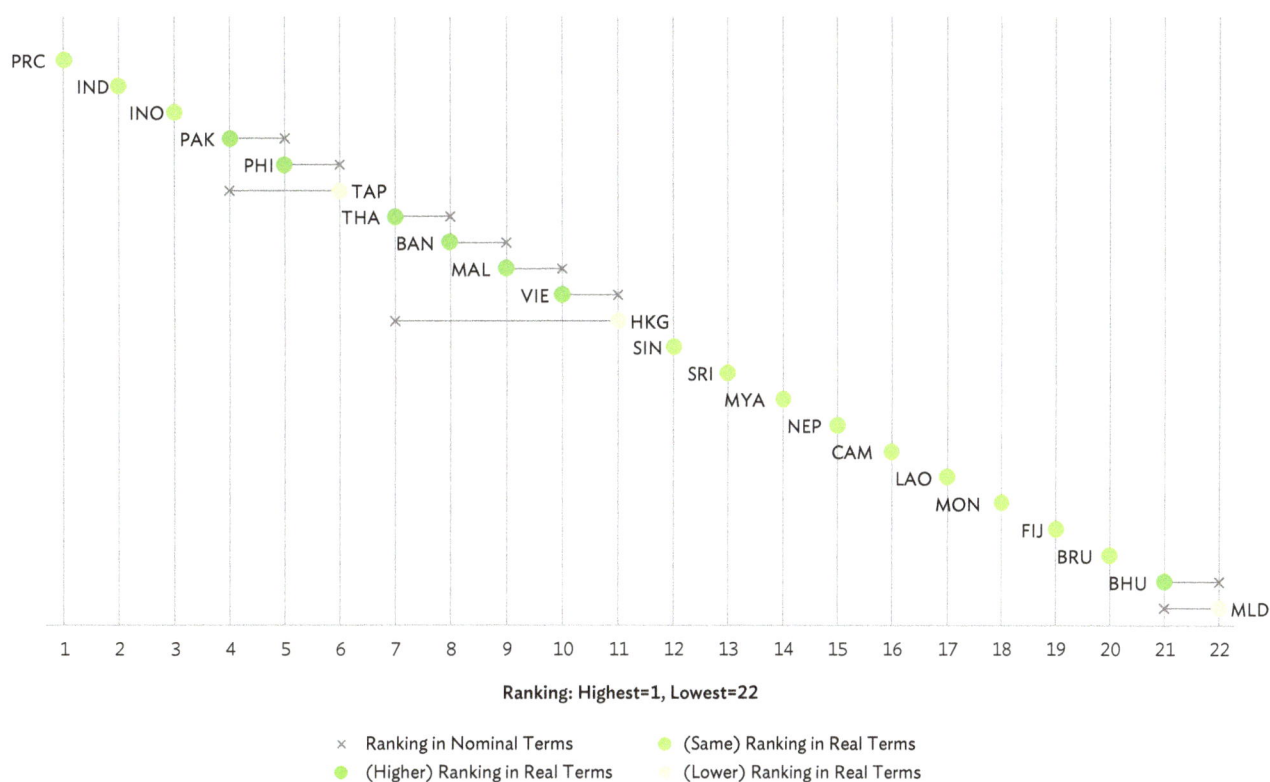

Ranking: Highest=1, Lowest=22

× Ranking in Nominal Terms   ● (Same) Ranking in Real Terms
● (Higher) Ranking in Real Terms   (Lower) Ranking in Real Terms

BAN = Bangladesh; BHU = Bhutan; BRU = Brunei Darussalam; CAM = Cambodia; FIJ = Fiji; HKG = Hong Kong, China; IND = India; INO = Indonesia; LAO = Lao People's Democratic Republic; MAL = Malaysia; MLD = Maldives; MON = Mongolia; MYA = Myanmar; NEP = Nepal; PAK = Pakistan; PHI = Philippines; PRC = People's Republic of China; SIN = Singapore; SRI = Sri Lanka; TAP = Taipei,China; THA = Thailand; VIE = Viet Nam.
Note: In this figure, individual consumption expenditure by households (ICEH) includes expenditures by nonprofit institutions serving households (NPISH).
Source: Asian Development Bank estimates.

The top five ranked economies in terms of real ICEH from highest to lowest are the People's Republic of China, India, Indonesia, Pakistan, and the Philippines; meanwhile, the bottom ranked economies from lowest to highest are Maldives, Bhutan, Brunei Darussalam, and Fiji. Differences in rankings based on nominal and real ICEH are generally small, except for Hong Kong, China, which has a much lower ranking in real terms.

The per capita ICEH are important when it comes to comparing material well-being of the economies. In Table 4.2, except for reference economy (Hong Kong, China), each economy's per capita nominal ICEH (column 7) is lower than its per capita real ICEH (column 6) arising from the fact that each PPP for ICEH (column 2) is lower than the exchange rate (column 3). This further implies that the reference economy has the highest price level for ICEH (columns 15 and 16). For the region, per capita nominal ICEH is HK$17,846, while per capita real ICEH is HK$30,933.

Rankings of the economies based on per capita real ICEH differ significantly from the rankings based on total real ICEH. By per capita real and nominal ICEH, the top ranked economies are Hong Kong, China; Singapore; Taipei,China; Malaysia; and Brunei Darussalam, as Figure 4.8 shows. The People's Republic of China has a somewhat lower rank of 14th compared to its rank based on per capita real GDP. India is ranked 17th based on per capita real ICEH, the same as its per capita rank for per capita real GDP.

Figure 4.8: Per Capita Real and Nominal Individual Consumption Expenditure by Households, 2017 (HK$)

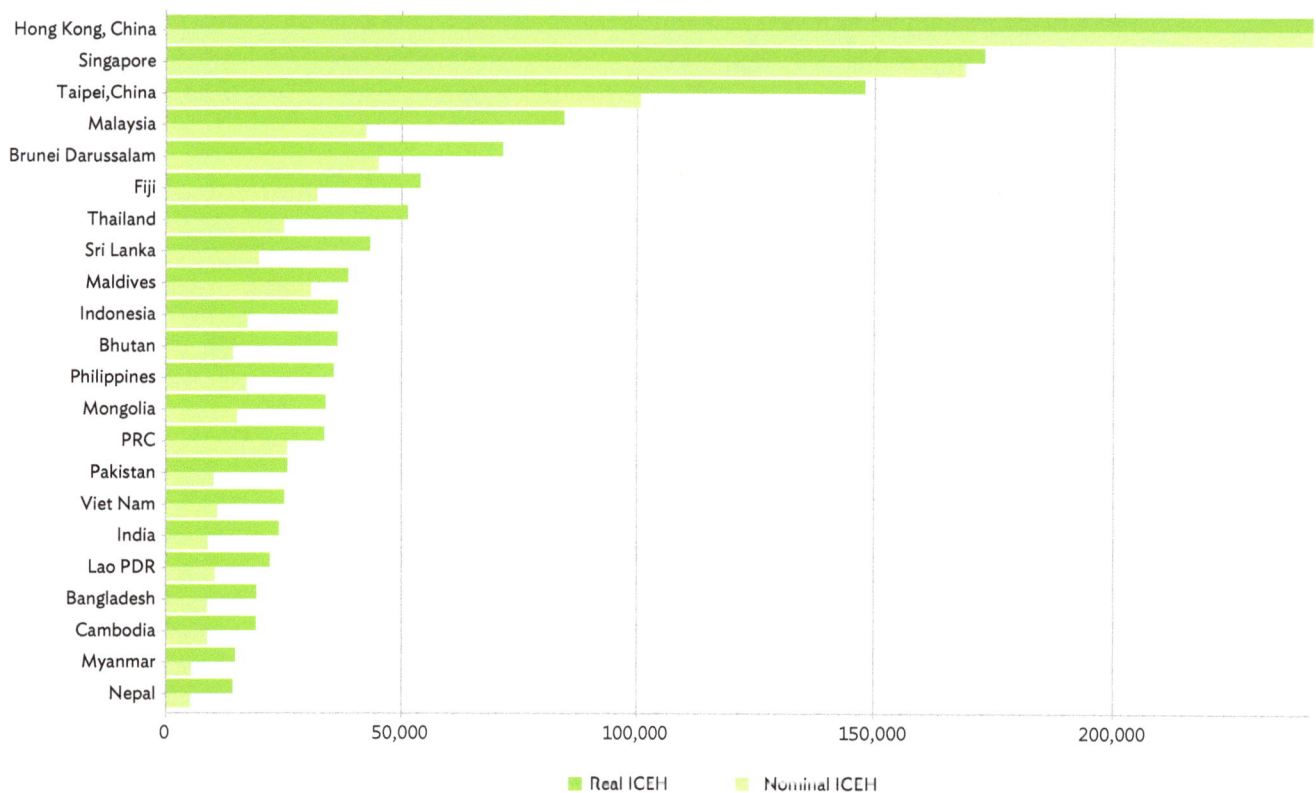

HK$ = Hong Kong dollar, ICEH = individual consumption expenditure by households, Lao PDR = Lao People's Democratic Republic, PRC = People's Republic of China.
Note: In this figure, individual consumption expenditure by households (ICEH) includes expenditures by nonprofit institutions serving households (NPISH).
Source: Table 4.2.

A comparison of the results in Table 4.1 and Table 4.2 respectively for GDP and ICEH suggests that there are economies where per capita GDP is high but per capita ICEH is relatively low. Figure 4.9 shows per capita real GDP and ICEH for the 22 participating economies. By definition, per capita ICEH is always lower than per capita GDP. However, from the figure it can be seen that per capita ICEH is significantly lower for Brunei Darussalam and Singapore. The People's Republic of China and Maldives follow a similar pattern, but of relatively lower magnitude. Economies with a significant trade balance or with large investment outlays in their GDPs, relatively have lower levels of ICEH. Economies with a large GFCF may have higher potential for future growth.

The many possible explanations for these differences require further analysis.

Actual Individual Consumption by Households

A comprehensive measure of goods and services consumed by the households is the actual individual consumption by households (AICH), which includes ICEH and NPISH on behalf of individuals, as well as government expenditure on behalf of households, or ICEG. Therefore, AICH is a better measure of material well-being than the overall GDP as this includes all goods and services consumed by the households to meet their individual consumption needs.

Figure 4.9: Per Capita Real Gross Domestic Product and Individual Consumption Expenditure by Households, 2017 (HK$)

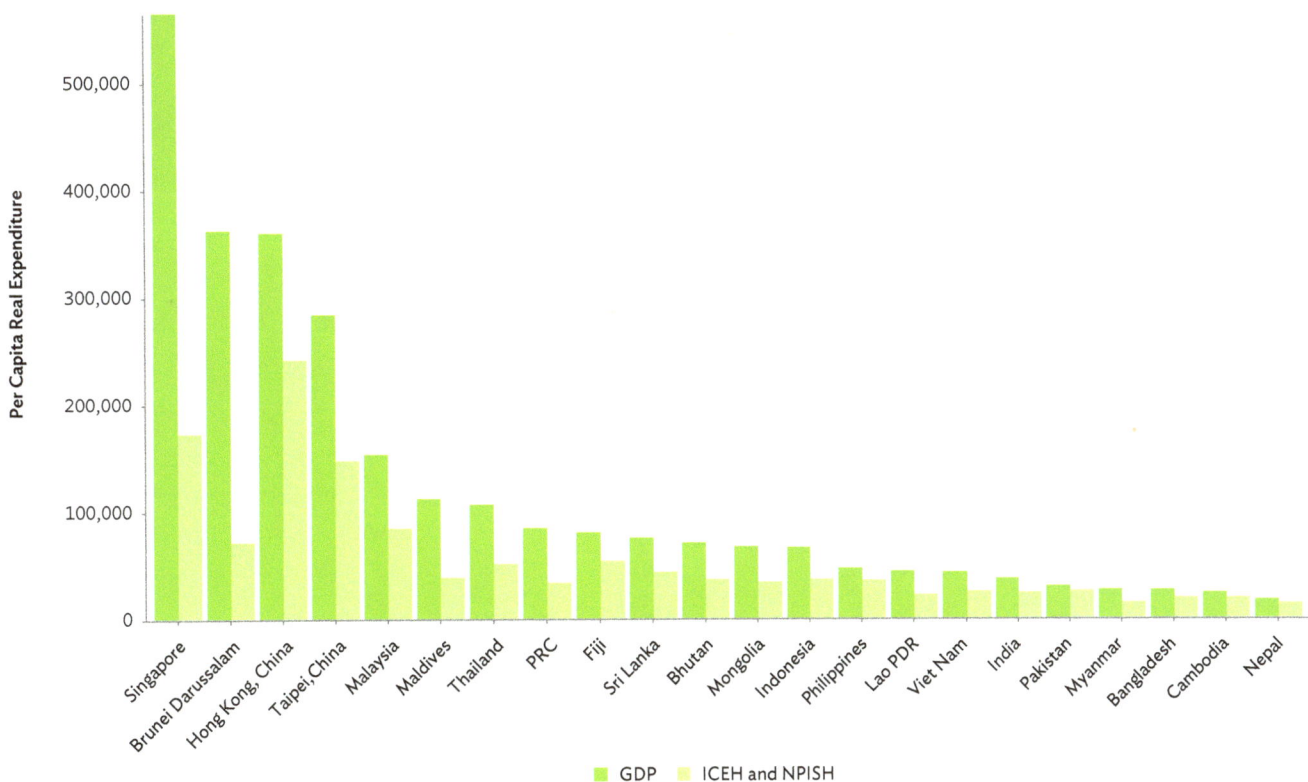

GDP = gross domestic product, HK$ = Hong Kong dollar, ICEH = individual consumption expenditure by households, Lao PDR = Lao People's Democratic Republic, NPISH = nonprofit institutions serving households, PRC = People's Republic of China.
Note: In this figure, individual consumption expenditure by households (ICEH) includes expenditures by nonprofit institutions serving households (NPISH).
Source: Tables 4.1 and 4.2.

Table 4.3 shows estimates of per capita real AICH for the participating economies.

The last column shows that the ratio (expressed as a percentage) of per capita real AICH to per capita real GDP varies from a very high of 92.29% to a low of 26.80%.[14] This ratio is likely to be high for low-income economies. The highest ratios are 92.29% in Pakistan, 88.72% in Cambodia, 86.29% in Nepal, and 83.29% in the Philippines. Brunei Darussalam has the lowest ratio of 26.80%, as expected for a resource-rich economy with a significant contribution from net exports to GDP. While Singapore has a low ratio of 34.09%; Hong Kong, China has a relatively higher ratio of 70.87%.

Table 4.3: Per Capita Real Actual Individual Consumption by Households, 2017
(Hong Kong, China as base)

Economy	Per Capita Real GDP	Per Capita Real AICH		Ratio of per Capita Real AICH to GDP
	Levels (HK$)	Levels (HK$)	Index (Asia and the Pacific =100)	
(1)	(2)	(3)	(4)	(5)
Bangladesh	26,401	20,301	57	76.89
Bhutan	70,855	43,196	122	60.96
Brunei Darussalam	362,379	97,121	274	26.80
Cambodia	23,853	21,161	60	88.72
China, People's Republic of	85,061	41,613	117	48.92
Fiji	80,772	60,057	169	74.35
Hong Kong, China	360,247	255,310	720	70.87
India	36,965	25,118	71	67.95
Indonesia	66,419	40,391	114	60.81
Lao People's Democratic Republic	43,944	25,055	71	57.02
Malaysia	153,532	95,858	270	62.43
Maldives	112,187	47,964	135	42.75
Mongolia	67,241	41,482	117	61.69
Myanmar	26,519	16,267	46	61.34
Nepal	17,431	15,041	42	86.29
Pakistan	29,905	27,599	78	92.29
Philippines	46,721	38,916	110	83.29
Singapore	564,960	192,614	543	34.09
Sri Lanka	75,587	51,965	146	68.75
Taipei,China	283,878	173,917	490	61.26
Thailand	106,892	62,106	175	58.10
Viet Nam	43,179	28,955	82	67.06
Asia and the Pacific	61,375	35,472	100	57.80

AICH = actual individual consumption by households, GDP = gross domestic product, HK$ = Hong Kong dollar.
Source: Asian Development Bank estimates.

---

14 A degree of caution needs to be exercised here as these aggregates are not additive; the sum of components of GDP in real terms do not add up to real GDP.

The Lorenz curves for real GDP, ICEH, and AICH show that the distribution of real ICEH and NPISH is more equal than the distribution of GDP and the distribution of AICH (Figure 4.10).

Figure 4.10: Lorenz Curves for Per Capita Real Gross Domestic Product and Per Capita Real Consumption by Households, 2017

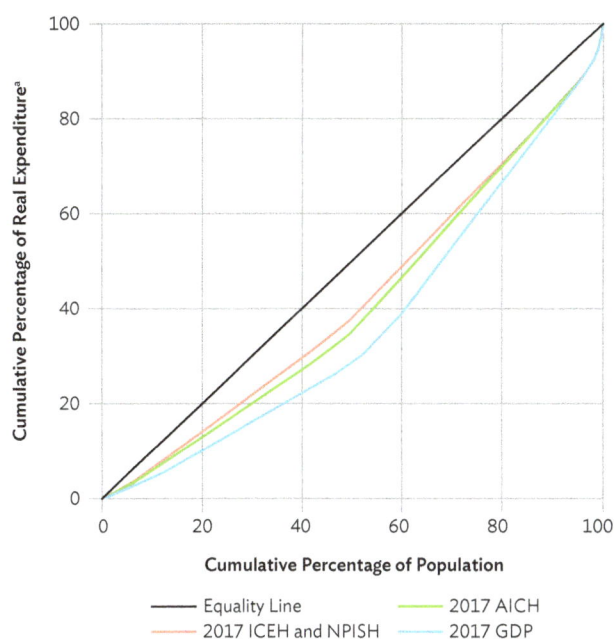

AICH = actual individual consumption by households, GDP = gross domestic product, ICEH = individual consumption expenditure by households, NPISH = nonprofit institutions serving households.
a Expenditure is represented by the economy-specific per capita expenditure (GDP, ICEH and NPISH, AICH.)
Source: Asian Development Bank estimates.

Government Final Consumption Expenditure

The government final consumption expenditure (GFCE) is the sum of ICEG on individual services such as health and education, and collective consumption expenditure by government on collective services such as general administration, defense, police, firefighting, and environmental protection. Comparative analysis of per capita real GFCE and its components provide useful insights into how different governments play different roles in their respective economies.

Table 4.4 presents PPPs, PLIs, and per capita (real and nominal) government expenditure for all the participating economies, with PPPs (column 2), which are generally quite low compared to exchange rates (column 3). PPPs for the general government are driven in large part by wages and salaries for government employees and, considering productivity differences across economies, adjustment factors were applied following Inklaar (2019) (see Appendix 1 for details). Despite adjusting for productivity levels of government employees in different economies, PPPs for government tend to be low compared with PPPs for GDP, and PLIs are accordingly low. The PLIs for all economies are lower than Hong Kong, China (set at 100). The lowest PLI of 17 belongs to Sri Lanka, followed by 19 for Bhutan, and 20 for Mongolia. Low PPPs for government imply relatively large per capita real expenditures. In terms of per capita real GFCE, Brunei Darussalam (HK$149,626) is the highest, followed by Singapore (HK$66,233) with less than half the per capita real GFCE of Brunei Darussalam. Brunei Darussalam's per capita real GFCE is almost 17 times that of region's per capita real GFCE.

Gross Fixed Capital Formation

GFCF is an important component of GDP from a policy perspective. GFCF represents investments, which comprises the acquisition and disposals of following categories of assets: machinery and equipment, construction, and other products. The 2017 ICP cycle introduced a few changes to the classification of GFCF components, combining the basic headings of "motor vehicles, trailers and semi-trailers" and "other road transport" of 2011 into a single basic heading, "road transport equipment," in 2017. In addition, the heading "other manufactured goods not elsewhere classified" of 2011 was combined with "other products" in 2017 (see Appendix 6, Figure A6.1).

Table 4.4: Summary Results for Government Final Consumption Expenditure, 2017
(Hong Kong, China as base)

Economy	PPPs (HK$ = 1.00)	Exchange Rates (HK$ = 1.00)	Expenditure (HK$ billion)		Expenditure per Capita (HK$)		Expenditure per Capita Indexes				Shares (Asia and the Pacific = 100.00)			PLIs		Reference Data	
			Based on PPPs	Based on XRs	Based on PPPs	Based on XRs	Asia and the Pacific = 100		HKG = 100		Expenditure		Population	Asia and the Pacific = 100	HKG = 100	Population (million)	Expenditure in LCU (billion)
							Based on PPPs	Based on XRs	Based on PPPs	Based on XRs	Based on PPPs	Based on XRs					
(1)	(2)	(3)	(4)	(5)	(6)	(7)	(8)	(9)	(10)	(11)	(12)	(13)	(14)	(15)	(16)	(17)	(18)
Bangladesh	4.11	10.32	318	127	1,966	783	22	14	6	2	0.94	0.60	4.27	64	40	161.80	1,308
Bhutan	1.62	8.36	17	3	22,991	4,453	258	80	65	13	0.05	0.02	0.02	31	19	0.73	27
Brunei Darussalam	0.07	0.18	64	25	149,626	58,267	1,680	1,046	423	165	0.19	0.12	0.01	62	39	0.43	4
Cambodia	183.79	519.75	41	15	2,592	917	29	16	7	3	0.12	0.07	0.42	57	35	15.85	7,552
China, People's Republic of	0.67	0.87	19,609	15,042	14,144	10,850	159	195	40	31	58.17	71.34	36.62	123	77	1,386.40	13,046
Fiji	0.13	0.27	15	7	17,113	8,176	192	147	48	23	0.04	0.03	0.02	76	48	0.88	2
Hong Kong, China	1.00	1.00	261	261	35,374	35,374	397	635	100	100	0.78	1.24	0.20	160	100	7.39	261
India	4.15	8.36	4,312	2,144	3,294	1,637	37	29	9	5	12.79	10.17	34.58	79	50	1,309.20	17,911
Indonesia	550.85	1,716.98	2,241	719	8,558	2,746	96	49	24	8	6.65	3.41	6.92	51	32	261.89	1,234,554
Lao People's Democratic Republic	236.96	1,071.64	88	20	12,806	2,832	144	51	36	8	0.26	0.09	0.18	35	22	6.90	20,941
Malaysia	0.23	0.55	712	298	22,237	9,319	250	167	63	26	2.11	1.42	0.85	67	42	32.02	165
Maldives	0.96	1.97	12	6	24,196	11,825	272	212	68	33	0.04	0.03	0.01	78	49	0.49	11
Mongolia	61.22	313.06	58	11	18,416	3,601	207	65	52	10	0.17	0.05	0.08	31	20	3.15	3,550
Myanmar	42.51	174.56	374	91	7,046	1,716	79	31	20	5	1.11	0.43	1.40	39	24	53.15	15,918
Nepal	5.05	13.41	59	22	2,035	766	23	14	6	2	0.17	0.10	0.76	60	38	28.83	296
Pakistan	5.27	13.53	727	283	3,649	1,420	41	26	10	4	2.16	1.34	5.26	62	39	199.11	3,827
Philippines	2.88	6.47	617	275	5,882	2,619	66	47	17	7	1.83	1.30	2.77	71	45	104.92	1,777
Singapore	0.13	0.18	372	277	66,233	49,384	744	887	187	140	1.10	1.31	0.15	119	75	5.61	49
Sri Lanka	3.26	19.56	347	58	16,177	2,696	182	48	46	8	1.03	0.27	0.57	27	17	21.44	1,131
Taipei,China	2.07	3.91	1,191	630	50,555	26,747	568	480	143	76	3.53	2.99	0.62	85	53	23.56	2,462
Thailand	1.67	4.36	1,487	569	21,978	8,414	247	151	62	24	4.41	2.70	1.79	61	38	67.65	2,479
Viet Nam	733.48	2,870.44	788	201	8,358	2,136	94	38	24	6	2.34	0.95	2.49	41	26	94.24	577,719
Asia and the Pacific	n.a.	n.a.	33,711	21,085	8,905	5,570	100	100	25	16	100.00	100.00	100.00	100	n.a.	3,785.65	n.a.

n.a. = not applicable; HK$ = Hong Kong dollar; HKG = Hong Kong, China; LCU = local currency unit; PLI = price level index; PPP = purchasing power parity; XR = exchange rate.
Note: Government compensation data for 2017 for Thailand is estimated by extrapolating government compensation data for 2011 with the deflator of government final consumption expenditure in accordance with the recommendations of the 2017 International Comparison Program Asia and the Pacific Experts Group and the Regional Advisory Board.
Sources: Asian Development Bank estimates. For exchange rates: International Monetary Fund. International Financial Statistics. http://data.imf.org/ (accessed 17 September 2019). Data for population refers to mid-year estimates supplied by the participating economies for the 2017 International Comparison Program.

Table 4.5 summarizes the results for GFCF. PPPs for GFCF are lower but relatively closer to exchange rates than what was observed for other aggregates. For the region, the per capita real GFCF (HK$19,795) is 36% higher than the nominal GFCF (HK$14,512). In comparison, the per capita real GDP (HK$61,375) is 56% higher than per capita nominal GDP (HK$39,326).

Table 4.5: Summary of Expenditure on Gross Fixed Capital Formation, 2017
(Hong Kong, China as base)

Economy	Population (thousand)	Exchange Rates (LCU per HK$)	Purchasing Power Parity (HK$ = 1.00)	Per Capita Nominal GFCF (HK$)	Per Capita Real GFCF (HK$)	Per Capita Real Expenditure Index (Asia and the Pacific=100)
(1)	(2)	(3)	(4)	(5)	(6)	(7)
Bangladesh	161,800	10.32	6.10	3,909	6,616	33
Bhutan	727	8.36	4.53	13,903	25,672	130
Brunei Darussalam	430	0.18	0.12	90,377	132,105	667
Cambodia	15,850	519.75	273.33	1,178	2,240	11
China, People's Republic of	1,386,395	0.87	0.74	29,253	34,209	173
Fiji	877	0.27	0.16	8,460	13,726	69
Hong Kong, China	7,392	1.00	1.00	77,924	77,924	394
India	1,309,200	8.36	3.86	4,315	9,339	47
Indonesia	261,891	1,716.98	830.33	9,720	20,099	102
Lao People's Democratic Republic	6,901	1,071.64	565.52	6,355	12,042	61
Malaysia	32,023	0.55	0.29	19,329	37,035	187
Maldives	492	1.97	1.26	32,266	50,477	255
Mongolia	3,149	313.06	166.96	6,968	13,066	66
Myanmar	53,150	174.56	71.07	2,861	7,026	35
Nepal	28,830	13.41	7.14	2,149	4,033	20
Pakistan	199,110	13.53	7.08	1,835	3,505	18
Philippines	104,921	6.47	3.85	5,826	9,799	50
Singapore	5,612	0.18	0.15	124,067	151,506	765
Sri Lanka	21,444	19.56	10.70	8,349	15,270	77
Taipei,China	23,560	3.91	2.93	38,947	51,992	263
Thailand	67,654	4.36	2.34	11,906	22,173	112
Viet Nam	94,240	2,870.44	1,497.52	4,401	8,435	43
Asia and the Pacific	3,785,647	n.a.	n.a.	14,512	19,795	100

n.a. = not applicable, GFCF = gross fixed capital formation, HK$ = Hong Kong dollar, LCU = local currency unit.
Sources: Asian Development Bank estimates. For exchange rates: International Monetary Fund. International Financial Statistics. http://data.imf.org/ (accessed 17 September 2019).
Data for population refers to mid-year estimates supplied by the participating economies for the 2017 International Comparison Program.

Shares of real and nominal GFCFs of the economies in the GFCF of Asia and the Pacific are shown in Figure 4.11. Twelve economies shown in Figure 4.11 account for nearly 99.0% of the share of GFCF in the region with 10 smaller economies accounting for only about 1.0% share. The nominal share for the People's Republic of China is greater than its real share. In both nominal and real terms, the People's Republic of China's share is quite high, and is more than 60% of the GFCF for the region. Though India is second ranked in GFCF share, its share in real GFCF is roughly one-fourth of the share of the People's Republic of China; and in nominal terms India's share is only about 14% of the share of the People's Republic of China. Indonesia, ranked third, has a greater share than Taipei,China and other middle- to high-income economies.

Figure 4.11: Nominal and Real Shares for Gross Fixed Capital Formation, 2017 (%)

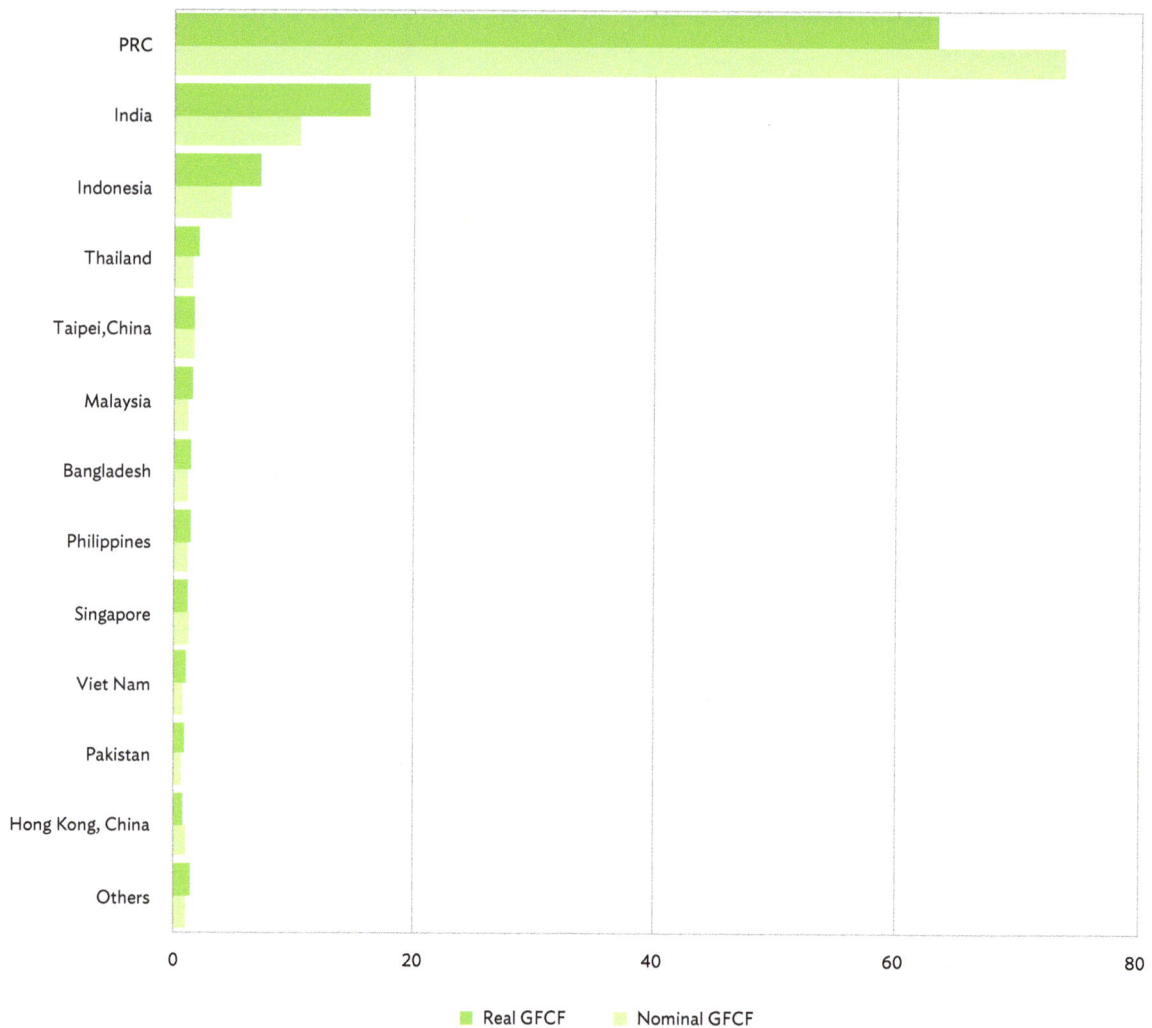

GFCF = Gross Fixed Capital Formation, PRC = People's Republic of China.
Source: Asian Development Bank estimates.

5. Consistency between the 2011 and 2017 Comparisons

This chapter examines consistency of the 2017 International Comparison Program (ICP) results with the 2011 ICP results. In order to provide a meaningful comparison with results from the 2017 ICP, it was considered necessary to revise the 2011 ICP results by taking into account: revisions in national accounts data; minor changes in classification used in 2017; and minor refinements to methodology introduced during the 2017 ICP cycle. The next section explains the process of updating and revising the 2011 ICP results. The last section examines consistency by comparing results from the 2017 benchmark with extrapolations from the revised 2011 results derived using appropriate indicators.

Updating and Revising the 2011 Cycle Results

The ICP primarily uses data on annual average prices of a basket of goods and services, gross domestic product (GDP) broken down by 155 expenditure basic headings, and to a lesser degree, population data compiled by the participating economies. As 2011 ICP price comparisons reflect prices in 2011, the price data used in estimating the purchasing power parities (PPPs) for the basic headings remain fixed. Thus, the major sources for the 2011 update are revised population data, revised expenditure data at the GDP and basic heading levels, changes in basic headings used for reference PPPs, refinements introduced in 2017 to productivity adjustment methodology for government compensation, and the effects of those changes on comparisons of government compensation.

Revisions to population and gross domestic product data. Table 5.1 shows the revisions in the population and GDP estimates for 2011. Generally, population data remains stable and is revised only when new information from a more recent population census or a demographic survey serves as the basis for adjusting or revising population estimates. Changes in population size do not affect the PPPs but obviously do affect per capita figures.

Revisions to the population figures for 2011 are minimal for most of the economies, except for a big spike in the population of Maldives, due to a revised counting system where expatriates are now included in the resident population, and a downward revision of population in Myanmar based on new data from the Population and Housing Census of 2014—the first population census held in 30 years.

REVISIONS IN 2011 ICP RESULTS

- Revised population data
- Revised expenditure data at the GDP and basic heading levels
- Refinements made to productivity adjustment methodology in 2017
- Changes in basic headings used for reference PPPs

Table 5.1 also reflects revisions in the estimates of GDP for economies participated in the 2011 ICP Asia and the Pacific. Most of the observed revisions are upward and some economies have reported significant changes to GDP estimates and the underlying structure. Maldives has the biggest upward revision, about 28%, mainly due to rebasing and implementing the 2008 System of National Accounts, along with improved methodology and data sources. Other economies with revisions exceeding 5% are Brunei Darussalam, Fiji, the Lao People's Democratic Republic, Indonesia, and Sri Lanka. GDP revisions stem from a range of

factors, including implementation of the 2008 System of National Accounts, reclassifications in national accounts, more exhaustive coverage of the economy, and more importantly, new input data from various censuses, including economic censuses and household and enterprise surveys in different economies.

Revisions due to changes in productivity adjustment methodology. During the 2017 ICP cycle, the Technical Advisory Group and the Inter-Agency Coordination Group considered the methodology proposed in Inklaar and Timmer (2013a) and the practical proposal

Table 5.1: Comparison of Original and Revised Population, Gross Domestic Product, Productivity Adjustment Factors, and Purchasing Power Parities, 2011

Economy	Population (thousands)			GDP in LCU (billions)			Productivity Adjustment Factors (HKG=1.00)			Purchasing Power Parities (HK$=1.00)		
	Original	Revised	Ratio of Revised to Original	Original	Revised	Ratio of Revised to Original	ADB (revised) Method	Inklaar Method	Ratio of Inklaar to ADB	Original	Revised	Ratio of Revised to Original
(1)	(2)	(3)	(4)	(5)	(6)	(7)	(8)	(9)	(10)	(11)	(12)	(13)
Bangladesh	149,700	149,700	1.00	9,703	9,855	1.02	0.33	0.21	0.62	4.24	4.47	1.06
Bhutan	708	680	0.96	86	85	0.99	0.72	0.44	0.61	3.09	3.13	1.02
Brunei Darussalam	393	393	1.00	21	23	1.11	1.30	1.21	0.93	0.13	0.13	1.03
Cambodia	14,226	14,307	1.01	52,069	52,069	1.00	0.26	0.12	0.48	246.65	262.06	1.06
China, People's Republic of	1,341,981	1,344,130	1.00	47,310	48,930	1.03	0.66	0.39	0.59	0.64	0.67	1.05
Fiji	854	854	1.00	7	7	1.09	0.68	0.32	0.47	0.19	0.18	0.95
Hong Kong, China	7,072	7,072	1.00	1,936	1,934	1.00	1.00	1.00	1.00	1.00	1.00	1.00
India	1,215,957	1,216,147	1.00	86,993	85,256	0.98	0.48	0.30	0.62	2.77	2.97	1.07
Indonesia	241,038	241,991	1.00	7,422,781	7,831,726	1.06	0.65	0.49	0.75	660.35	671.29	1.02
Lao People's Democratic Republic	6,385	6,117	0.96	64,727	71,544	1.11	0.41	0.20	0.49	451.84	509.59	1.13
Macau, China	557	553	0.99	295	294	1.00	1.13	1.08	0.96	0.84	0.85	1.01
Malaysia	28,964	29,062	1.00	884	912	1.03	0.81	0.58	0.71	0.27	0.28	1.05
Maldives	325	406	1.25	32	41	1.28	0.37	0.36	1.00	1.56	1.50	0.96
Mongolia	2,679	2,786	1.04	12,547	13,174	1.05	0.64	0.49	0.76	98.35	101.97	1.04
Myanmar	60,380	49,663	0.82	45,128	43,900	0.97	0.34	0.12	0.35	43.02	50.03	1.16
Nepal	26,494	26,490	1.00	1,450	1,441	0.99	0.24	0.14	0.58	4.51	4.83	1.07
Pakistan	177,110	177,100	1.00	19,188	19,161	1.00	0.39	0.24	0.62	4.46	4.77	1.07
Philippines	94,185	94,185	1.00	9,706	9,708	1.00	0.50	0.33	0.66	3.27	3.46	1.06
Singapore	5,184	5,184	1.00	334	351	1.05	1.14	1.08	0.95	0.16	0.16	0.99
Sri Lanka	20,869	20,195	0.97	6,543	7,219	1.10	0.63	0.46	0.72	7.08	7.51	1.06
Taipei,China	23,225	23,190	1.00	13,709	14,312	1.04	1.02	0.72	0.70	2.77	2.90	1.05
Thailand	67,597	66,214	0.98	11,121	11,307	1.02	0.67	0.48	0.73	2.26	2.37	1.05
Viet Nam	87,840	88,110	1.00	2,779,880	2,779,880	1.00	0.43	0.20	0.45	1,228.43	1,321.50	1.08

ADB = Asian Development Bank; GDP = gross domestic product; HK$ = Hong Kong dollar; HKG = Hong Kong, China; LCU = local currency unit.
Source: Asian Development Bank estimates.

for productivity adjustment made by Inklaar (2019) and recommended that the methodology proposed by Inklaar (2019) be used uniformly at the regional level and for global linking. The Inklaar methodology introduces further refinements to the methodology used by the Asian Development Bank (ADB) in 2011. In particular, the Inklaar approach provides productivity adjustment factors that are transitive and base invariant. The second refinement concerns data: Inklaar's estimates are based on improved estimates of capital stock (in PPP terms) and economically meaningful labor shares. The ADB approach in the 2011 ICP cycle used only three levels for labor shares—0.5, 0.6 and 0.7—for three different groups of participating economies divided based on per capita real GDP. In contrast, Inklaar's approach provides properly estimated and calibrated labor shares for individual economies. Upon the recommendation of the Regional Advisory Board, the regional implementing agency (RIA) for Asia and the Pacific implemented the Inklaar method for productivity adjustments in the 2017 ICP cycle as well as for updating adjustment factors in the compilation of revised 2011 ICP results. For further details of the Inklaar methodology, see Appendix 1. The effect of this shift in methodology on productivity adjustment factors for 2011 is shown in Table 5.1.

Table 5.1 shows significant revisions to productivity adjustment factors of 2011, expressed relative to Hong Kong, China. Productivity in most economies is lower under the Inklaar methodology (column 9) than in the estimates used by ADB in 2011 (column 8), with the exception of Maldives, where the change is negligible. For many economies, productivity estimates were revised significantly downward. These revisions imply higher price levels and lower real government expenditures. This downward revisions in real government expenditure in turn affected a downward revision in the real GDP for these economies. The refined methodology for productivity adjustment is used for 2011 revisions as well as for 2017, thus, ensuring consistency for comparison across the two benchmarks.

Revisions to purchasing power parities in 2011. The basic price data that underpins the computation and revision of PPPs for 2011 remain unchanged. Therefore, any revisions to 2011 PPPs stem from changes in national accounts data (which alters the weighting structure), adoption of refinements to productivity adjustment, and changes in the 2017 ICP (applied to 2011 as well) for some reference basic headings. From Table 5.1, it is clear that adopting Inklaar data and methodology has resulted in an upward adjustment in PPPs for the regional economies. Table 5.1 also presents the ratio of revised 2011 PPPs to the original PPPs at the GDP level (column 13). As expected, due to upward revisions in the PPPs for government final consumption expenditure (GFCE), revised PPPs for GDP are greater than the original PPPs for most of the economies, with the exception of Fiji, Maldives, and Singapore. Maldives was not affected by changes to productivity adjustment methodology. For Myanmar and the Lao People's Democratic Republic, under Inklaar methodology, PPPs were revised significantly upward, more than 10%, and productivity was revised significantly downward. The PPPs for Maldives were revised downward, mainly because of GDP revisions in national accounts, because the productivity adjustment factor did not change significantly under the new approach.

Consistency between the 2017 Cycle and Extrapolations from Revised 2011 Benchmark Comparisons

Given the considerable lags between successive benchmarks for the ICP—six years between the 2005, 2011, and 2017 cycles—users of PPPs tend to extrapolate PPPs from one ICP cycle until the results from the next cycle become available. Users, analysts, and international organizations who need PPPs on an annual basis are likely to extrapolate the 2011 results for the years between 2011 and 2017 and beyond, using relevant indicators to update PPPs for different aggregates. For example, PPPs at the GDP level are likely to be extrapolated using GDP deflators, whereas PPPs for individual consumption expenditure by households (ICEH) are likely to be extrapolated using consumer price index (CPI) movements over time. This type of extrapolation is perfectly defensible and represents common practice.

When the new set of PPPs is released for a new benchmark year, the new PPPs and real expenditures can be compared with extrapolations from the previous benchmark. Users expect consistency between the extrapolated and the benchmark PPPs. At the release of 2005 results, analysts were surprised at the big systematic upward revisions of PPPs compared to extrapolations from benchmark. Similarly, there was considerable discussion when the 2011 benchmark PPPs represented a significant systematic downward shift in PPPs compared to extrapolations from 2005.

Divergence between benchmark and extrapolated PPPs is to be expected on several grounds especially when there is a long gap between two benchmarks. McCarthy (2013) offers several reasons for such divergence: differences in baskets of goods and services used for ICP and the deflators used in extrapolation; different index number methods and computational schemes; differences in weighting patterns; and differences in the changes in the structure of economies over time in comparison with the structure of reference economy. Also, as the economy becomes richer, the quality of goods and services priced in 2017 compared with the quality of well-known products in 2011 might be higher, leading to "quality creep" in comparison over time. Thus, for example, a well-known brand specification for trousers is likely to have higher quality in 2017 compared with the quality of the same brand of trousers priced in 2011. In addition, major changes in the methodology used for the ICP are also likely to produce discernible differences in

PPPs. Inklaar and Rao (2017) demonstrated that once they accounted for differences in the methodology—by constructing a counterfactual for 2005 using 2005 data but 2011 methodology—no systematic differences were evident between the 2005 and 2011 benchmarks. The methodology, however, remained stable between the 2017 ICP cycle and the revised 2011 ICP.

The reliability of extrapolated PPPs hinges heavily on the quality of indicators used in the extrapolation process. Further, differences in the treatment of net exports in the ICP and in national accounts may also cause major divergence in the case of economies with large net exports, because the ICP uses exchange rates as the PPPs for net exports, whereas national accounts use deflators derived from export and import prices for deflating net exports. Thus, users should exercise caution when there is divergence between extrapolated and benchmark PPPs and real expenditures.

Are the results from the 2017 ICP cycle broadly consistent with extrapolations from 2011? Here comparisons between actual and extrapolated PPPs for 2011 are presented only for the GDP and ICEH for which GDP deflators and CPIs are respectively used for extrapolating 2011 revised PPPs to 2017.

Figure 5.1 shows that there are differences, sizable in some instances, between the actual and extrapolated PPPs for GDP, but there are no systematic patterns in these differences. In the low- to middle-income level, some economies have actual 2017 PPP estimates that are higher than extrapolations from revised 2011; in other cases, the estimates are lower. For Hong Kong, China, by definition, there is no difference. The differences are small for Singapore and Taipei,China, possibly because of the reliability of their GDP deflators and high data quality in these economies. These various differences notwithstanding, there is no systematic pattern in the differences with ratios being scattered randomly above and below 1.

Figure 5.1: Ratio of 2017 Purchasing Power Parities for Gross Domestic Product to Extrapolations from 2011 (Revised)

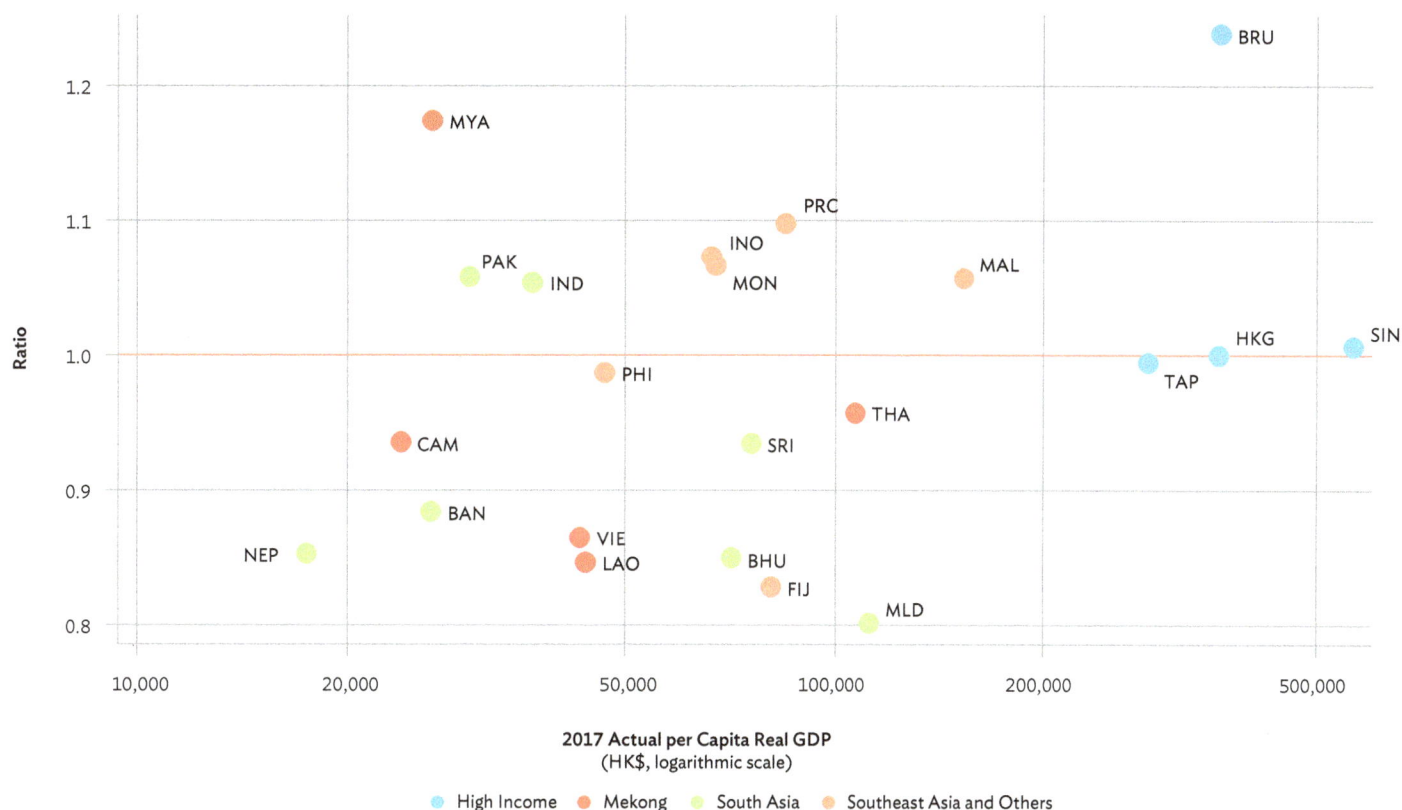

BAN = Bangladesh; BHU = Bhutan; BRU = Brunei Darussalam; CAM = Cambodia; FIJ = Fiji; GDP = gross domestic product; HK$ = Hong Kong dollar; HKG = Hong Kong, China; IND = India; INO = Indonesia; LAO = Lao People's Democratic Republic; MAL = Malaysia; MLD = Maldives; MON = Mongolia; MYA = Myanmar; NEP = Nepal; PAK = Pakistan; PHI = Philippines; PRC = People's Republic of China; SIN = Singapore; SRI = Sri Lanka; TAP = Taipei,China; THA = Thailand; VIE = Viet Nam.
Source: Asian Development Bank estimates.

A similar conclusion emerges in the case of extrapolations of PPPs for ICEH presented in Figure 5.2. These figures again show no systematic patterns in the differences between the actual and extrapolated PPPs and real expenditures. While the differences are scattered randomly above and below 1, low income economies show higher variability, possibly reflecting the reliability of the CPI or national accounts deflators used for extrapolations. Further, in many low-income economies, the CPI focuses on capital cities or urban areas, whereas coverage for the ICP is economy-wide.

Overall, the PPPs for GDP and ICEH, the two key aggregates, estimated from the 2017 ICP cycle are broadly consistent with extrapolations from 2011, with no systematic patterns observed.

**Figure 5.2: Ratio of 2017 Purchasing Power Parities to Extrapolations
from 2011 (Revised) for Individual Consumption Expenditures by Households**

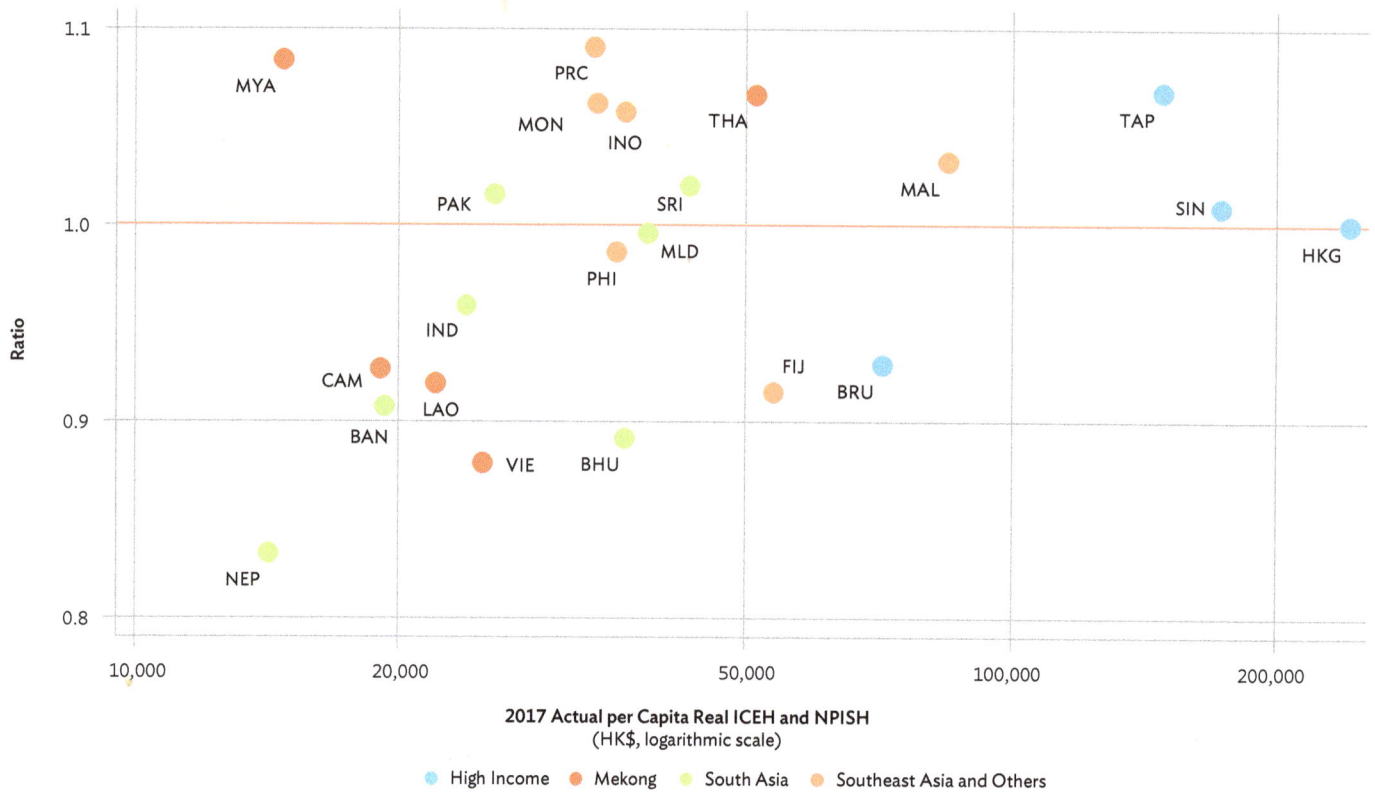

BAN = Bangladesh; BHU = Bhutan; BRU = Brunei Darussalam; CAM = Cambodia; FIJ = Fiji; HK$ = Hong Kong dollars; HKG = Hong Kong, China; ICEH = individual consumption expenditure for households; IND = India; INO = Indonesia; LAO = Lao People's Democratic Republic; MAL = Malaysia; MLD = Maldives; MON = Mongolia; MYA = Myanmar; NEP = Nepal; NPISH = nonprofit institutions serving households; PAK = Pakistan; PHI = Philippines; PRC = People's Republic of China; SIN = Singapore; SRI = Sri Lanka; TAP = Taipei,China; THA = Thailand; VIE = Viet Nam.
Note: Individual consumption expenditure by households (ICEH) includes expenditure by nonprofit institutions serving households (NPISH).
Source: Asian Development Bank estimates.

6. Summary and Future Directions

The 2017 International Comparison Program (ICP) in Asia and the Pacific produced a wealth of information on the state of the economies in the region. Estimates of purchasing power parities of currencies, price levels, PPP-converted (real) gross domestic product and its components, combined with the results at a more detailed level provide ample information for researchers and government policy makers. This chapter summarizes key results and lessons learned and discusses future directions for the ICP in the region.

Key Results and Conclusions

The 2017 ICP followed the same methodology as in 2011 albeit with minor refinements (see Chapter 5). All the results reported here use Hong Kong dollar as the reference currency and Hong Kong, China as the base economy. The total GDP, in real (or PPP) terms, for the 22 participating economies in 2017 ICP in Asia and the Pacific is HK$232.34 trillion. Major contributors to the total size of the economy of the region are the People's Republic of China, India, and

Figure 6.1: Economy Shares of Real Gross Domestic Product and its Main Components, 2017 (%)

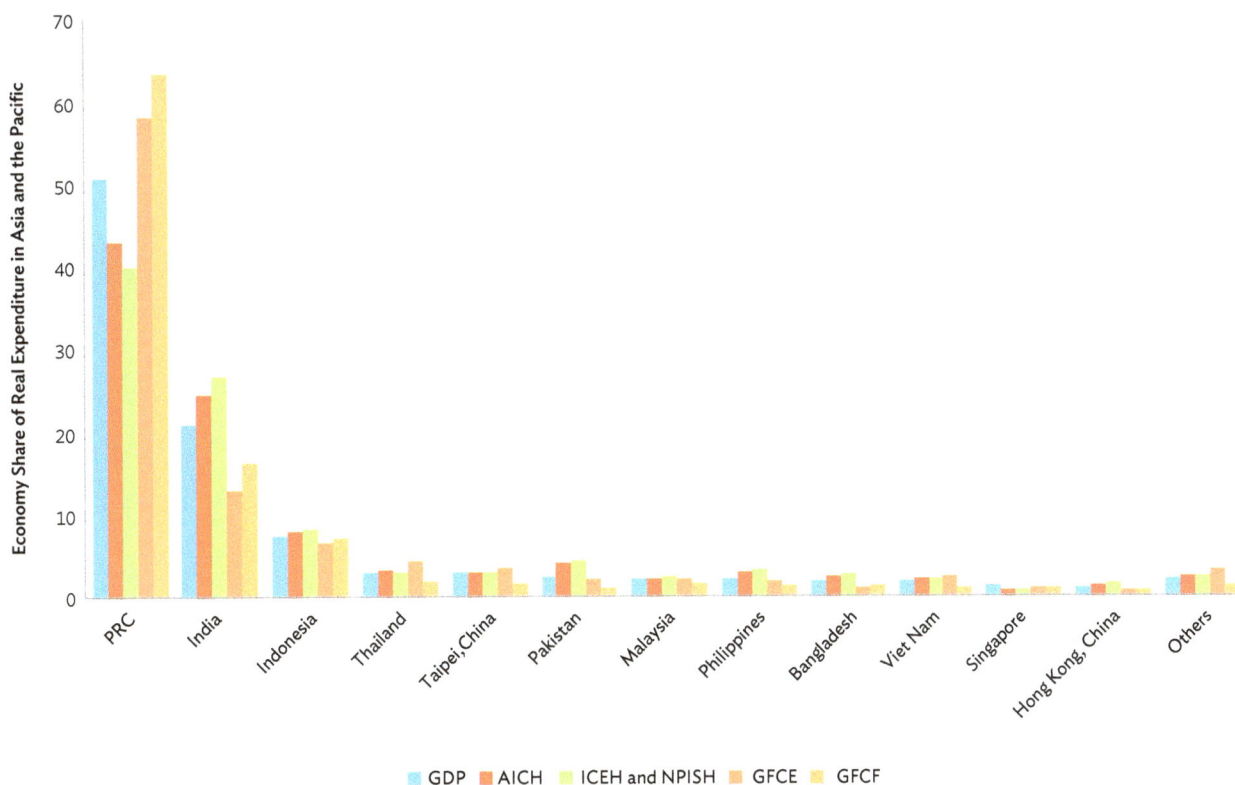

AICH = actual individual consumption expenditure by households, GDP = gross domestic product, GFCE = government final consumption expenditure, GFCF = gross fixed capital formation, ICEH = individual consumption expenditure by households, NPISH = nonprofit institutions serving households, PRC= People's Republic of China.
Source: Asian Development Bank estimates.

Indonesia. These economies are also the three most populous economies in the region. In terms of size of real GDP, the economies in the region exhibit a large range. Figure 6.1 presents the percentage shares of the top 12 economies and others for total real GDP, individual consumption expenditure by households (ICEH), actual individual consumption by households (AICH), government final consumption expenditure (GFCE), and gross fixed capital formation (GFCF). The People's Republic of China is the largest economy, with 50.76% share in the regional real GDP, with India ranking second at 20.83% and Indonesia third at 7.49%. The top 12 economies account for nearly 98.0%, while the other 10 have a combined share of about 2.0% of real GDP in the region. The rankings of the top and bottom economies remain the same whether the size of the economy is measured in real or nominal terms. A similar picture and rankings emerge for the components of GDP namely, AICH, ICEH, GFCE, and GFCF, with the People's Republic of China, India, and Indonesia, in that order, dominating the real expenditures. Hong Kong, China and Singapore are ranked sixth and seventh largest when GDP is measured in nominal terms but slip down to 12th and 11th respectively when GDP is measured in real terms.

Figure 6.2 shows per capita real GDP which exhibits significant diversity among the participating economies. The per capita real income of Singapore, which is highest in the region, is more than 32 times that of Nepal, which has the lowest per capita real GDP. The three largest economies in terms of overall

Figure 6.2: Per Capita Real Gross Domestic Product and its Main Components, 2017

(Hong Kong, China as base)

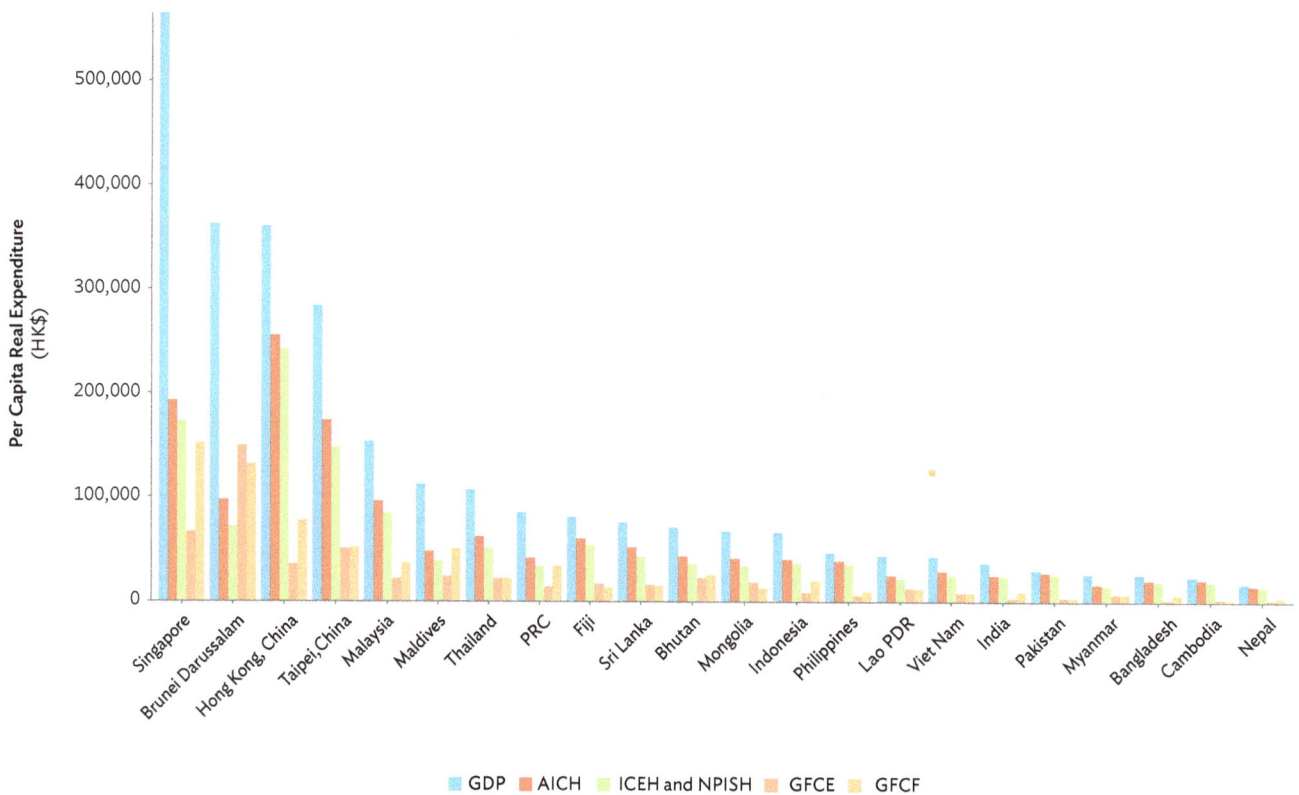

AICH = actual individual consumption expenditure by households, GDP = gross domestic product, GFCE = government final consumption expenditure, GFCF = gross fixed capital formation, HK$ = Hong Kong dollar, ICEH = individual consumption expenditure by households, Lao PDR = Lao People's Democratic Republic, NPISH = nonprofit institutions serving households, PRC = People's Republic of China.
Source: Asian Development Bank estimates.

GDP also have large populations, resulting in lower ranks in terms of their per capita real GDP: the People's Republic of China is 8th, Indonesia is 13th, and India is 17th among the 22 economies. Singapore has the highest per capita real GDP at HK$564,960, followed by Brunei Darussalam (HK$362,379); Hong Kong, China (HK$360,247); and Taipei,China (HK$283,878). At the other end of the spectrum, the economies with the lowest per capita real GDP are Nepal (HK$17,431), Cambodia (HK$23,853), Bangladesh (HK$26,401), and Myanmar (HK$26,519). While Singapore has a per capita real GDP that is 1.5 times that of Hong Kong, China, the per capita AICH for Hong Kong, China is 1.3 times that of Singapore, indicating higher consumption for households in

Hong Kong, China. Singapore, on the other hand, has much higher per capita expenditures on GFCF, almost twice that of Hong Kong, China.

The price level indexes (PLI) in Figure 6.3 exhibit several patterns depending on the aggregate under consideration. First, the price level for Hong Kong, China is always the highest among the 22 participating economies for all the aggregates; this implies that PPPs for all the aggregates of the other 21 economies are less than their respective exchange rates. Second, the PLIs for GDP and ICEH tend to be quite similar—this reflects the fact that ICEH is a major component of GDP.[15] The PLI for government expenditure for almost all the economies is lower than

Figure 6.3: Price Level Indexes for Gross Domestic Product and Its Main Components, 2017
(Hong Kong, China = 100)

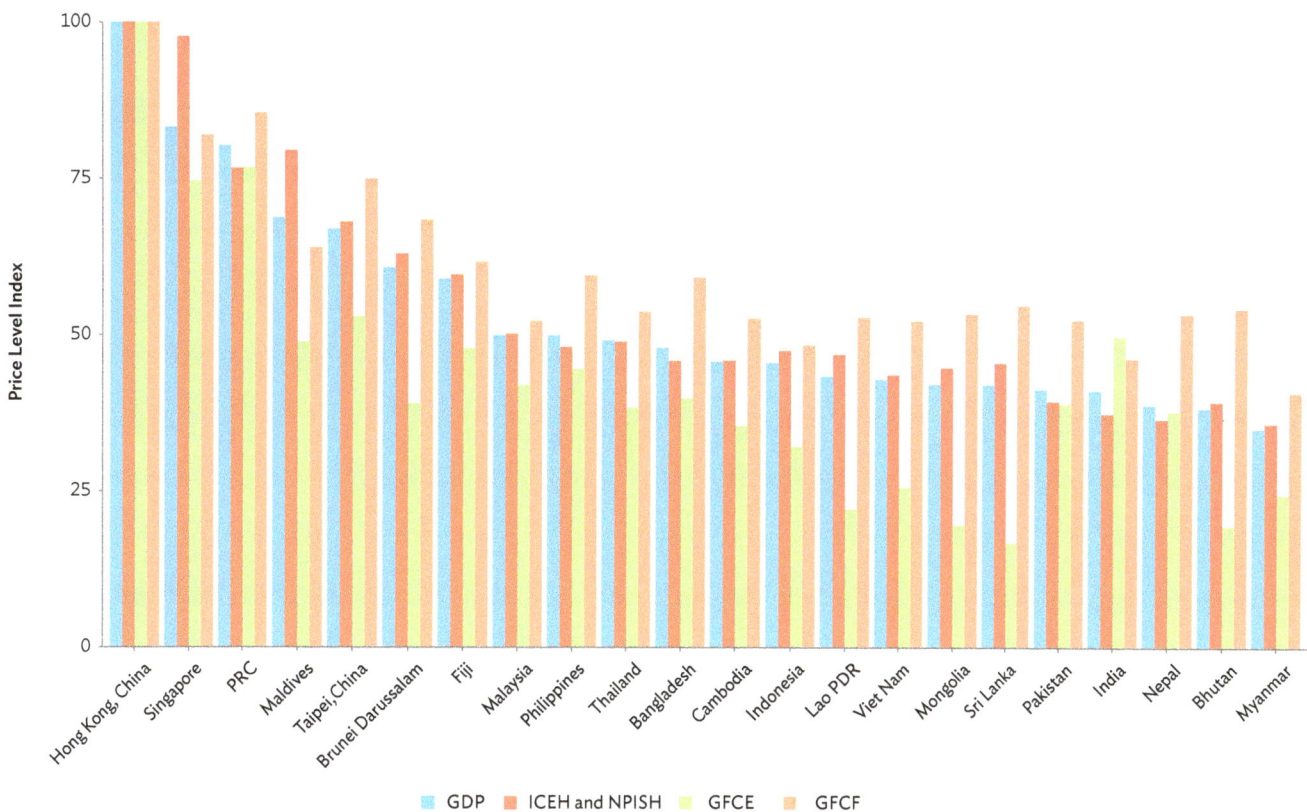

GDP = gross domestic product, GFCE = government final consumption expenditure, GFCF = gross fixed capital formation, ICEH = individual consumption expenditure by households, Lao PDR = Lao People's Democratic Republic, NPISH = nonprofit institutions serving households, PRC= People's Republic of China.
Source: Asian Development Bank estimates.

---

15   In Figure 6.3, ICEH includes expenditures by nonprofit institutions serving households (NPISH).

the PLI for GDP, which reflects significant differences in wages and salaries for government compensation and low salaries in low-income economies. Third, the PLI for GFCF is above the PLI for GDP and ICEH for all the economies except for Hong Kong, China; Maldives; and Singapore. Price levels for machinery and equipment are likely to be close to one because most products priced under machinery and equipment are internationally traded. The People's Republic of China has consistently high PLIs relative to what may be expected for a middle-income economy.

The availability of results from the 2011 (revised) and the 2017 cycles—both calculated using the same methods—makes it possible to check consistency of the 2017 actual results with extrapolations from the 2011 benchmark (revised) results. While divergence between benchmark and extrapolated PPPs is expected for several reasons, the general finding is that the 2017 results are broadly consistent and observed differences between actual and extrapolated PPPs are random and do not exhibit any systematic pattern.

The reader is advised to refer to the main report for 2017 ICP in Asia and the Pacific for further details on the conceptual framework and governance of the ICP; item selection and price surveys; data validation procedures; special methods used in dealing with comparison resistant services such as dwellings, and government compensation; index number methods used in aggregating price data collected; and procedures for linking Asia and the Pacific with the rest of the world.

Lessons from 2017

At the Regional Level

Regional workshops. Through bilateral consultations with economies and through the regional workshops, ADB strengthened (i) statistical capacity in conducting ICP price surveys, (ii) rigorous data validation that

improved the quality of data for PPP estimation, and (iii) knowledge on estimating GDP expenditures for the required 155 basic heading weights at the economy level.

One of the major achievements in ICP implementation is the camaraderie and friendship built through personal interaction during the regional meetings, which was crucial in collectively achieving the milestones of this large and intensive statistical undertaking and fostered a culture of learning from each other's experiences.

Rigorous data mining with the cooperation of the national implementing agencies. At the regional level, ADB noted that rigorous data mining from (i) existing censuses and surveys and (ii) administrative data allowed implementing agencies to collect complete and high quality data on indicators of quantity and quality for dwelling surveys. Thus, ADB encouraged the economies to search for all possible sources of data from various housing censuses and surveys, such as the Demographic and Health Survey, Household Socio Economic Survey, Living Standards and Measurement Survey, Living Standards Survey, Multiple Indicator Cluster Survey, National Family Health Survey, National Sample Survey, and Social Indicator Sample Survey. At the same time, ADB rigorously validated the housing rental survey data to create good quality and comparable rental prices for the list of dwellings. These high-quality datasets led to successful research that developed an improved methodology for comparison of dwelling services in the region. With the positive recommendations from the Technical Advisory Group and Regional Advisory Board, the new methodology will be implemented in the 2020 ICP cycle and will replace the reference volume approach currently used.

Not all participating economies used the Classification of Individual Consumption According to Purpose. In Asia and the Pacific, price survey operations for household products started in April 2017 in 14 economies and during May–July 2017 in the remaining eight participating economies. Because the prices collected did not represent the prices for calendar year 2017, average item prices for the 12-month collection period were converted to 2017 annual average prices for PPP computation using monthly basic heading-level (or the closest aggregate available) consumer price indexes (CPIs).

Toward this end, ADB developed an approach for adjusting the prices to the 2017 calendar year, using monthly price indexes from the CPI to meet the PPP computation requirements for 2017 calendar year average prices. This exercise revealed that many economies still have not adopted the Classification of Individual Consumption According to Purpose. More standardization of CPIs is needed when economies undertake any CPI revisions in future. Similar issues exist in the GDP expenditures on housing services, where estimation methods need to be improved and data gaps must be addressed.

Guiding principles in 2017 and previous cycles. As in the 2005 and 2011 rounds, the guiding principles in implementing the 2017 ICP have been transparency, ownership, and bottom-up approach. These principles are fundamental to the success of the ICP in Asia and the Pacific.

At the Economy Level

Best practices applied to consumer price index methods. The ICP helped build capacity in economies that are now adopting best practices from ICP to improve their CPI whenever there is a base year revision exercise. Maldives is already integrating the use of structured product descriptions in revising CPI product baskets, while Thailand has indicated it will use structured product descriptions for CPI price collection. Bangladesh plans to include those ICP items (along with structured product descriptions) that are important to them in their CPI price collection. Further, ICP data validation procedures are also being applied in the CPI price validation. These help in fostering greater synergy between CPI and ICP operations, while also improving CPIs.

The inclusion of ICP items in the CPI item list or use of CPI prices for matching ICP products greatly facilitated ICP price collection in some economies and led to a greater integration of ICP and CPI activities.

Continued participation over several cycles among national teams. ICP teams from the participating economies have continued to participate in several ICP rounds, leading to more efficient ICP operations at the economy level. The experience that these teams gained in implementing the ICP at regular intervals maintained the momentum in ICP implementation at the economy level. The shorter 3-year cycle introduced since the 2017 ICP cycle will help strengthen institutional and technical capacity and enable the implementing agencies in the economies to carry out the 2020 ICP and future rounds.

Machinery and equipment and construction price surveys. Local experts provided highly valuable assistance in collecting prices for machinery, equipment, and construction in some economies. Meanwhile, some specified models of machinery and equipment items were difficult to find, especially in smaller economies, and in some cases more popular and up-to-date models for electronic products were available for pricing. Because the ICP requires pricing of exact matches in equipment for price comparison, for future ICP rounds it is desirable to consider a wider range of comparable models for equipment items. The guidance and recommendations of the international experts on price validations and specifications of construction and machinery and equipment items helped the economies substantially improve quality of their data.

Future Directions

As the 2017 ICP cycle in Asia and the Pacific is drawing to a conclusion, ADB in its role as the regional implementing agency (RIA) is placing administrative structures to conduct the 2020 ICP cycle in the region. Timing of the 2020 cycle was largely determined by the United Nations Statistical Commission (UNSC), which has recommended that frequency of the ICP be increased and mandated 2020 as the next benchmark year. Funding to proceed with the 2020 cycle has been secured and ADB has initiated various activities. ADB has recently held the inception workshop for the 2020 ICP, where the Framework of Partnership between ADB and the national implementing agencies for participation in ICP was discussed. Work on the product lists has begun with household product list already finalized and price surveys for household initiated.

The UNSC has endorsed and strongly encouraged participating economies to introduce the rolling price survey approach, which is designed to evenly distribute the burden of price surveys over a period of 3 years. The ICP Global Office has commissioned a task force to prepare a report on the feasibility of implementing the rolling price survey approach in different regions in near future.

Appendixes

Appendix 1: Methodology for the 2017 Cycle in Asia and the Pacific

This appendix introduces the methodology and framework that underpins the International Comparison Program (ICP). The 2017 ICP final report for the region will include a more detailed presentation of the methodology. The following section describes the index number foundations for the ICP and international comparisons of national accounts aggregates. Section A1.1 establishes a link between (i) the national accounts practice of compiling gross domestic product (GDP) at current and constant prices for comparisons over time and (ii) the notion of purchasing power parities (PPPs) and real expenditures for spatial comparisons across economies. Section A1.2 discusses the hierarchical structure used to implement the ICP; section A1.3 describes the index number methods used to aggregate item level price data, leading to estimates of PPPs for aggregates at various levels. Section A1.4 focuses on more practical aspects of the ICP including preparing item lists; the survey framework for price collection; and the subsequent data validation and editing. Section A1.5 describes the refinements in the methodology for productivity adjustments for comparisons of government compensation; and finally, section A1.6 sketches the linking approach that the ICP Global Office uses to combine results from all the participating regions leading to estimates of PPPs and real expenditures at the global level. The global comparisons are presented with United States as the base economy and US dollar as the reference currency.

A1.1 Index Number Foundations for International Comparisons

Index number theory for price and quantity comparisons over time provides the foundation for the ICP framework and methodology for compiling PPPs.

In particular, the fundamental notion of decomposing changes in value into price change and quantity change is critical in building the conceptual framework for the ICP. In the System of National Accounts, the chapter on Price and Volume Measures states: "The index numbers of interest within the SNA [System of National Accounts] are designed to decompose changes in value aggregates into their overall change in price and volume components" (United Nations 2009, p. 297). The national statistical agencies use this framework in their decomposition of changes in GDP over two periods, s and t:

$$\text{Change in GDP from period } s \text{ to } t = \frac{GDP_t}{GDP_s}$$

$$= P_{st} \times Q_{st}$$

where P_{st} represents price change and Q_{st} represents quantity (or volume) change component. In national accounts parlance, P_{st} is the GDP deflator for period t with base period s; the quantity index, Q_{st}, is the volume index for period t with base period s. From this equation, the volume measure can be obtained from an observed change in GDP and a suitably measured GDP deflator P_{st}, that is:

$$\text{Volume change from period } s \text{ to } t = Q_{st}$$

$$= \frac{\frac{GDP_t}{GDP_s}}{P_{st}}$$

This volume change measure can be expressed, equivalently, as:

$$\text{Volume change from period } s \text{ to } t = Q_{st} = \frac{\frac{GDP_t}{P_{st}}}{GDP_s}$$

$$= \frac{\text{GDP in period } t \text{ at constant period } s \text{ prices}}{\text{GDP in period } s \text{ in period } s \text{ prices}}$$

Here, GDP at constant prices, on the right-hand side of the equation, is obtained by deflating the observed GDP in a period with the corresponding GDP deflator.

The framework for international comparisons is analogous to the temporal decomposition described above. Now consider GDP in economies j and k, denoted by GDP_j and GDP_k, observed at a given period of time, for example the year 2017 for the current ICP cycle. Usually, these two GDPs would be expressed in respective domestic currencies. The index number decomposition of relative levels of GDP, the ratio of GDPs, can be expressed as the ratio of real GDP in each economy converted using an appropriate measure of price level differences across the two economies. In order to distinguish between temporal and international comparisons, let PPP_{jk} represent the level of prices in economy k relative to prices in economy j while accounting for the currency units in which GDP's are expressed. Thus, the fundamental index decomposition gives:

$$\text{Relative levels of GDP} = \frac{GDP_k}{GDP_j}$$

$$= PPP_{jk} \times Q_{jk}$$

Then, the volume comparison between economies j and k is given by:

$$Q_{jk} = \frac{\frac{GDP_k}{GDP_j}}{PPP_{jk}} = \frac{\frac{GDP_k}{PPP_{jk}}}{\frac{GDP_j}{GDP_j}} = \frac{\frac{GDP_k}{PPP_{jk}}}{\frac{GDP_j}{PPP_{jj}}}$$

where $\frac{GDP_k}{PPP_{jk}}$ is a measure of real GDP or volume of economy k, expressed in currency units of economy j after accounting for differences in levels of prices in these two economies. Similarly, if $PPP_{jj} = 1$, GDP_j presents the volume or real GDP of economy j in currency units of economy j. Here j is base or reference economy.

Thus, volume comparisons of GDP and other aggregates across participating economies require estimates of PPPs for the currencies of all the economies, $\{PPP_j: j = 1,2,...,22\}$, all expressed relative to a reference or base economy currency. For the ICP in Asia and the Pacific, Hong Kong, China is the base economy and the Hong Kong dollar is the reference currency. The following subsections discuss the steps involved in compiling PPPs for ICP in the Asia and Pacific region.

A1.2 Hierarchical Approach to Compilation of Purchasing Power Parities

The ICP uses a bottom-up approach to aggregate price data collected for individual items, moving progressively to higher-level aggregates, ultimately leading to estimates of PPPs at the GDP level. The approach is essentially the same whether price comparisons are regional or global.[1] Details of this hierarchical approach are outlined in World Bank (2013) and Rao (2013). Figure A1.1 depicts the pyramid structure for the aggregation of price data.

Figure A1.1: Pyramid Structure for the Aggregation of Price Data

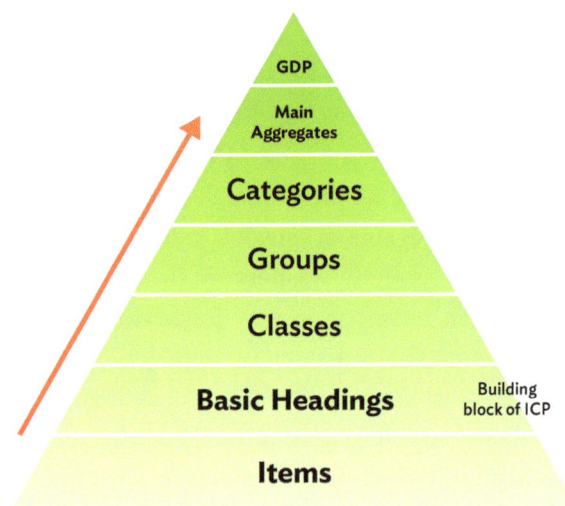

GDP = gross domestic product, ICP = International Comparison Program.
Source: Rao, D.S. Prasada. 2013. "The Framework of the International Comparison Program." In *Measuring the Real Size of the World Economy*, edited by World Bank. Washington, DC: World Bank.

At the base of this structure lies the most important input into PPP computation, the national annual average prices for a large number of items (goods and services) provided by the participating economies. The next section discusses the processes involved in identifying and preparing the list of products to be priced by the participating economies.

---

1   Section A1.6 describes the process used by the ICP Global Office in linking regional comparisons leading to global comparisons.

Basic Headings

In the first stage of aggregating price data, individual items at the base of the pyramid are grouped into 155 groups of homogeneous goods and services referred to as the *basic headings*. These basic headings have three important features. First, products within a basic heading should be homogeneous, each covering a group of similar well-defined goods or services. For example, in the ICP in Asia and the Pacific, the basic heading of rice includes 20 different items of rice consumed across the participating economies. Second, the relative prices of goods or services within a basic heading are expected to be similar across economies. Third, basic headings are the lowest level of aggregation of items in the GDP breakdown at which expenditures

and expenditure shares are available. This feature of the basic headings is similar to the elementary groups of items used to compute elementary indexes in the process of consumer price index (CPI) compilation.

Higher Level Aggregates

Once the basic headings are identified, then these are aggregated to form 126 *classes*. For example, the bread and cereals class comprises the basic headings of rice; other cereals, flour, and other cereal products; bread; other bakery products; and pasta products and couscous.

At the next level, these 126 classes are clustered into 63 *groups*. For example, the food group comprises the

Table A1.1 Composition of Classes, Groups, Categories, and Main Aggregates, 2017 Cycle in Asia and the Pacific

Main Aggregates and Categories		Category	Group	Class	Basic Heading
Gross Domestic Product		**28**	**63**	**126**	**155**
1100000	**Individual Consumption Expenditure by Households**	13	44	91	110
1101000	Food and non-alcoholic beverages		2	11	29
1102000	Alcoholic beverages, tobacco and narcotics		3	5	5
1103000	Clothing and footwear		2	5	5
1104000	Housing, water, electricity, gas and other fuels		5	8	8
1105000	Furnishings, household equipment and routine household maintenance		6	12	13
1106000	Health		3	7	7
1107000	Transport		3	13	13
1108000	Communication		3	3	3
1109000	Recreation and culture		6	13	13
1110000	Education		1	1	1
1111000	Restaurants and hotels		2	2	2
1112000	Miscellaneous goods and services		7	10	10
1113000	Net purchases abroad		1	1	1
1200000	**Individual Consumption Expenditure by NPISHs**	5	5	5	5
1201000	Housing		1	1	1
1202000	Health		1	1	1
1203000	Recreation and culture		1	1	1
1204000	Education		1	1	1
1205000	Social protection and other services		1	1	1
1300000	**Individual Consumption Expenditure by Government**	5	7	16	21
1301000	Housing		1	1	1
1302000	Health		2	7	12
1303000	Recreation and culture		1	1	1
1304000	Education		2	6	6
1305000	Social protection		1	1	1
1400000	**Collective Consumption Expenditure by Government**	1	1	5	5
1500000	**Gross Capital Formation**	3	5	8	12
1501000	Gross fixed capital formation		3	6	10
1502000	Changes in inventories		1	1	1
1503000	Acquisitions less disposals of valuables		1	1	1
1600000	**Balance of Exports and Imports**	1	1	1	2

NPISH = nonprofit institutions serving households.
Source: Asian Development Bank based on World Bank. 2016b. *International Comparison Program: Classification of Final Expenditure on GDP*. Washington, DC. http://pubdocs.worldbank.org/en/708531575560035925/pdf/ICP-Classification-description-2019-1205.pdf.

classes of bread and cereals; meat; fish and seafood; milk, cheese, and eggs; oils and fats; fruits; vegetables; sugar, jam, honey, chocolate, and confectionery; and food products not elsewhere classified.

The 63 groups are then grouped into 28 *categories*. For example, the category of food and non-alcoholic beverages comprises the groups (i) food and (ii) non-alcoholic beverages.

At the next level, the 28 categories are grouped into six main aggregates which together make up the GDP. Table A1.1 shows the composition of the six main aggregates under GDP which are critically important to users and policy makers.

Expenditure Weights

In order to compute PPPs for classes and corresponding real expenditure aggregates, first prices of individual goods and services belonging to the basic headings within that class are aggregated leading to PPPs at the basic heading level (see Section A1.3 for a description of the method used for this purpose). Then, these basic heading PPPs are aggregated upward using expenditure share weights associated with corresponding basic headings. Weights at the basic heading level are computed using final expenditures for each basic heading from national accounts data made available by the implementing agencies of the participating economies. For example, for computing PPPs for the "bread and cereals" class, it is necessary to have (i) PPPs for the five basic headings that make up this class; and (ii) basic heading level expenditures from national accounts.

A1.3 Index Number Methods for Computing Purchasing Power Parities of Currencies

Properties of Index Number Formulas for International Comparisons

Many index number formulas are available for making price comparisons. Some of the well-known formulas

include Jevons; Dutot; Laspeyres, Paasche, Fisher; Tornqvist; Lowe; and the geometric Young index. Only formulas which satisfy several important criteria can be used for the purpose of international comparisons. Of these several properties, three most important are: transitivity, economy symmetry or economy base invariance, and characteristicity.

Transitivity. Transitivity is an internal consistency requirement that states that PPPs computed using a given index number formula must satisfy the following equation for any three economies, for example j, k, and l:

$$PPP_{jk} = PPP_{jl} \cdot PPP_{lk} \quad \text{for all } j,k,l = 1,2,...,22$$

This property requires that a PPP for economy k with reference economy j must be identical to a PPP computed indirectly through link economy l. For example, if three economies of interest are: Hong Kong, China; India; and Malaysia, then transitivity implies that:

$$PPP_{\text{HKG,India}} = PPP_{\text{HKG,Malaysia}} \cdot PPP_{\text{Malaysia,India}}$$

To compute PPPs, the ICP uses only index number formulas that satisfy this property. With transitivity satisfied, it is sufficient to publish PPPs with one selected economy as the base or reference economy, thus the ICP publishes only PPPs with Hong Kong, China as the reference. All other PPPs can be computed using PPPs with Hong Kong, China as the base. Continuing from the example above, the PPP for India with Malaysia as base can be computed as:

$$PPP_{\text{Malaysia,India}} = \frac{PPP_{\text{HKG,India}}}{PPP_{\text{HKG,Malaysia}}}$$

Exchange rates also satisfy transitivity, implying absence of any possibility for arbitrage—the activity of buying and selling a currency for pure profit arising from the differences in exchange rates for the same currency.

Economy symmetry or base economy invariance. For international comparisons, it is important that all the participating economies are treated symmetrically, without giving a special place or significance to any one of the economies. Economy symmetry is satisfied if the relativities in PPPs between any two economies are not affected by either the choice of reference economy or currency.

Characteristicity. The property of transitivity necessarily implies that a PPP between two economies, say India and Malaysia, would be influenced by price and expenditure data from all the remaining 20 economies. Therefore, a bilateral comparison between these two economies (when transitivity is not required) will differ from a bilateral comparison when transitivity is imposed. The property of characteristicity advocates that PPPs satisfying transitivity in multilateral comparisons must be as close as possible to direct bilateral comparisons between pairs of economies. The *Gini-Èltetö-Köves-Szulc* (GEKS) method is specially formulated to maintain a high degree of characteristicity in a multilateral context.

Following the hierarchical scheme outlined above, PPPs can, in principle, be compiled at three different levels: (i) the item level; (ii) the basic heading level; and (3) at all levels of aggregation above the basic heading level. Different index number methods are used for price comparisons at different levels of aggregation, reflecting the nature of data available at each level.

Item Level Price Comparisons

At the item level there is no index number problem. The PPP for the currency of a given economy with currency of a reference economy based on a single item is simply the ratio of prices of the item observed in the two economies. The Big Mac index discussed in the main text of this report is a good example of an item level comparison.

The ICP does not publish item level PPPs because such PPPs cannot be defined unless the product is priced in both economies. For example, the Big Mac is not available in Cambodia, hence it is not meaningful to have a PPP for the Big Mac for Cambodia with Hong Kong, China as the reference economy.

Basic Heading Level Price Comparisons: The Country-Product-Dummy Method

In calculating PPPs for each basic heading, the only data available are the prices of items included in the basic heading. It is almost impossible to collect data on expenditures or quantities consumed in the whole economy at the item-level. Also, not all items in the basic heading are priced in all economies. Economies usually price only a subset of items in a basic heading, generally those items which are representative of expenditures for that basic heading.

The ICP uses the country-product-dummy (CPD) method—recommended by the Technical Advisory Group since the 2005 cycle—for aggregating item-level price data to compute PPPs at the basic heading level. Details of the method along with a comparison of its properties with other methods are in Rao (2013). The method regresses the logarithm of observed prices on country-specific and product-specific dummy variables, hence the label country-product-dummy method.

Consider a basic heading which has N items. For example, the basic heading of rice contains 20 items, $N = 20$. Let p_{ij} be the observed or reported price of commodity i in j-th economy $\{i = 1,2,...,N; j = 1,2,....,22\}$. Conceptually, every p_{ij} may be decomposed into an commodity-specific factor, η_i; an economy-specific factor, π_j; and a factor of ε_{ij} to account for the deviation of $\eta_i \times \pi_j$ from the actual price p_{ij}:

$$p_{ij} = \pi_j \times \eta_i \times \varepsilon_{ij}$$

Taking the natural logarithm of both sides and invoking the property of logarithm, we have:

$$ln\ p_{ij} = ln\ \pi_j + ln\ \eta_i + ln\ \varepsilon_{ij}$$

Because $ln\ \pi_j$ is economy-specific and $ln\ \eta_i$ is product-specific, they can be estimated by the CPD method using the following regression model with economy and product fixed effects using dummy variables:

$$ln\ p_{ij} = \sum_{k=1}^{22} \pi_k D_k + \sum_{n=1}^{N} \eta_n D_n^* + u_{ij}$$

where p_{ij} is the price of the i-th item reported by economy j. D_k is the country or economy dummy variable such that $D_k = 1$ if $k = j$ and $D_k = 0$ if $k \neq j$; and D_i is the commodity dummy variable such that $D_n^* = 1$ if $n = i$; and $D_n^* = 0$ if $n \neq i$. The last, u_{ij}, is a random disturbance. The goal is to estimate $ln p_j$ with the estimator $\hat{\pi}_k$, $ln p_i$, with the estimator $\hat{\eta}_n$, and $ln\varepsilon_{ij}$ with the estimator $\hat{u}_{ij}$.

The CPD method estimates this regression model using price data for the basic headings by ordinary least squares after imposing one parameter restriction.[2] Since Hong Kong, China is the base economy, this model is estimated after imposing the restriction that $\pi_{HKG} = 0$. Any standard statistical package such as Stata can be used to implement the estimation of this model. Let the estimated values of the parameters be denoted by $\{\hat{\pi}_k : k = 1,2,....,22\}$ and $\{\hat{\eta}_n : n = 1,2,....,N\}$. Then a $PPP_{HKG,j}$ for economy j with Hong Kong, China as the base is given by:

$$PPP_{HKG,j} = \exp(\hat{\pi}_j)\ \ j = 1,2,....,22$$

Note that the PPP for Hong Kong, China is equal to 1 since $\exp(\hat{\pi}_{HKG}) = \exp(0) = 1$.

The CPD method is fairly simple but has many useful properties:

1.   If all the items are priced in all the economies, then the PPP formula simply reduces to the Jevons index used as the elementary index in CPI computations. The PPP is given by the unweighted geometric average of the price ratios:

$$PPP_{HKG,j} = \prod_{n=1}^{N}\left[\frac{p_{ij}}{p_{i,HK}}\right]^{1/N}$$

2.   The method can be applied in the practical scenario where not all commodities are priced in all the economies, provided there is connectivity in the observed price matrix.[3]

3.   With the CPD method, it is possible to attach weights to individual price observations. In the CPD method described here, all the items have the same weight equal to 1. Note that not all the items priced by an economy in the basic heading would be representative or equally important in the basic heading expenditure of the economy. If the national implementing agencies can meaningfully identify products which are important, such products may be given a higher weight. The issue of whether to attach weights and, if so, what weights should be selected, were discussed at several meetings of the Technical Advisory Group during the 2011 ICP cycle. After serious deliberations, the group finally recommended assigning a weight of 3 to products labeled as important and a weight of 1 to the remaining products.

4.   Identifying important products is not straightforward and is subject to interpretation by the national implementing agencies. Uncertainty regarding what constitutes the importance of an item may create unnecessary bias when this information is used in giving weights to products in the CPD method. The 2017 ICP in Asia and the Pacific, similar to the 2005 and 2011 ICP, opted not to use weights for products priced. Notwithstanding, the regional implementing agency (RIA) collects this information for the global core products and submits it to the ICP Global Office for use in global linking.

---

2   The model as specified suffers from perfect multicollinearity and therefore can be estimated only after imposing restriction on one of the parameters.
3   Connectivity here simply means that price data are such that it is not possible to group the economies into two sets such that no item priced in one set of economies is priced in the other. In such cases, there is no basis for making price comparisons.

5. Finally, residuals of the estimated CPD models form the basis for Dikhanov tables, which are used in identifying outliers and data validation.

Reference Purchasing Power Parities for Some Basic Headings

Out of the 155 basic headings used in the ICP, there are some basic headings for which it is difficult to (i) specify the products and (ii) collect product prices that can be used in the CPD model. In such instances, PPPs of other basic headings which are considered similar are used as proxies or reference PPPs. For example, PPPs for the basic heading "maintenance and repair of dwelling" serve as a reference PPP for repair of household appliances. A full list of reference PPPs is in Appendix 7.

Computing Purchasing Power Parities for Higher Level Aggregates: The Gini-Èltetö-Köves-Szulc Method

After computing PPPs for the 155 basic headings, the RIA compiles a complete table of PPPs for 155 basic headings for the 22 participating economies, along with expenditure or expenditure share data from national accounts corresponding to each basic heading for all the economies.[4] *The basic heading PPPs are treated like price data associated with the composite group of items which the basic heading represents.* To implement the index number formulas below, the following data structure is available:

$$\{ p_{ij}, e_{ij} : i = 1,2,...,155; \text{ and } j = 1,2,...,22 \}$$

where p_{ij} and e_{ij} are, respectively, price (PPP) and expenditure (in local currency units) for i-th basic heading in j-th economy.

To compute PPPs at higher levels of aggregation, it is necessary to identify the aggregate of interest first and then consider all the basic headings that make up this aggregate. If the aggregate "food and non-alcoholic beverages" is of interest, then it is necessary to include all the 29 basic headings that comprise this aggregate. Similarly, if GDP is of interest, then all the 155 basic headings are included. The formulas given below are for the whole GDP, but the same formula applied to different sub-classes of basic headings can be used for other aggregates.

Since the 2005 ICP cycle, the Technical Advisory Group has recommended using the GEKS method as the index number method to compute PPPs for higher level aggregates above the basic heading. The GEKS method builds on the well-known Fisher binary index number formula, chosen because it satisfies a number of axiomatic and economic theoretic properties, including the country reversal test, factor reversal test, and commensurability test. The Fisher index is also known to be superlative from an economic theoretic viewpoint (Diewert 2013).

The GEKS PPPs are computed in two stages. In the first stage, the Fisher binary index, denoted by F_{jk}, is computed for each pair of economies as the geometric mean of the Laspeyres and Paasche price indexes denoted, respectively, L_{jk} and P_{jk}. Therefore

$$\text{Fisher index} = F_{jk} = [L_{jk} \cdot P_{jk}]^{\frac{1}{2}}$$

$$= \left[\left(\sum_{i=1}^{155} \frac{P_{ik}}{P_{ij}} \cdot e_{ij} \right) \times \frac{1}{\left(\sum_{i=1}^{155} \frac{P_{ij}}{P_{ik}} \cdot e_{ik} \right)} \right]^{1/2}$$

where $e_{ij} = \frac{P_{ij} \cdot q_{ij}}{\sum_{i=1}^{155} P_{ij} \cdot q_{ij}}$ is the national accounts' expenditure share of i-th basic heading in j-th economy.

This Fisher index is not transitive and therefore cannot be used for international comparisons. The GEKS formula for computing PPP for economy k with economy j as the base is:

$$PPP_{jk} = \prod_{l=1}^{22} \left[F_{jl} \cdot F_{lk} \right]^{1/22} \quad j, k = 1,2,...,22$$

---

4   Since GDP is known, if expenditure shares are known then expenditure associated with each basic heading can be computed. Similarly, if expenditure for each basic heading is given, shares can be computed.

The GEKS index provides PPPs that are transitive and base invariant and at the same time, by construction, close to the Fisher binary index. Therefore, the GEKS index also possesses the property of characteristicity. It is due to these desirable properties that this index has been the main aggregation procedure used in Eurostat and Organisation for Economic Co-operation and Development (OECD) comparisons since 1990. During the 2005 ICP cycle, the technical advisory group considered a number of alternative methods and recommended the use of the GEKS procedure.

Non-Additivity of Sub-Aggregates in Real Terms

From the national accounts, it is clear that all the sub-aggregates expressed in local currency units add up to higher level aggregates. For example, the sum of the values of the six main aggregates add up to GDP: this is known as the additivity property. When these aggregates are converted using exchange rates, the resulting nominal aggregates are also additive: for example, nominal values of the six main aggregates also sum to nominal GDP. This is because the exchange rate used to convert each component is same across all aggregates. However, *the additivity property does not hold for real aggregates obtained by converting aggregates in local currency units into a common currency unit using PPPs.* This is because each aggregate has its own corresponding PPP which is different across aggregates. For example, nominal individual consumption expenditure by households (ICEH) is converted into real expenditures by using a PPP specific for household consumption, which is estimated using data on PPPs and expenditures for 110 basic headings. The gross fixed capital formation (GFCF) is converted using 10 PPPs and corresponding expenditures of headings. However, GDP is converted using PPP which is calculated by aggregating PPPs and expenditures data for all the 155 basic headings. *Users of real or volume comparisons from the ICP must be aware of lack of additivity when PPPs are used in deriving real expenditures and, therefore, refrain from using the real aggregates to study the structure of GDP or computing shares of each real aggregate in real GDP.*

A1.4 Product Lists, Survey Framework, and Data Validation and Editing

The most critical and resource intensive activities within the ICP are: determining the lists of items, goods, and services to be priced; establishing the principles and survey framework for price surveys; collecting actual prices; and, finally, validating and editing price data. Once price data are finalized, they are combined with national accounts expenditure data in the compilation of PPPs.

Preparation of Product Lists

Since 2005, the ICP has adopted a regional approach where each region is responsible for implementing ICP in the economies in their respective regions. The ICP Global Office at the World Bank is responsible for linking regional results and compiling the global results. The 2017 ICP uses the linking methodology established during the 2011 ICP cycle, discussed in Section A1.6. The linking methodology uses prices collected by all the 176 participating economies for a common list of products, referred to as the global core list, that was developed by the ICP Global Office.

The ICP therefore relies on regionally determined product lists and the global list of products. These lists are determined after an extensive process of consultation between all the stakeholders. At the regional level, the RIA prepared the 2017 lists, starting from the 2011 ICP product lists and updated global products lists from the World Bank. Extensive consultations with coordinators from the participating economies, who considered their CPI lists and other relevant product lists, provided valuable suggestions regarding inclusion, exclusion, and the structured product descriptions of the items. The RIA facilitated and moderated in the preparation of the lists. At the global level, the ICP Global Office consulted with all the regional coordinators through its Inter-Agency Coordination Group meetings in its preparation of the global core lists. Both the regional and global lists are prepared in accordance with a set of common principles:

- **Consistency with national accounts practices.** Because the ultimate purpose for compiling PPPs is to convert expenditure aggregates in national accounts to facilitate volume or real expenditure comparisons, it is necessary to examine the coverage of the particular aggregate in the national accounts and then identify product lists for ICP price surveys. For example, if national accounts use the rental approach to derive the aggregate for dwelling services, then for ICP price surveys, the ICP needs to consider rental prices for dwellings typical in the participating economies.

- **Comparability.** Comparability of products priced is an essential requirement for meaningful price comparisons across economies. The general principle of comparing like with like underpins the ICP price comparisons. Consequently, specification of the products is an important task undertaken at the time of preparation of product lists. Comparability is achieved through the use of *structured product descriptions* (SPDs).

- **Representativity.** The items included in the product list must be representative of the products that are purchased in an economy and are included in the national accounts aggregate under consideration. Comparability and representativity are two competing requirements that need to be balanced when preparing item lists. For example, a branded men's shirt with specifications such as 100% cotton and full sleeves would be perfectly comparable across all the economies. However, such a specified branded shirt may not be representative of the shirts purchased in many of the participating economies. The Big Mac is another item that is comparable but may not be representative of household consumption in all economies where it is available. The task of compiling a list of representative products is particularly challenging in a diverse region like Asia and the Pacific. Consequently, the ICP took an inclusive approach that includes products representative of various subregions and encourages participating economies to price as many available and representative items as possible to ensure a sufficient degree of overlap of items between economies.

- **Importance indicators.** To address the issue of representativity of the product list, participating economies are encouraged to indicate whether or not a product priced in their economy is considered important, where importance is expected to be determined on the basis of its expenditure share within the basic heading. Importance indicator information can be incorporated into PPP computation by giving different weights for important and less important products.

- **Structured product descriptions.** SPDs are essentially a set of price-determining characteristics used to specify the products to be priced. Identifying SPDs for each of the items included in the product list is a major task, but SPDs provide a way of achieving a fine balance between comparability and representativity. SPDs, for example, include details of the package size, the type of outlet, and whether the product is branded or unbranded. SPDs ensure that the quality of products priced are the same across the economies when the specifications in the SPDs are followed diligently. The ICP Global Office determines the SPDs of global product lists for household consumption, government compensation of employees, machinery and equipment, and construction, and these are used across all the participating regions with minor deviations that may be specific to each region.

Product Lists for Major Aggregates

Household consumption. Household consumption is the most significant aggregate in the national accounts with an average share, over the 22 participating economies, of approximately 45% of GDP. It comprises 110 basic headings out of 155 basic headings for the GDP. The items in the product list for household consumption comprise (i) the regional product list with goods and services considered representative of consumption in the participating economies of the region and (ii) the global core list of products prepared by the ICP Global Office. A degree of overlap between the regional and global lists is desirable. The regional list for Asia and the Pacific comprises 887 goods and services whereas the global list comprises 415 items; the two lists share 296 products in common. The combined list of regional and global items comprises in total 1006 items, which are then priced by the participating economies.

Health and education. These are two components of household consumption where one part of the expenditure is incurred by the individuals and another through government provision. Across the 22 participating economies in the region, there is a diverse mix of government provision and the degrees to which these services are subsidized. The basic principle is that prices used for converting health and education expenditures should reflect market prices, regardless of who provides these services and at what price. The product list for health includes 174 goods and services and the global core list has 77 items. Similar to the 2011 ICP, pharmaceutical products from the ICP Global Office were split according to the brands priced for originator products, and the origin for the generic products. This resulted in 133 child items in the regional list from 57 parent pharmaceutical items in the global list. Therefore, participating economies had a total of 174 goods and services to price under the health category. For education, the product list consists of seven items and coincides with the global core list.

Housing or dwelling expenditure. It is difficult to make international price and volume comparisons for dwellings. Differences in national accounts practices in the treatment of owner-occupied housing and the lack of well-established rental markets make the task particularly complex. At the conclusion of extensive data collection and analysis by the RIA in Asia and the Pacific and at the recommendation of the Regional Advisory Board and Technical Advisory Group, the ICP decided that in the 2017 cycle, it will continue to use the *reference volume approach* used in the 2005 and 2011 cycles. During 2017 ICP cycle, the participating economies conducted rental surveys for use in

implementing the *rental approach*. In parallel, data on a range of quantity measures of dwelling volumes and associated quality indicators were collected for use in the *quantity approach*. To implement the rental approach, rents were collected for 21 types of dwellings, of which 9 were houses (7 from global list and 2 specific to the Asia and Pacific region); 10 were apartments (5 global and 5 regional specifications); and 2 were traditional dwellings both with regional specifications. On the volume side, the standard volume indicators were used: number of dwellings per 100 people, number of rooms per 100 people, and square meters of usable floor space per person. In addition, quality indicators were used, measured by the proportion of dwellings with electricity, safe water, inside toilets, and several other quality indicators collected from United Nations sources on Sustainable Development Goals. The RIA developed a new approach that combined the rental and quantity approaches recommended for estimating PPPs for dwelling, and this approach will be implemented after further testing during the 2020 ICP.

Government compensation. The list of standard occupations used in the ICP for this aggregate is determined at the global level. There are a total of 35 occupations, of which 34 are from the global list; the occupation of "medical imaging and therapeutic equipment technicians" was added in Asia and the Pacific. However, after considering the problem of comparability of some occupations across economies of the region, the occupation of "senior government official" was dropped. The final list included 9 occupations from health, 5 occupations from education, and 20 occupations from collective services of the government.

Machinery and equipment. Machinery and equipment is a component of GFCF, along with construction. The list for machinery and equipment is global and includes 196 products, 93 of which are unspecified and 103 of which are specified with details of make, manufacturer, and technical specifications. After evaluating variability in prices reported, the RIA and NIA agreed to drop 16 out of 196 items from the list for which the price data was evaluated as not comparable in consultation with an expert on machinery and equipment. Further analysis of price data for unspecified items, led to a decision to split 26 unspecified items into two groups following established criteria based on price clustering.

Construction. Construction consists of residential buildings, non-residential buildings, and civil engineering works. The input approach is used for construction in the region. For Asia and the Pacific, the region uses a regional list, which covers material inputs, equipment rental, and labor. The regional list is composed of 40 items for materials, 10 items for equipment rental, and 8 items for labor inputs. Out of 58 items, 55 items are from the global list and 3 are regional items. Indicators of relevance of material inputs in the different types of construction were used to identify the relevance of construction inputs for each type of construction. For example, only 30 material inputs out of 40 are considered relevant for residential buildings, 34 for non-residential buildings and 21 for civil engineering works.

Survey Framework

The ICP Global Office designed the survey framework used in the price surveys conducted by the participating economies to meet the basic principles of the ICP. The RIA applied the global framework after undertaking modifications suitable for the region.

National coverage. Surveys collected prices that are representative of national averages by covering both rural and urban markets of the participating economies and did not concentrate only on urban areas or capital cities. However, for certain aggregates, the surveys necessarily focused on major cities. For dwellings, surveys focused on areas where rental markets are prevalent; for machinery and equipment, surveys were limited to capital cities.

Calendar year. The ICP requires that prices used in PPP computation must represent annual average prices, observed during the calendar year 2017. Due to delays in starting 2017 ICP activities and competing statistical priorities in some economies, not all economies conducted simultaneous household price collection. The collection of prices for household items was spread over a period of twelve months during 2017 and 2018, with the starting month of price collection varying from April to July 2017. Thus, the 12-month average prices for household items were estimated by the national implementing agencies for the calendar year 2017 using the most detailed consumer price index. Surveys for government compensation, construction, and machinery and equipment were conducted during 2017 and 2018 and referenced to the calendar year 2017. For some economies, rental data was estimated for 2017 based on rental fees collected for 2018. The national accounts data for economies where the accounting year differs from the calendar year were adjusted to the calendar year.

Survey design. All the participating economies were encouraged to implement a self-weighing sampling design in selecting the number of quotations from different outlets, urban and rural areas, towns, and cities. An advantage of such a design is that a simple average of all the price quotations collected would be a reliable estimator of the national average price.

Data Editing and Validation

The quality of price and national accounts data is paramount in compiling reliable PPPs and real expenditures. The RIA and the ICP Global Office take data validation quite seriously.

Validation at the Economy Level

The national implementing agencies are responsible for checking price quotations for outliers and ensuring consistency in following the SPDs. The national agencies used software supplied by ADB, the ICP Asia and the Pacific Software Suite, which has extensive functionalities including the generation of survey questionnaires, data entry, basic data, validations, and diagnostics. The software also helped identify non-sampling errors such as units of measurement and data entry errors. Different price capture tools were also provided for data entry and basic validation on compensation, rental, machinery and equipment and construction surveys, and national accounts expenditure estimates.

Validation at the Regional Level

The RIA employs a number of sophisticated statistical tools at the regional level to conduct checks on price data provided by participating economies.

Quaranta tables. Eurostat first introduced these tables in the 1990s for data validation in EU regional comparisons. These tables provide an overview of the extent of variability, across the participating economies, in the price data at the item level as well as at the basic heading level. Quaranta tables use the coefficient of variation and the range in price ratios, among other measures, for validating economy data.

Dikhanov tables. Dikhanov tables use residuals from the CPD regressions discussed in the section on index number methods for computing PPPs. These tables make use of residuals from CPD regression at the basic heading level; and residuals from CPD regressions for higher level aggregates such as whole household consumption, government compensation, construction, and machinery and equipment to identify outliers among the PPP ratios and provide measures of price variations for products and economies.

Price changes in the consumer price index versus the International Comparison Program. The RIA developed this novel technique for Asia and the Pacific during the 2011 ICP cycle and further refined and used it to its full potential during the 2017 ICP cycle. Basically, the tool exploits the fact that there are a large number of goods and services in common in the product lists of 2011 and 2017. For each economy, there are prices for a common set of items in 2011 and 2017 which can be used in computing an estimate of price change based on ICP products, labeled *ICP inflation*. During the same period, domestic inflation data based on CPI, *CPI inflation,* is available as an independent measure of price change from 2011 to 2017. While the ICP and CPI inflations would not be identical, there is an expectation that these two measures not diverge widely. Based on this, the RIA used differences between ICP and CPI inflation as a validation tool and urged participating economies to verify these differences and document the source of deviation as a part of data editing and checking.

A1.5 Productivity Adjustment Method for Wages and Salaries of Government Employees

The RIA at ADB championed the need for productivity adjustment for comparisons of government compensation. In the 2005 ICP in Asia and the Pacific, the RIA observed that wages and salaries of government employees in many low income economies of the region were too low, resulting in lower price levels and higher volume or real expenditure measures of government expenditure. In some instances, the real per capita government expenditure in some low income economies were at implausibly high levels, most likely because the low wages in fact reflect low productivity levels of employees in these economies, which in turn reflect low levels of capital employed per labor unit. In 2011, the RIA used the methodology described below, which represents a refinement used in the method of 2005.

Labor productivity in the government sector is difficult to measure because of a variety of measurement issues, including obtaining suitable measures of capital stock in the government sector. The ADB approach makes the simplifying assumption that productivity of labor in the government sector is at a constant proportion to productivity of labor in the whole economy across all the participating economies. This means that if labor productivity in Malaysia is 50% of that in Hong Kong, China at the economy level, then productivity of labor in government sector is also assumed to be 50% of productivity in the sector in Hong Kong, China.

Productivity levels in different economies are estimated under the assumption that all of them follow a Cobb-Douglas production function with constant returns to scale.[5] For economy j, the production function with capital and labor as inputs is given by:

$$Y_j = A \cdot K_j^{\alpha_j} \cdot L_j^{\beta_j} \text{ with } \alpha_j + \beta_j = 1 \text{ (constant returns to scale)}$$

where Y_j is output (GDP), K_j is capital stock, and L_j is labor input in economy j. Coefficients α_j and β_j represent respectively income shares of capital and labor in j-th economy. This equation can be rewritten to express labor productivity as a function of capital–labor ratio:

$$\frac{Y_j}{L_j} = A \left(\frac{K_j}{L_j}\right)^{\alpha_j}$$

To compare labor productivity across economies, the estimate of capital stock of economy j must be expressed in a common currency unit converted using a suitable PPP. Labor is measured in physical units, such as the number of hours worked. If the income share of capital is known, then this formula can compute labor productivity for different economies. If k_j represents the capital–labor ratio in j-th economy, then labor productivity (LPROD) can be written as:

$$\text{LPROD}_j = \frac{Y_j}{L_j} = A \left(k_j\right)^{\alpha_j} \text{ where } k_j = \frac{K_j}{L_j}$$

Then the productivity adjustment is made by dividing wages and salaries with the productivity ratio relative to the base economy of Hong Kong, China:

$$\frac{\text{LPROD}_j}{\text{LPROD}_{HKG}} = \frac{A \left(k_j\right)^{\alpha_j}}{A \left(k_{HKG}\right)^{\alpha_{HKG}}} = \frac{\left(k_j\right)^{\alpha_j}}{\left(k_{HKG}\right)^{\alpha_{HKG}}}$$

This is the productivity ratio used for adjustment in 2011.[6] In order to implement this, it is necessary to have estimates of capital shares in different economies. It was assumed that (i) income shares of labor takes the values 0.5, 0.6, and 0.7 for three groups characterized as low-, middle-, and high-income economies as given below and (ii) the capital share is one minus the labor share.

Labor share of 0.5 and capital share of 0.5 were assumed for Bangladesh, Bhutan, Cambodia, India, the Lao People's Democratic Republic, Maldives, Mongolia, Myanmar, Nepal, Pakistan, and Sri Lanka.

Labor share of 0.6 and capital share of 0.4 were assumed for Fiji, Indonesia, the People's Republic of China, the Philippines, and Viet Nam.

Labor share of 0.7 and capital share of 0.3 were assumed for Brunei Darussalam; Hong Kong, China; Macau, China; Malaysia; Singapore; Taipei,China; and Thailand.[7]

Productivity Adjustment Method for 2017: The Inklaar Method

The Inklaar method (Inklaar, 2019) represents a further refinement to the productivity adjustment method introduced and implemented by ADB in the 2005 and 2011 ICP cycles. It addresses two critical deficiencies of the ADB method described above. First, although the ADB method of 2011 provided a set of transitive labor productivity adjustment factors, it is not base invariant: use of PPPs relative to a reference currency other than the Hong Kong dollar would give a different set of adjustment factors. Second, in the ADB method, the estimates of income shares of labor and capital were somewhat ad hoc and broadly based. The Inklaar productivity adjustments make use of properly estimated and calibrated labor shares (Inklaar and Timmer 2013a; and Inklaar 2019).

---

5   The Cobb-Douglas production function reflects the relationship between the output produced and the corresponding inputs: physical capital and labor.
6   While this is essentially the method used in 2011, the actual implementation was slightly more complicated.
7   Macau, China participated in the 2011 cycle of the ICP but not the 2017 cycle.

The transitive and base-invariant measures of labor productivity from the Inklaar method are given by:

$$LPROD_j = \left(\frac{k_j}{\bar{k}}\right)^{\frac{\alpha_j + \bar{\alpha}}{2}} \text{ where } \bar{k} = \prod_{j=1}^{22}\left(k_j\right)^{1/22}$$

$$\text{and } \bar{\alpha} = \frac{1}{22}\sum_{j=1}^{22}\alpha_j$$

Productivity of economy j relative to the economy of Hong Kong, China is simply the ratio of labor productivities in economy j and in Hong Kong, China.

The income shares of labor used in the application of the Inklaar methodology for Asia and the Pacific are in Table A1.2.

Table A1.2: Income Shares of Labor: ADB and Estimated Shares from Inklaar, 2011

Economy	Inklaar	ADB
Bangladesh	0.4370	0.5000
Bhutan	0.4380	0.5000
Brunei Darussalam	0.4680	0.7000
Cambodia	0.3860	0.5000
China, People's Republic of	0.5500	0.6000
Fiji	0.4886	0.6000
Hong Kong, China	0.5156	0.7000
India	0.5127	0.5000
Indonesia	0.4592	0.6000
Lao People's Democratic Republic	0.3976	0.5000
Macau, China	0.3383	0.7000
Malaysia	0.3571	0.7000
Maldives	0.4170	0.5000
Mongolia	0.3778	0.5000
Myanmar	0.4550	0.5000
Nepal	0.4040	0.5000
Pakistan	0.4200	0.5000
Philippines	0.3622	0.6000
Singapore	0.4395	0.7000
Sri Lanka	0.3104	0.5000
Taipei,China	0.6675	0.7000
Thailand	0.3928	0.7000
Viet Nam	0.4390	0.6000

ADB = Asian Development Bank.
Note: Shaded cells indicate that Inklaar estimates are not available and show labor shares from the International Labour Organization.
Sources: Asian Development Bank. 2014. *Purchasing Power Parities and Real Expenditures*. Manila. 131; Groningen Growth and Development Centre. Penn World Table version 9.1. https://www.rug.nl/ggdc/productivity/pwt/ (accessed 9 December 2019); Robert C. Feenstra et al. 2015. The Next Generation of the Penn World Table. *American Economic Review*. 105 (10). pp. 3150–3182. www.ggdc.net/pwt; and International Labour Organization. SDG Labour Market Indicators. https://www.ilo.org/shinyapps/bulke xplorer20/?lang=en&segment=indicator&id=SDG_1041_NOC_RT_A (accessed 28 November 2019).

The Inklaar method, along with the new income shares of labor and capital, resulted in significant downward revisions to productivity estimates of all the economies (except for the reference economy,

Hong Kong, China). As a result, price level indexes (PLIs) for all the economies have increased and real expenditures were adjusted downward (see Chapter 5).

A1.6 Methodology for Global Linking: Linking Asia and the Pacific to the Rest of the World

The most important task performed by the ICP Global Office in any given ICP cycle is to bring together price and real expenditure comparisons from different regions and produce global comparisons expressed relative to a selected reference economy. As in the past, the United States is the reference economy and the US dollar is the reference currency. This section briefly explains the methodology used by the ICP Global Office to produce global PPPs and results using PPPs and other data finalized by the regional agencies. The linking procedure used in the 2017 ICP cycle is the same as that used in 2011.

All the 176 participating economies in the 2017 cycle belong to the following six regions: Africa, Asia and the Pacific, the Commonwealth of Independent States, Latin America and the Caribbean, Western Asia, and Eurostat-OECD. Some countries, like Egypt, are included in two different regions, but the description below does not go into all the technical details; rather, it provides an overall picture of the linking method and how linking works.

Stage I. All the regional implementing agencies implement the ICP in their respective regions, using procedures similar to those outlined in this appendix, then compile the following results and submit them to the ICP Global Office:

- **Purchasing power parities.** The PPPs for the currencies of all the participating economies (22 in the case of Asia and the Pacific) are at the basic heading level, for all the 155 basic headings. These PPPs are expressed relative to the reference currency of the respective regions; in Asia and the Pacific, all the PPPs are relative to the Hong Kong dollar.

- **National accounts data.** The data include GDP and expenditure share weights for all 155 basic headings.
- **Additional data.** All the regions provide prices of all the goods and services included in the *global core product lists* for household consumption including education and health, government compensation, dwellings, machinery and equipment, and construction.

Stage II. The ICP Global Office links all the regional price comparisons using price data for the global core products. The linking method used is the *country aggregation and reallocation of volumes* (CAR-Volume) method. This method satisfies the *fixity* principle.

The fixity principle ensures that the global comparisons, compiled by linking all the regional comparisons, will maintain the same relative price levels and real expenditures or volumes between participating economies of the regions compiled at the regional level. For example, if the size of real GDP of the People's Republic of China is 2.44 times that of India in the comparisons for Asia and the Pacific (in Hong Kong dollars), the relative size of People's Republic of China would still be 2.44 times that of India in the global comparisons (expressed in US dollars).

The following steps are involved in the linking process, though there are deviations from this process when aggregates such as construction, education, health, and housing are linked.[8]

1. Basic heading PPPs from different regions are linked using *linking factors* computed using global core prices collected by all the economies in the ICP. First, global core prices of items collected in a given region are converted into the units of the reference currency of the region

using PPPs for that basic heading. For example, for the basic heading of rice, global core prices collected by the 22 economies are converted into Hong Kong dollars using PPPs for the basic heading of rice in the region. The same procedure is used to convert global core prices from the other regions.

2. Linking factors for a given basic heading are then estimated by running a CPD regression on the global core prices expressed in the reference currencies of the six regions. For example, for Asia and the Pacific, the linking factor shows the number of Hong Kong dollars that are equivalent to one US dollar for that basic heading.

3. The basic heading PPPs for all the 155 basic headings supplied by all the regions are expressed relative to the US dollar using the estimated linking factors. This results in a matrix with 155 rows, with one row for each basic heading such as rice, and each row with 176 entries that correspond to each of the participating economies.

4. These basic heading PPPs are combined with national accounts data on expenditure shares using the GEKS method, resulting in globally linked PPPs for GDP. Using these PPPs, the total real GDP is computed for each region and then redistributed using shares of economies computed at the regional level. This is the *redistribution* step in the CAR-Volume method.

5. Once the real GDP of each economy in each region is computed, then PPPs for the currencies of each economy is expressed relative to the reference currency, the US dollar.

6. Steps (1) to (5) are repeated for computing PPPs and real expenditures for other aggregates like ICEH and NPISH, GFCE, and GFCF.

The ICP Global Office compiles results for all the desired aggregates and publishes them in their report for the 2017 ICP cycle.

---

8   Slightly different procedures are used for these aggregates since the Eurostat-OECD economies' procedure are different from those used in other regions. Details can be obtained from the final report for the 2011 ICP cycle (World Bank 2015).

Appendix 2: Membership of the Regional Advisory Board in the International Comparison Program for Asia and the Pacific

Members from Implementing Agencies

Commissioner, Census and Statistics Department, Hong Kong, China
Chief Statistician of India and Secretary, Ministry of Statistics and Programme Implementation
Chief Statistician, Badan Pusat Statistik, Indonesia
Head, Lao Statistics Bureau, Lao People's Democratic Republic
Director General, International Statistical Information Center, National Bureau of Statistics of China, People's Republic of China
Director General, Department of Census and Statistics, Sri Lanka
Director General, General Statistics Office, Viet Nam

Institutional Members

Chief Economist, Asian Development Bank
General Manager, Macroeconomic Statistics Division, Australian Bureau of Statistics
Director, Statistics Division, United Nations Economic and Social Commission for Asia and the Pacific
Director, United Nations Statistical Institute for Asia and the Pacific

Ex-Officio Members

Advisor, Office of the Chief Economist and Director General and Head, Statistics and Data Innovation Unit, Asian Development Bank[1]
Director, Development Data Group, World Bank

Member Secretary   Regional Coordinator, International Comparison Program (ICP) Asia and the Pacific, Asian Development Bank

Secretariat   Asian Development Bank ICP Team

[1] Effective 3 February 2020 onward. Formerly, Director of Development Indicators and Policy Research Division, Economic Research and Regional Cooperation Department.
Source: 2017 International Comparison Program for Asia and the Pacific.

Appendix 3: Participating Economies: Implementing Agencies and Local Currency Units

Economy	Implementing Agency	Local Currency Units
Bangladesh	Bangladesh Bureau of Statistics	taka (Tk)
Bhutan	National Statistics Bureau	ngultrum (Nu)
Brunei Darussalam	Department of Economic Planning and Statistics	Brunei dollar(s) (B$)
Cambodia	National Institute of Statistics	riel(s) (KR)
China, People's Republic of	National Bureau of Statistics of China	yuan (CNY)
Fiji	Fiji Bureau of Statistics	Fiji dollar(s) (F$)
Hong Kong, China	Census and Statistics Department	Hong Kong dollar(s) (HK$)
India	Ministry of Statistics and Programme Implementation	Indian rupee(s) (₹)
Indonesia	Badan Pusat Statistik	rupiah (Rp)
Lao People's Democratic Republic	Lao Statistics Bureau	kip (KN)
Malaysia	Department of Statistics	ringgit (RM)
Maldives	National Bureau of Statistics	rufiyaa (Rf)
Mongolia	National Statistics Office	togrog (MNT)
Myanmar	Central Statistical Organization	kyat(s) (MK)
Nepal	Central Bureau of Statistics	Nepalese rupee(s) (NRe)
Pakistan	Pakistan Bureau of Statistics	Pakistani rupee(s) (PRe/PRs)
Philippines	Philippine Statistics Authority	peso(s) (₱)
Singapore	Department of Statistics	Singapore dollar(s) (S$)
Sri Lanka	Department of Census and Statistics	Sri Lankan rupee(s) (SLRe/SLRS))
Taipei,China	Directorate-General of Budget, Accounting, and Statistics	NT dollar(s) (NT$)
Thailand	Trade Policy and Strategy Office	baht (B)
Viet Nam	General Statistics Office	dong (D)

Source: 2017 International Comparison Program for Asia and the Pacific.

Appendix 4: Detailed Tables: Purchasing Power Parities and Real Expenditures, 2017

The succeeding tables present the 2017 key results for Asia and the Pacific for broad aggregates of gross domestic product (GDP). These include the actual individual consumption by household (AICH), individual consumption expenditure by household (ICEH) and nonprofit institutions serving households (NPISH), collective consumption expenditure by government, government final consumption expenditure (GFCE), gross fixed capital formation (GFCF), change in inventories and net acquisitions of valuables, and balance of exports and imports. These aggregates were derived using the Gini-Elteto-Köves-Szulc (GEKS) method, so real expenditures are not additive within a particular economy. The results presented in these tables are produced by the ICP Asia Pacific regional implementing agency, based on data supplied by all the participating economies, and in accordance with the methodology recommended by the ICP Technical Advisory Group and approved by the Asia and the Pacific Regional Advisory Board. As such, these results are not produced by participating economies as part of the economies' official statistics.

Table A4.1: Purchasing Power Parities, 2017
(Hong Kong, China as base)

Expenditure Category	BAN	BHU	BRU	CAM	FIJ	HKG	IND	INO	LAO	MAL	MLD	MON	MYA	NEP	PAK	PHI	PRC	SIN	SRI	TAP	THA	VIE
Gross Domestic Product	4.95	3.20	0.11	237.61	0.16	1.00	3.43	781.12	463.97	0.28	1.36	131.66	61.00	5.20	5.59	3.22	0.70	0.15	8.22	2.62	2.14	1,230.21
Actual Individual Consumption by Households[a]	4.58	3.05	0.11	227.84	0.15	1.00	3.15	780.92	462.27	0.27	1.48	125.77	59.20	4.74	5.25	3.06	0.67	0.17	7.91	2.58	2.05	1,174.31
Food and non-alcoholic beverages	5.42	3.92	0.12	274.33	0.17	1.00	3.30	1,029.47	594.80	0.28	1.22	147.76	77.44	5.79	6.35	3.35	0.67	0.15	11.10	3.20	2.31	1,399.93
Food	5.38	3.83	0.12	270.90	0.17	1.00	3.24	1,021.42	581.49	0.28	1.19	144.20	76.57	5.68	6.26	3.37	0.66	0.15	10.98	3.20	2.28	1,387.67
Bread and cereals	6.17	4.50	0.12	276.89	0.18	1.00	3.51	1,209.55	629.01	0.30	1.26	177.53	89.63	6.06	6.61	4.01	0.79	0.16	10.74	3.68	2.52	1,512.19
Meat and fish	5.57	3.58	0.11	288.16	0.17	1.00	3.64	882.61	577.90	0.27	0.76	109.06	73.77	6.74	5.85	2.78	0.61	0.16	10.05	3.08	2.06	1,348.70
Fruits and vegetables	3.88	3.92	0.16	268.30	0.15	1.00	2.65	1,110.52	549.54	0.30	2.02	232.70	70.00	4.36	5.52	3.65	0.58	0.15	10.78	3.42	2.42	1,339.90
Other food and non-alcoholic beverages	5.74	3.78	0.12	270.59	0.18	1.00	3.57	998.10	613.14	0.27	1.26	158.03	78.05	6.03	6.77	3.25	0.73	0.12	11.96	2.74	2.28	1,440.01
Clothing and footwear	5.74	3.87	0.20	287.62	0.20	1.00	3.13	1,070.50	519.63	0.33	1.40	183.41	77.71	5.73	7.10	4.88	1.29	0.17	8.86	2.59	2.13	1,398.93
Clothing	5.55	3.46	0.18	291.31	0.19	1.00	3.04	1,091.62	503.79	0.31	1.32	170.43	75.07	5.63	6.86	4.30	1.27	0.16	8.53	2.49	2.02	1,339.04
Housing, water, electricity, gas and other fuels	3.30	2.02	0.06	219.78	0.09	1.00	2.56	451.72	360.00	0.19	2.15	124.18	34.45	3.56	3.93	2.43	0.56	0.19	5.72	2.59	1.41	1,204.73
Health and education	2.66	1.29	0.07	94.01	0.11	1.00	1.69	417.68	132.09	0.21	0.80	51.50	25.97	1.90	2.76	1.84	0.47	0.15	2.11	1.58	1.21	542.92
Health	2.47	1.13	0.09	116.49	0.09	1.00	1.49	423.42	173.04	0.21	0.70	56.57	28.03	2.14	3.11	2.20	0.39	0.18	2.78	1.32	1.37	653.21
Education	2.80	1.42	0.06	77.49	0.11	1.00	1.91	403.71	107.48	0.21	0.89	46.25	24.07	1.74	2.42	1.59	0.58	0.13	1.57	1.94	1.07	456.55
Transportation and communication	5.07	4.35	0.16	306.87	0.15	1.00	3.76	934.30	705.03	0.32	1.97	162.25	89.23	6.88	6.11	3.79	0.56	0.21	10.91	2.49	2.53	1,535.26
Transportation	5.16	4.06	0.14	315.26	0.16	1.00	3.95	906.71	710.98	0.28	1.82	150.30	83.40	8.38	6.46	3.55	0.52	0.22	11.32	2.58	2.46	1,624.48
Recreation and culture	6.34	5.14	0.19	354.03	0.20	1.00	4.56	1,284.49	740.90	0.40	2.30	201.62	93.98	5.39	8.00	4.11	0.86	0.15	13.60	3.28	3.27	1,657.38
Restaurants and hotels	4.76	3.18	0.10	242.71	0.19	1.00	3.98	787.72	703.55	0.24	1.13	163.06	72.50	4.50	6.38	3.54	0.74	0.14	10.93	2.47	1.99	1,133.87
Other consumption expenditure items	5.42	3.62	0.10	227.68	0.20	1.00	4.29	887.71	521.69	0.33	1.46	139.40	64.70	6.56	6.13	3.29	0.82	0.20	9.85	2.85	2.54	1,230.12
Individual Consumption Expenditure by Government	3.51	1.50	0.07	140.26	0.11	1.00	3.71	491.78	173.85	0.22	0.89	46.91	32.26	3.60	4.77	2.72	0.60	0.15	2.51	1.89	1.40	609.30
Collective Consumption Expenditure by Government	4.60	1.74	0.07	233.89	0.14	1.00	4.54	598.80	277.70	0.24	1.03	75.18	49.33	5.99	5.72	3.00	0.72	0.12	3.99	2.25	1.91	839.84
Gross Fixed Capital Formation	6.10	4.53	0.12	273.33	0.16	1.00	3.86	830.33	565.52	0.29	1.26	166.96	71.07	7.14	7.08	3.85	0.74	0.15	10.70	2.93	2.34	1,497.52
Machinery and equipment	12.49	9.51	0.20	520.78	0.26	1.00	6.69	1,652.77	1,090.28	0.50	2.16	292.38	136.32	11.54	12.43	6.45	1.00	0.21	19.00	4.30	4.16	2,656.58
Construction	3.59	2.60	0.08	164.05	0.12	1.00	2.53	498.40	330.38	0.19	0.83	107.12	42.15	4.86	4.51	2.59	0.57	0.12	6.77	2.35	1.46	963.83
Change in Inventories and Net Acquisitions of Valuables	5.77	3.92	0.12	286.26	0.18	1.00	3.93	920.21	576.43	0.30	1.44	158.07	73.52	6.44	6.21	3.77	0.76	0.17	11.30	2.91	2.47	1,470.82
Balance of Exports and Imports	10.32	8.36	0.18	519.75	0.27	1.00	8.36	1,716.98	1,071.64	0.55	1.97	313.06	174.56	13.41	13.53	6.47	0.87	0.18	19.56	3.91	4.36	2,870.44
Individual Consumption Expenditure by Households and NPISH	4.73	3.28	0.11	238.51	0.16	1.00	3.12	815.39	502.05	0.28	1.57	139.95	62.45	4.89	5.33	3.11	0.66	0.17	8.89	2.66	2.13	1,250.81
Government Final Consumption Expenditure	4.11	1.62	0.07	183.79	0.13	1.00	4.15	550.85	236.96	0.23	0.96	61.22	42.51	5.05	5.27	2.88	0.67	0.13	3.26	2.07	1.67	733.48
Actual Individual Consumption by Households[a]	4.58	3.05	0.11	227.84	0.15	1.00	3.15	780.92	462.27	0.27	1.48	125.77	59.20	4.74	5.25	3.06	0.67	0.17	7.91	2.58	2.05	1,174.31
All goods	6.02	4.06	0.12	311.41	0.21	1.00	3.91	1,049.61	630.68	0.33	1.69	165.76	80.58	6.54	6.41	4.09	0.77	0.19	12.25	2.94	2.76	1,572.13
Non-durables	5.31	3.50	0.10	276.08	0.19	1.00	3.49	938.37	558.86	0.30	1.44	145.70	70.90	5.71	5.58	3.63	0.68	0.18	10.83	2.71	2.47	1,376.34
Semi-durables	6.18	4.43	0.18	312.78	0.21	1.00	3.76	1,035.20	589.17	0.33	1.61	195.04	81.83	5.77	7.37	4.79	1.26	0.17	11.72	2.71	2.76	1,585.95
Durables	9.44	6.33	0.22	478.31	0.28	1.00	5.79	1,488.51	946.61	0.43	3.12	226.71	133.71	12.21	9.74	5.33	0.80	0.28	18.18	3.73	3.83	2,413.51
Services	3.66	2.75	0.11	174.70	0.11	1.00	2.49	631.07	407.25	0.24	1.56	127.71	47.05	3.31	4.62	2.29	0.60	0.16	6.39	2.52	1.63	1,047.27

BAN = Bangladesh; BHU = Bhutan; BRU = Brunei Darussalam; CAM = Cambodia; FIJ = Fiji; HKG = Hong Kong, China; IND = India; INO = Indonesia; LAO = Lao People's Democratic Republic; MAL = Malaysia; MLD = Maldives; MON = Mongolia; MYA = Myanmar; NEP = Nepal; NPISH=nonprofit institutions serving households; PAK = Pakistan; PHI = Philippines; PRC = People's Republic of China; SIN = Singapore; SRI = Sri Lanka; TAP = Taipei,China; THA = Thailand; VIE = Viet Nam.

a Includes individual consumption expenditure by households, nonprofit institutions serving households, and government.

Source: Asian Development Bank estimates.

Table A4.2: Price Level Indexes, 2017
(Hong Kong, China = 100)

Expenditure Category	BAN	BHU	BRU	CAM	FIJ	HKG	IND	INO	LAO	MAL	MLD	MON	MYA	NEP	PAK	PHI	PRC	SIN	SRI	TAP	THA	VIE
Gross Domestic Product	48	38	61	46	59	100	41	45	43	50	69	42	35	39	41	50	80	83	42	67	49	43
Actual Individual Consumption by Households[a]	44	36	61	44	58	100	38	45	43	49	75	40	34	35	39	47	77	96	40	66	47	41
Food and non-alcoholic beverages	53	47	69	53	64	100	39	60	56	51	62	47	44	43	47	52	77	83	57	82	53	49
Food	52	46	68	52	62	100	39	59	54	51	60	46	44	42	46	52	77	84	56	82	52	48
Bread and cereals	60	54	69	53	68	100	42	70	59	54	64	57	51	45	49	62	92	92	55	94	58	53
Meat and fish	54	43	62	55	64	100	44	51	54	49	39	35	42	50	43	43	70	91	51	79	47	47
Fruits and vegetables	38	47	91	52	58	100	32	65	51	54	102	74	40	33	41	57	67	84	55	87	56	47
Other food and non-alcoholic beverages	56	45	65	52	67	100	43	58	57	48	64	50	45	45	50	50	84	69	61	70	52	50
Clothing and footwear	56	46	113	55	75	100	37	62	48	60	71	59	45	43	52	75	148	97	45	66	49	49
Clothing	54	41	104	56	70	100	36	64	47	56	67	54	43	42	51	67	146	91	44	64	46	47
Housing, water, electricity, gas and other fuels	32	24	35	42	34	100	31	26	34	34	109	40	20	27	29	37	64	109	29	66	32	42
Health and education	26	15	42	18	40	100	20	24	12	38	41	16	15	14	20	28	54	86	11	40	28	19
Health	24	14	50	22	36	100	18	25	16	37	36	18	16	16	23	34	45	99	14	34	31	23
Education	27	17	35	15	42	100	23	24	10	37	45	15	14	13	18	25	67	75	8	50	25	16
Transportation and communication	49	52	91	59	57	100	45	54	66	57	100	52	51	51	45	59	64	121	56	64	58	53
Transportation	50	49	79	61	60	100	47	53	66	52	92	48	48	63	48	55	60	123	58	66	57	57
Recreation and culture	61	62	107	68	77	100	55	75	69	73	116	64	54	40	59	63	99	85	70	84	75	58
Restaurants and hotels	46	38	57	47	71	100	48	46	66	44	57	52	42	34	47	55	85	79	56	63	46	40
Other consumption expenditure items	53	43	58	44	77	100	51	52	49	60	74	45	37	49	45	51	94	111	50	73	58	43
Individual Consumption Expenditure by Government	34	18	40	27	43	100	44	29	16	39	45	15	18	27	35	42	70	85	13	48	32	21
Collective Consumption Expenditure by Government	45	21	39	45	52	100	54	35	26	44	52	24	28	45	42	46	83	70	20	58	44	29
Gross Fixed Capital Formation	59	54	68	53	62	100	46	48	53	52	64	53	41	53	52	59	86	82	55	75	54	52
Machinery and equipment	121	114	115	100	100	100	80	96	102	90	109	93	78	86	92	100	116	118	97	110	96	93
Construction	35	31	45	32	44	100	30	29	31	34	42	34	24	36	33	40	65	68	35	60	34	34
Change in Inventories and Net Acquisitions of Valuables	56	47	69	55	69	100	47	54	54	55	73	50	42	48	46	58	88	93	58	75	57	51
Balance of Exports and Imports	100	100	100	100	100	100	100	100	100	100	100	100	100	100	100	100	100	100	100	100	100	100
Individual Consumption Expenditure by Households and NPISH	46	39	63	46	60	100	37	47	47	50	79	45	36	36	39	48	77	98	45	68	49	44
Government Final Consumption Expenditure	40	19	39	35	48	100	50	32	22	42	49	20	24	38	39	45	77	75	17	53	38	26
Actual Individual Consumption by Households[a]	44	36	61	44	58	100	38	45	43	49	75	40	34	35	39	47	77	96	40	66	47	41
All goods	58	49	70	60	79	100	47	61	59	61	85	53	46	49	47	63	89	108	63	75	63	55
Non-durables	51	42	55	53	71	100	42	55	52	55	73	47	41	43	41	56	78	99	55	69	57	48
Semi-durables	60	53	99	60	80	100	45	60	55	61	81	62	47	43	54	74	145	95	60	69	63	55
Durables	91	76	126	92	104	100	69	87	88	78	158	72	77	91	72	82	92	157	93	96	88	84
Services	35	33	62	34	42	100	30	37	38	43	79	41	27	25	34	35	69	90	33	64	37	36

BAN = Bangladesh; BHU = Bhutan; BRU = Brunei Darussalam; CAM = Cambodia; FIJ = Fiji; HKG = Hong Kong, China; IND = India; INO = Indonesia; LAO = Lao People's Democratic Republic; MAL = Malaysia; MLD = Maldives; MON = Mongolia; MYA = Myanmar; NEP = Nepal; NPISH=nonprofit institutions serving households; PAK = Pakistan; PHI = Philippines; PRC = People's Republic of China; SIN = Singapore; SRI = Sri Lanka; TAP = Taipei,China; THA = Thailand; VIE = Viet Nam.

a Includes individual consumption expenditure by households, nonprofit institutions serving households, and government.
Source: Asian Development Bank estimates.

Table A4.3: Price Level Indexes, 2017
(Asia and the Pacific = 100)

Expenditure Category	BAN	BHU	BRU	CAM	FIJ	HKG	IND	INO	LAO	MAL	MLD	MON	MYA	NEP	PAK	PHI	PRC	SIN	SRI	TAP	THA	VIE
Gross Domestic Product	75	60	95	71	92	156	64	71	68	78	107	66	55	60	64	78	125	130	66	105	77	67
Actual Individual Consumption by Households[a]	76	62	103	75	98	170	64	77	73	83	128	68	58	60	66	80	132	164	69	112	80	70
Food and non-alcoholic beverages	92	82	121	92	111	175	69	105	97	89	108	83	78	75	82	90	135	144	99	143	93	85
Food	92	81	121	92	110	177	69	105	96	90	107	81	78	75	82	92	136	149	99	145	93	86
Bread and cereals	97	87	112	86	110	162	68	114	95	87	103	92	83	73	79	101	148	149	89	153	94	85
Meat and fish	90	72	104	93	107	167	73	86	90	82	64	58	71	84	72	72	117	152	86	132	79	79
Fruits and vegetables	77	95	185	105	117	204	65	132	104	111	208	151	82	66	83	115	137	172	112	178	113	95
Other food and non-alcoholic beverages	98	80	115	92	119	177	75	103	101	85	113	89	79	79	88	89	148	122	108	124	92	89
Clothing and footwear	75	62	152	74	101	134	50	84	65	80	95	79	60	57	70	101	199	131	61	89	66	65
Clothing	75	58	145	78	98	139	51	89	65	78	93	76	60	58	71	93	203	126	61	89	65	65
Housing, water, electricity, gas and other fuels	68	51	74	89	71	211	65	56	71	73	230	84	42	56	61	79	135	231	62	140	68	89
Health and education	63	38	102	44	98	244	49	59	30	92	99	40	36	35	50	69	133	209	26	99	68	46
Health	64	36	133	60	95	267	48	66	43	100	95	48	43	43	61	91	119	264	38	90	84	61
Education	63	39	80	34	96	230	53	54	23	86	104	34	32	30	41	56	154	172	19	114	57	37
Transportation and communication	85	90	157	102	98	173	78	94	114	99	173	90	89	89	78	101	111	209	97	110	101	93
Transportation	89	87	141	108	107	178	84	94	118	92	164	86	85	111	85	98	108	219	103	118	101	101
Recreation and culture	70	70	122	78	88	114	62	85	79	83	133	73	61	46	67	72	113	97	79	96	86	66
Restaurants and hotels	71	59	89	72	110	155	74	71	102	69	88	81	64	52	73	85	131	123	86	98	71	61
Other consumption expenditure items	72	59	79	60	105	137	70	71	66	82	101	61	51	67	62	69	129	151	69	100	80	59
Individual Consumption Expenditure by Government	57	30	67	45	72	168	75	48	27	66	76	25	31	45	59	71	117	143	22	82	54	36
Collective Consumption Expenditure by Government	69	32	61	70	80	155	84	54	40	68	81	37	44	69	66	72	129	109	32	89	68	45
Gross Fixed Capital Formation	81	74	93	72	84	136	63	66	72	71	87	73	56	73	71	81	117	112	75	102	73	71
Machinery and equipment	115	108	110	95	95	95	76	91	97	85	104	89	74	82	87	95	110	112	92	105	91	88
Construction	64	57	84	58	81	185	56	54	57	63	77	63	45	67	62	74	121	125	64	111	62	62
Change in Inventories and Net Acquisitions of Valuables	85	72	106	84	106	153	72	82	82	83	111	77	64	73	70	89	134	142	88	114	87	78
Balance of Exports and Imports	100	100	100	100	100	100	100	100	100	100	100	100	100	100	100	100	100	100	100	100	100	100
Individual Consumption Expenditure by Households and NPISH	79	68	109	80	103	173	65	82	81	87	138	77	62	63	68	83	133	169	79	118	85	76
Government Final Consumption Expenditure	64	31	62	57	76	160	79	51	35	67	78	31	39	60	62	71	123	119	27	85	61	41
Actual Individual Consumption by Households[a]	76	62	103	75	98	170	64	77	73	83	128	68	58	60	66	80	132	164	69	112	80	70
All goods	85	71	102	87	115	146	68	89	86	89	125	77	67	71	69	92	130	158	91	110	92	80
Non-durables	87	71	93	90	120	169	71	92	88	93	123	79	69	72	70	95	133	168	94	117	96	81
Semi-durables	70	62	116	70	94	117	52	70	64	71	95	73	55	50	64	86	169	111	70	81	74	64
Durables	102	85	141	103	116	112	78	97	99	87	177	81	86	102	81	92	103	175	104	107	99	94
Services	71	66	124	67	85	199	59	73	76	86	157	81	54	49	68	70	137	179	65	128	75	73

BAN = Bangladesh; BHU = Bhutan; BRU = Brunei Darussalam; CAM = Cambodia; FIJ = Fiji; HKG = Hong Kong, China; IND = India; INO = Indonesia; LAO = Lao People's Democratic Republic; MAL = Malaysia; MLD = Maldives; MON = Mongolia; MYA = Myanmar; NEP = Nepal; NPISH=nonprofit institutions serving households; PAK = Pakistan; PHI = Philippines; PRC = People's Republic of China; SIN = Singapore; SRI = Sri Lanka; TAP = Taipei,China; THA = Thailand; VIE = Viet Nam.

a Includes individual consumption expenditure by households, nonprofit institutions serving households, and government.
Source: Asian Development Bank estimates.

Table A4.4: Real Expenditure, 2017
(billion Hong Kong dollars)

Expenditure Category	BAN	BHU	BRU	CAM	FIJ	HKG	IND	INO	LAO	MAL	MLD	MON	MYA	NEP	PAK	PHI	PRC	SIN	SRI	TAP	THA	VIE	AP
Gross Domestic Product	4,272	52	156	378	71	2,663	48,395	17,394	303	4,916	55	212	1,409	503	5,954	4,902	117,929	3,171	1,621	6,688	7,232	4,069	232,344
Actual Individual Consumption by Households[a]	3,285	31	42	335	53	1,887	32,884	10,578	173	3,070	24	131	865	434	5,495	4,083	57,692	1,081	1,114	4,097	4,202	2,729	134,284
Food and non-alcoholic beverages	1,412	8	5	123	14	192	8,316	2,335	56	606	4	31	352	208	1,458	1,460	8,641	77	216	417	881	656	27,470
Food	1,415	8	4	119	14	180	8,343	2,100	48	587	4	29	346	208	1,407	1,328	8,422	67	215	389	775	637	26,645
Bread and cereals	551	2	1	37	3	19	1,762	469	12	78	1	4	65	70	327	422	1,250	11	69	81	150	174	5,558
Meat and fish	263	1	2	35	3	92	706	726	20	191	2	13	117	29	158	542	3,391	22	32	126	208	272	6,951
Fruits and vegetables	266	2	1	18	4	26	2,972	328	8	128	1	1	93	54	249	142	2,419	14	33	109	269	96	7,233
Other food and non-alcoholic beverages	306	3	2	32	4	55	3,028	833	16	215	2	14	79	58	710	359	1,788	31	82	101	252	111	8,082
Clothing and footwear	156	2	1	5	2	90	2,236	255	3	71	1	5	25	11	319	27	1,384	29	37	155	64	114	4,992
Clothing	144	1	1	3	2	59	1,829	215	3	65	1	4	23	9	266	21	1,094	26	35	141	65	100	4,104
Housing, water, electricity, gas and other fuels	743	6	8	54	6	295	5,408	1,545	26	614	4	18	205	71	1,469	571	9,596	141	162	627	533	587	22,692
Health and education	516	10	16	111	11	278	8,246	2,521	51	540	9	52	208	92	1,387	784	22,460	217	357	1,172	1,348	1,080	41,467
Health	218	7	3	45	3	157	4,124	859	15	220	6	18	104	39	738	212	15,269	99	149	795	574	436	24,090
Education	298	4	14	66	8	121	4,075	1,707	38	325	4	36	104	52	630	614	8,110	118	216	415	787	661	18,405
Transportation and communication	137	4	5	19	7	170	4,680	1,516	9	518	2	13	31	13	336	435	7,850	146	172	567	472	277	17,379
Transportation	121	3	4	18	5	125	3,984	1,222	7	361	1	10	23	7	232	373	5,931	112	158	432	416	248	13,794
Recreation and culture	38	1	1	6	1	194	199	280	2	127	1	3	7	13	147	51	2,169	128	76	277	127	85	3,933
Restaurants and hotels	72	1	2	15	1	167	491	961	12	325	2	2	34	8	123	135	2,089	122	30	310	376	125	5,402
Other consumption expenditure items	254	3	4	28	11	501	4,980	1,464	34	443	3	19	55	28	604	698	9,166	209	154	797	670	353	20,481
Individual Consumption Expenditure by Government	81	6	15	30	5	102	1,523	961	20	378	6	32	69	15	312	316	12,874	113	220	693	883	405	19,058
Collective Consumption Expenditure by Government	222	10	49	14	9	160	2,701	1,273	63	341	6	27	278	40	409	305	7,283	258	145	512	652	394	15,152
Gross Fixed Capital Formation	1,070	19	57	36	12	576	12,227	5,264	83	1,186	25	41	373	116	698	1,028	47,428	850	327	1,225	1,500	795	74,936
Machinery and equipment	153	3	11	8	5	161	2,130	434	12	203	5	8	83	15	138	224	6,465	175	95	327	489	104	11,250
Construction	1,276	22	51	32	5	360	9,603	6,588	63	1,045	23	28	306	102	469	750	43,267	399	226	548	812	879	66,852
Change in Inventories and Net Acquisitions of Valuables	6	-0	-3	2	1	11	2,058	61	0	14	1	12	16	56	86	5	1,935	56	122	-14	-20	95	4,499
Balance of Exports and Imports	-144	-4	13	-0	-1	29	-573	80	-3	170	1	2	-38	-66	-250	-241	1,643	665	-49	571	491	49	2,344
Individual Consumption Expenditure by Households and NPISH	3,120	26	31	303	47	1,785	31,360	9,551	152	2,707	19	107	784	410	5,135	3,738	46,611	969	929	3,484	3,466	2,364	117,100
Government Final Consumption Expenditure	318	17	64	41	15	261	4,312	2,241	88	712	12	58	374	59	727	617	19,609	372	347	1,191	1,487	788	33,711
Actual Individual Consumption by Households[a]	3,285	31	42	335	53	1,887	32,884	10,578	173	3,070	24	131	865	434	5,495	4,083	57,692	1,081	1,114	4,097	4,202	2,729	134,284
All goods	1,893	16	14	163	25	641	14,128	4,587	92	1,305	9	55	474	239	2,766	1,886	21,720	271	364	1,497	1,582	1,390	55,119
Non-durables	1,845	13	10	162	22	322	12,433	3,738	86	1,103	8	50	496	245	2,626	1,914	16,025	132	291	915	1,350	1,149	44,934
Semi-durables	172	2	2	7	2	160	2,072	574	5	123	1	6	26	14	318	71	2,229	55	103	309	144	134	6,528
Durables	55	1	2	8	3	158	702	479	7	143	1	3	7	7	76	80	3,821	70	6	289	166	162	6,248
Services	849	8	12	100	17	1,061	17,359	4,457	57	1,453	10	43	228	120	2,051	1,705	23,753	717	649	1,890	1,755	1,018	59,314

0 = magnitude is less than half of unit employed; AP = Asia and the Pacific; BAN = Bangladesh; BHU = Bhutan; BRU = Brunei Darussalam; CAM = Cambodia; FIJ = Fiji; HKG = Hong Kong, China; IND = India; INO = Indonesia; LAO = Lao People's Democratic Republic; MAL = Malaysia; MLD = Maldives; MON = Mongolia; MYA = Myanmar; NEP = Nepal; NPISH=nonprofit institutions serving households; PAK = Pakistan; PHI = Philippines; PRC = People's Republic of China; SIN = Singapore; SRI = Sri Lanka; TAP = Taipei,China; THA = Thailand; VIE = Viet Nam.

Note: Each real aggregate value is derived by using a purchasing power parity that is specific to that aggregate, so real aggregates may not sum up to the total of their real components for an economy.

a Includes individual consumption expenditure by households, nonprofit institutions serving households, and government.

Source: Asian Development Bank estimates.

Table A4.5: Economy Shares of Real Expenditure to Asia and the Pacific, 2017
(%)

Expenditure Category	BAN	BHU	BRU	CAM	FIJ	HKG	IND	INO	LAO	MAL	MLD	MON	MYA	NEP	PAK	PHI	PRC	SIN	SRI	TAP	THA	VIE	AP
Gross Domestic Product	1.84	0.02	0.07	0.16	0.03	1.15	20.83	7.49	0.13	2.12	0.02	0.09	0.61	0.22	2.56	2.11	50.76	1.36	0.70	2.88	3.11	1.75	100.00
Actual Individual Consumption by Households[a]	2.45	0.02	0.03	0.25	0.04	1.41	24.49	7.88	0.13	2.29	0.02	0.10	0.64	0.32	4.09	3.04	42.96	0.81	0.83	3.05	3.13	2.03	100.00
Food and non-alcoholic beverages	5.14	0.03	0.02	0.45	0.05	0.70	30.27	8.50	0.21	2.21	0.02	0.11	1.28	0.76	5.31	5.32	31.46	0.28	0.79	1.52	3.21	2.39	100.00
Food	5.31	0.03	0.02	0.45	0.05	0.68	31.31	7.88	0.18	2.20	0.01	0.11	1.30	0.78	5.28	4.98	31.61	0.25	0.81	1.46	2.91	2.39	100.00
Bread and cereals	9.92	0.03	0.02	0.67	0.05	0.34	31.70	8.44	0.22	1.41	0.01	0.07	1.18	1.25	5.88	7.60	22.49	0.19	1.24	1.45	2.70	3.14	100.00
Meat and fish	3.79	0.01	0.02	0.50	0.04	1.32	10.16	10.45	0.29	2.74	0.02	0.19	1.69	0.42	2.28	7.79	48.79	0.32	0.46	1.81	2.99	3.91	100.00
Fruits and vegetables	3.68	0.03	0.01	0.25	0.06	0.36	41.09	4.53	0.11	1.77	0.01	0.02	1.29	0.75	3.44	1.97	33.45	0.20	0.45	1.50	3.71	1.33	100.00
Other food and non-alcoholic beverages	3.78	0.04	0.02	0.39	0.06	0.68	37.46	10.31	0.19	2.67	0.02	0.17	0.98	0.71	8.78	4.44	22.13	0.38	1.02	1.25	3.12	1.38	100.00
Clothing and footwear	3.13	0.04	0.01	0.10	0.04	1.81	44.78	5.11	0.06	1.43	0.01	0.10	0.51	0.21	6.39	0.54	27.72	0.57	0.74	3.11	1.29	2.29	100.00
Clothing	3.51	0.04	0.02	0.06	0.04	1.45	44.57	5.23	0.06	1.59	0.01	0.10	0.55	0.22	6.48	0.51	26.65	0.63	0.85	3.43	1.58	2.43	100.00
Housing, water, electricity, gas and other fuels	3.27	0.02	0.04	0.24	0.03	1.30	23.83	6.81	0.12	2.71	0.02	0.08	0.91	0.31	6.47	2.52	42.29	0.62	0.72	2.76	2.35	2.59	100.00
Health and education	1.24	0.02	0.04	0.27	0.03	0.67	19.89	6.08	0.12	1.30	0.02	0.12	0.50	0.22	3.35	1.89	54.16	0.52	0.86	2.83	3.25	2.60	100.00
Health	0.90	0.03	0.01	0.19	0.01	0.65	17.12	3.57	0.06	0.91	0.02	0.07	0.43	0.16	3.07	0.88	63.38	0.41	0.62	3.30	2.38	1.81	100.00
Education	1.62	0.02	0.08	0.36	0.04	0.66	22.14	9.28	0.21	1.77	0.02	0.19	0.57	0.28	3.43	3.33	44.07	0.64	1.18	2.25	4.28	3.59	100.00
Transportation and communication	0.79	0.02	0.03	0.11	0.04	0.98	26.93	8.72	0.05	2.98	0.01	0.07	0.18	0.07	1.94	2.50	45.17	0.84	0.99	3.26	2.72	1.59	100.00
Transportation	0.88	0.02	0.03	0.13	0.03	0.91	28.88	8.86	0.05	2.62	0.01	0.07	0.17	0.05	1.68	2.70	43.00	0.81	1.14	3.13	3.01	1.80	100.00
Recreation and culture	0.96	0.01	0.04	0.15	0.02	4.94	5.06	7.13	0.05	3.23	0.01	0.08	0.17	0.32	3.75	1.30	55.14	3.27	1.93	7.05	3.24	2.16	100.00
Restaurants and hotels	1.34	0.01	0.04	0.28	0.01	3.09	9.08	17.79	0.22	6.02	0.04	0.04	0.64	0.15	2.28	2.50	38.67	2.26	0.55	5.74	6.96	2.31	100.00
Other consumption expenditure items	1.24	0.02	0.02	0.14	0.05	2.45	24.32	7.15	0.16	2.16	0.02	0.09	0.27	0.13	2.95	3.41	44.75	1.02	0.75	3.89	3.27	1.72	100.00
Individual Consumption Expenditure by Government	0.43	0.03	0.08	0.16	0.03	0.53	7.99	5.04	0.11	1.98	0.03	0.17	0.36	0.08	1.63	1.66	67.55	0.59	1.15	3.64	4.64	2.13	100.00
Collective Consumption Expenditure by Government	1.47	0.07	0.32	0.09	0.06	1.05	17.83	8.40	0.41	2.25	0.04	0.18	1.83	0.27	2.70	2.01	48.06	1.70	0.96	3.38	4.30	2.60	100.00
Gross Fixed Capital Formation	1.43	0.02	0.08	0.05	0.02	0.77	16.32	7.02	0.11	1.58	0.03	0.05	0.50	0.16	0.93	1.37	63.29	1.13	0.44	1.63	2.00	1.06	100.00
Machinery and equipment	1.36	0.02	0.10	0.08	0.04	1.43	18.94	3.86	0.11	1.80	0.05	0.07	0.74	0.14	1.23	1.99	57.47	1.55	0.84	2.90	4.35	0.93	100.00
Construction	1.91	0.03	0.08	0.05	0.01	0.54	14.36	9.85	0.09	1.56	0.03	0.04	0.46	0.15	0.70	1.12	64.72	0.60	0.34	0.82	1.21	1.31	100.00
Change in Inventories and Net Acquisitions of Valuables	0.13	-0.00	-0.06	0.04	0.02	0.24	45.74	1.35	0.00	0.32	0.02	0.26	0.34	1.25	1.91	0.12	43.01	1.25	2.71	24.37	20.94	2.12	100.00
Balance of Exports and Imports	-6.16	-0.17	0.56	-0.01	-0.06	1.23	-24.46	3.43	-0.15	7.26	0.03	0.09	-1.61	-2.81	-10.68	-10.27	70.11	28.36	-2.09	-0.31	-0.45	2.09	100.00
Individual Consumption Expenditure by Households and NPISH	2.66	0.02	0.03	0.26	0.04	1.52	26.78	8.16	0.13	2.31	0.02	0.09	0.67	0.35	4.39	3.19	39.80	0.83	0.79	2.98	2.96	2.02	100.00
Government Final Consumption Expenditure	0.94	0.05	0.19	0.12	0.04	0.78	12.79	6.65	0.26	2.11	0.04	0.17	1.11	0.17	2.16	1.83	58.17	1.10	1.03	3.53	4.41	2.34	100.00
Actual Individual Consumption by Households[a]	2.45	0.02	0.03	0.25	0.04	1.41	24.49	7.88	0.13	2.29	0.02	0.10	0.64	0.32	4.09	3.04	42.96	0.81	0.83	3.05	3.13	2.03	100.00
All goods	3.43	0.03	0.02	0.30	0.05	1.16	25.63	8.32	0.17	2.37	0.02	0.10	0.86	0.43	5.02	3.42	39.41	0.49	0.66	2.72	2.87	2.52	100.00
Non-durables	4.11	0.03	0.02	0.36	0.05	0.72	27.67	8.32	0.19	2.45	0.02	0.11	1.10	0.55	5.84	4.26	35.66	0.29	0.65	2.04	3.00	2.56	100.00
Semi-durables	2.63	0.03	0.03	0.11	0.03	2.46	31.74	8.79	0.08	1.88	0.02	0.09	0.39	0.22	4.87	1.09	34.15	0.84	1.58	4.73	2.20	2.05	100.00
Durables	0.89	0.02	0.03	0.13	0.05	2.53	11.24	7.67	0.11	2.29	0.01	0.05	0.12	0.11	1.22	1.28	61.15	1.12	0.09	4.62	2.66	2.60	100.00
Services	1.43	0.01	0.02	0.17	0.03	1.79	29.27	7.51	0.10	2.45	0.02	0.07	0.38	0.20	3.46	2.87	40.05	1.21	1.09	3.19	2.96	1.72	100.00

0.00 = magnitude of less than half of the unit employed; AP = Asia and the Pacific; BAN = Bangladesh; BHU = Bhutan; BRU = Brunei Darussalam; CAM = Cambodia; FIJ = Fiji; HKG = Hong Kong, China; IND = India; INO = Indonesia; LAO = Lao People's Democratic Republic; MAL = Malaysia; MLD = Maldives; MON = Mongolia; MYA = Myanmar; NEP = Nepal; NPISH=nonprofit institutions serving households; PAK = Pakistan; PHI = Philippines; PRC = People's Republic of China; SIN = Singapore; SRI = Sri Lanka; TAP = Taipei,China; THA = Thailand; VIE = Viet Nam.

Note: Each real aggregate value is derived by using a purchasing power parity that is specific to that aggregate, so real aggregates may not sum up to the total of their real components for an economy.

a Includes individual consumption expenditure by households, nonprofit institutions serving households, and government.

Source: Asian Development Bank estimates.

Table A4.6: Per Capita Real Expenditure, 2017
(Hong Kong dollars)

Expenditure Category	BAN	BHU	BRU	CAM	FIJ	HKG	IND	INO	LAO	MAL	MLD	MON	MYA	NEP	PAK	PHI	PRC	SIN	SRI	TAP	THA	VIE	AP
Gross Domestic Product	26,401	70,855	362,379	23,853	80,772	360,247	36,965	66,419	43,944	153,532	112,187	67,241	26,519	17,431	29,905	46,721	85,061	564,960	75,587	283,878	106,892	43,179	61,375
Actual Individual Consumption by Households[a]	20,301	43,196	97,121	21,161	60,057	255,310	25,118	40,391	25,055	95,858	47,964	41,482	16,267	15,041	27,599	38,916	41,613	192,614	51,965	173,917	62,106	28,955	35,472
Food and non-alcoholic beverages	8,727	11,369	10,950	7,758	16,471	25,959	6,352	8,916	8,180	18,930	8,650	9,899	6,614	7,206	7,322	13,918	6,233	13,644	10,075	17,712	13,023	6,966	7,256
Food	8,748	10,702	9,993	7,527	15,796	24,354	6,373	8,019	6,990	18,342	7,589	9,169	6,509	7,230	7,066	12,656	6,075	11,938	10,006	16,504	11,450	6,758	7,038
Bread and cereals	3,407	2,535	2,219	2,357	3,012	2,525	1,346	1,791	1,786	2,443	1,312	1,207	1,232	2,412	1,641	4,027	902	1,922	3,219	3,430	2,219	1,850	1,468
Meat and fish	1,627	1,367	3,936	2,186	3,229	12,392	539	2,773	2,944	5,952	3,529	4,258	2,204	1,011	796	5,162	2,446	3,959	1,497	5,349	3,072	2,881	1,836
Fruits and vegetables	1,643	2,791	1,349	1,141	5,122	3,557	2,270	1,251	1,172	3,994	1,116	394	1,750	1,876	1,249	1,358	1,745	2,542	1,525	4,616	3,971	1,020	1,911
Other food and non-alcoholic beverages	1,889	4,591	3,662	1,994	5,093	7,484	2,313	3,182	2,277	6,729	3,130	4,381	1,494	2,003	3,565	3,423	1,290	5,459	3,828	4,294	3,730	1,182	2,135
Clothing and footwear	967	2,564	1,688	313	2,021	12,229	1,708	974	461	2,224	1,507	1,537	479	365	1,601	258	998	5,114	1,721	6,594	951	1,211	1,319
Clothing	891	2,059	1,517	158	1,802	8,043	1,397	820	379	2,032	1,168	1,288	425	314	1,335	198	789	4,621	1,620	5,971	961	1,057	1,084
Housing, water, electricity, gas and other fuels	4,591	7,690	19,297	3,398	7,159	39,868	4,131	5,901	3,826	19,182	8,083	5,717	3,865	2,474	7,376	5,444	6,922	25,209	7,577	26,629	7,885	6,230	5,994
Health and education	3,190	14,074	36,636	6,973	12,291	37,648	6,299	9,626	7,319	16,858	18,690	16,427	3,916	3,179	6,967	7,477	16,200	38,718	16,662	49,759	19,927	11,458	10,954
Health	1,345	9,103	7,943	2,866	3,822	21,294	3,150	3,280	2,145	6,878	11,501	5,666	1,947	1,353	3,709	2,019	11,014	17,683	6,937	33,725	8,487	4,622	6,363
Education	1,845	5,470	32,719	4,151	8,565	16,354	3,113	6,519	5,541	10,159	7,803	11,362	1,958	1,812	3,166	5,850	5,850	21,049	10,092	17,606	11,637	7,012	4,862
Transportation and communication	848	4,862	11,210	1,193	8,291	22,991	3,574	5,789	1,308	16,178	4,350	4,139	588	439	1,689	4,143	5,662	26,027	8,017	24,070	6,982	2,938	4,591
Transportation	747	4,244	9,967	1,124	5,410	16,963	3,043	4,667	997	11,273	2,426	3,282	438	256	1,166	3,555	4,278	20,003	7,362	18,335	6,146	2,630	3,644
Recreation and culture	233	730	3,471	368	762	26,263	152	1,070	269	3,972	1,179	973	127	441	740	488	1,564	22,894	3,538	11,760	1,882	899	1,039
Restaurants and hotels	447	887	4,774	939	579	22,555	375	3,668	1,710	10,152	4,447	766	646	280	617	1,288	1,507	21,731	1,393	13,164	5,556	1,322	1,427
Other consumption expenditure items	1,570	4,355	9,726	1,787	12,524	67,796	3,804	5,589	4,882	13,844	6,712	6,067	1,041	957	3,035	6,655	6,611	37,263	7,202	33,822	9,910	3,747	5,410
Individual Consumption Expenditure by Government	502	8,087	34,673	1,899	6,002	13,756	1,163	3,668	2,900	11,798	11,761	10,191	1,293	516	1,565	3,014	9,286	20,109	10,255	29,420	13,057	4,302	5,034
Collective Consumption Expenditure by Government	1,374	14,383	113,259	898	10,782	21,618	2,063	4,860	9,112	10,660	12,499	8,637	5,225	1,405	2,056	2,909	5,253	45,883	6,778	21,714	9,640	4,178	4,003
Gross Fixed Capital Formation	6,616	25,672	132,105	2,240	13,726	77,924	9,339	20,099	12,042	37,035	50,477	13,066	7,026	4,033	3,505	9,799	34,209	151,506	15,270	51,992	22,173	8,435	19,795
Machinery and equipment	946	3,588	26,197	535	5,300	21,838	1,627	1,657	1,763	6,329	10,950	2,566	1,556	529	695	2,137	4,663	31,125	4,416	13,862	7,234	1,109	2,972
Construction	7,884	29,896	119,441	1,991	5,913	48,761	7,335	25,156	9,128	32,637	46,048	8,850	5,754	3,541	2,354	7,146	31,208	71,169	10,519	23,251	11,997	9,326	17,659
Change in Inventories and Net Acquisitions of Valuables	35	-31	-6,342	106	778	1,485	1,572	233	0	451	1,383	3,767	292	1,957	431	50	1,396	9,994	5,693	-600	-300	1,012	1,188
Balance of Exports and Imports	-892	-5,544	30,743	-12	-1,707	3,910	-438	307	-499	5,317	1,293	669	-709	-2,282	-1,257	-2,294	1,185	118,442	-2,282	24,246	7,253	519	619
Individual Consumption Expenditure by Households and NPISH	19,282	36,422	71,556	19,097	53,908	241,555	23,954	36,471	22,065	84,526	38,688	33,862	14,750	14,212	25,791	35,630	33,620	172,694	43,335	147,894	51,232	25,088	30,933
Government Final Consumption Expenditure	1,966	22,991	149,626	2,592	17,113	35,374	3,294	8,558	12,806	22,237	24,196	18,416	7,046	2,035	3,649	5,882	14,144	66,233	16,177	50,555	21,978	8,358	8,905
Actual Individual Consumption by Households[a]	20,301	43,196	97,121	21,161	60,057	255,310	25,118	40,391	25,055	95,858	47,964	41,482	16,267	15,041	27,599	38,916	41,613	192,614	51,965	173,917	62,106	28,955	35,472
All goods	11,698	21,596	31,484	10,314	29,034	86,686	10,792	17,516	13,357	40,741	17,900	17,452	8,926	8,303	13,890	17,975	15,667	48,365	16,977	63,539	23,390	14,754	14,560
Non-durables	11,403	18,025	24,238	10,222	24,927	43,557	9,496	14,272	12,487	34,442	15,477	15,771	9,330	8,505	13,188	18,242	11,558	23,554	13,557	38,848	19,956	12,195	11,870
Semi-durables	1,062	3,009	4,026	445	2,098	21,704	1,582	2,191	787	3,826	2,099	1,908	483	491	1,598	676	1,608	9,765	4,812	13,103	2,121	1,421	1,724
Durables	342	1,760	3,745	524	3,305	21,425	537	1,830	1,037	4,474	1,457	984	136	237	384	760	2,756	12,510	260	12,261	2,452	1,722	1,650
Services	5,246	11,584	28,852	6,289	18,955	143,607	13,259	17,019	8,330	45,363	19,598	13,528	4,294	4,174	10,301	16,250	17,133	127,775	30,285	80,239	25,942	10,800	15,668

0 = magnitude of less than half of the unit employed; AP = Asia and the Pacific; BAN = Bangladesh; BHU = Bhutan; BRU = Brunei Darussalam; CAM = Cambodia; FIJ = Fiji; HKG = Hong Kong, China; IND = India; INO = Indonesia; LAO = Lao People's Democratic Republic; MAL = Malaysia; MLD = Maldives; MON = Mongolia; MYA = Myanmar; NEP = Nepal; NPISH=nonprofit institutions serving households; PAK = Pakistan; PHI = Philippines; PRC = People's Republic of China; SIN = Singapore; SRI = Sri Lanka; TAP = Taipei,China; THA = Thailand; VIE = Viet Nam.

Note: Each real aggregate value is derived by using a purchasing power parity that is specific to that aggregate, so real aggregates may not sum up to the total of their real components for an economy.

a Includes individual consumption expenditure by households, nonprofit institutions serving households, and government.

Source: Asian Development Bank estimates.

Table A4.7: Per Capita Real Expenditure Index, 2017
(Asia and the Pacific = 100)

Expenditure Category	BAN	BHU	BRU	CAM	FIJ	HKG	IND	INO	LAO	MAL	MLD	MON	MYA	NEP	PAK	PHI	PRC	SIN	SRI	TAP	THA	VIE	AP
Gross Domestic Product	43	115	590	39	132	587	60	108	72	250	183	110	43	28	49	76	139	921	123	463	174	70	100
Actual Individual Consumption by Households[a]	57	122	274	60	169	720	71	114	71	270	135	117	46	42	78	110	117	543	146	490	175	82	100
Food and non-alcoholic beverages	120	157	151	107	227	358	88	123	113	261	119	136	91	99	101	192	86	188	139	244	179	96	100
Food	124	152	142	107	224	346	91	114	99	261	108	130	92	103	100	180	86	170	142	234	163	96	100
Bread and cereals	232	173	151	161	205	172	92	122	122	166	89	82	84	164	112	274	61	131	219	234	151	126	100
Meat and fish	89	74	214	119	176	675	29	151	160	324	192	232	120	55	43	281	133	216	82	291	167	157	100
Fruits and vegetables	86	146	71	60	268	186	119	65	61	209	58	21	92	98	65	71	91	133	80	242	208	53	100
Other food and non-alcoholic beverages	88	215	172	93	239	351	108	149	107	315	147	205	70	94	167	160	60	256	179	201	175	55	100
Clothing and footwear	73	194	128	24	153	927	129	74	35	169	114	117	36	28	121	20	76	388	131	500	72	92	100
Clothing	82	190	140	15	166	742	129	76	35	187	108	119	39	29	123	18	73	426	149	551	89	98	100
Housing, water, electricity, gas and other fuels	77	128	322	57	119	665	69	98	64	320	135	95	64	41	123	91	115	421	126	444	132	104	100
Health and education	29	128	334	64	112	344	58	88	67	154	171	150	36	29	64	68	148	353	152	454	182	105	100
Health	21	143	125	45	60	335	50	52	34	108	181	89	31	21	58	32	173	278	109	530	133	73	100
Education	38	113	673	85	176	336	64	134	114	209	161	234	40	37	65	120	120	433	208	362	239	144	100
Transportation and communication	18	106	244	26	181	501	78	126	28	352	95	90	13	10	37	90	123	567	175	524	152	64	100
Transportation	21	116	274	31	148	466	84	128	27	309	67	90	12	7	32	98	117	549	202	503	169	72	100
Recreation and culture	22	70	334	35	73	2,528	15	103	26	382	113	94	12	42	71	47	151	2,204	341	1,132	181	87	100
Restaurants and hotels	31	62	335	66	41	1,581	26	257	120	711	312	54	45	20	43	90	106	1,523	98	923	389	93	100
Other consumption expenditure items	29	81	180	33	231	1,253	70	103	90	256	124	112	19	18	56	123	122	689	133	625	183	69	100
Individual Consumption Expenditure by Government	10	161	689	38	119	273	23	73	58	234	234	202	26	10	31	60	184	399	204	584	259	85	100
Collective Consumption Expenditure by Government	34	359	2,830	22	269	540	52	121	228	266	312	216	131	35	51	73	131	1,146	169	543	241	104	100
Gross Fixed Capital Formation	33	130	667	11	69	394	47	102	61	187	255	66	35	20	18	50	173	765	77	263	112	43	100
Machinery and equipment	32	121	882	18	178	735	55	56	59	213	368	86	52	18	23	72	157	1,047	149	466	243	37	100
Construction	45	169	676	11	33	276	42	142	52	185	261	50	33	20	13	40	177	403	60	132	68	53	100
Change in Inventories and Net Acquisitions of Valuables	3	-3	-534	9	65	125	132	20	0	38	116	317	25	165	36	4	117	841	479	-50	-25	85	100
Balance of Exports and Imports	-144	-895	4,966	-2	-276	632	-71	50	-81	859	209	108	-115	-369	-203	-371	191	19,132	-369	3,916	1,172	84	100
Individual Consumption Expenditure by Households and NPISH	62	118	231	62	174	781	77	118	71	273	125	109	48	46	83	115	109	558	140	478	166	81	100
Government Final Consumption Expenditure	22	258	1,680	29	192	397	37	96	144	250	272	207	79	23	41	66	159	744	182	568	247	94	100
Actual Individual Consumption by Households[a]	57	122	274	60	169	720	71	114	71	270	135	117	46	42	78	110	117	543	146	490	175	82	100
All goods	80	148	216	71	199	595	74	120	92	280	123	120	61	57	95	123	108	332	117	436	161	101	100
Non-durables	96	152	204	86	210	367	80	120	105	290	130	133	79	72	111	154	97	198	114	327	168	103	100
Semi-durables	62	175	234	26	122	1,259	92	127	46	222	122	111	28	28	93	39	93	566	279	760	123	82	100
Durables	21	107	227	32	200	1,298	33	111	63	271	88	60	8	14	23	46	167	758	16	743	149	104	100
Services	33	74	184	40	121	917	85	109	53	290	125	86	27	27	66	104	109	816	193	512	166	69	100

0 = magnitude of less than half of the unit employed; AP = Asia and the Pacific; BAN = Bangladesh; BHU = Bhutan; BRU = Brunei Darussalam; CAM = Cambodia; FIJ = Fiji; HKG = Hong Kong, China; IND = India; INO = Indonesia; LAO = Lao People's Democratic Republic; MAL = Malaysia; MLD = Maldives; MON = Mongolia; MYA = Myanmar; NEP = Nepal; NPISH=nonprofit institutions serving households; PAK = Pakistan; PHI = Philippines; PRC = People's Republic of China; SIN = Singapore; SRI = Sri Lanka; TAP = Taipei,China; THA = Thailand; VIE = Viet Nam.

Note: Each real aggregate value is derived by using a purchasing power parity that is specific to that aggregate, so real aggregates may not sum up to the total of their real components for an economy.

a Includes individual consumption expenditure by households, nonprofit institutions serving households, and government.

Source: Asian Development Bank estimates.

Table A4.8: Nominal Expenditure, 2017
(billion Hong Kong dollars)

Expenditure Category	BAN	BHU	BRU	CAM	FIJ	HKG	IND	INO	LAO	MAL	MLD	MON	MYA	NEP	PAK	PHI	PRC	SIN	SRI	TAP	THA	VIE	AP
Gross Domestic Product	2,047	20	95	173	42	2,663	19,893	7,913	131	2,453	38	89	493	195	2,459	2,444	94,638	2,637	681	4,480	3,548	1,744	148,874
Actual Individual Consumption by Households[a]	1,457	11	25	147	30	1,887	12,382	4,811	75	1,505	18	52	293	153	2,131	1,929	44,670	1,043	451	2,707	1,977	1,116	78,873
Food and non-alcoholic beverages	741	4	3	65	9	192	3,283	1,400	31	309	3	15	156	90	685	756	6,656	63	123	342	467	320	15,712
Food	738	4	3	62	9	180	3,234	1,249	26	298	2	13	152	88	651	693	6,452	56	120	318	406	308	15,063
Bread and cereals	329	1	1	20	2	19	740	330	7	42	0	2	34	31	160	262	1,144	10	38	76	87	92	3,426
Meat and fish	142	0	1	19	2	92	308	373	11	94	1	5	50	15	69	233	2,384	20	16	100	98	128	4,159
Fruits and vegetables	100	1	1	9	3	26	943	212	4	70	1	1	37	18	102	81	1,628	12	18	95	149	45	3,554
Other food and non-alcoholic beverages	170	2	1	16	3	55	1,292	484	9	104	1	7	35	26	355	180	1,501	21	50	71	132	56	4,573
Clothing and footwear	87	1	1	3	1	90	838	159	2	43	1	3	11	5	167	20	2,053	28	17	103	31	56	3,719
Clothing	78	1	1	1	1	59	665	136	1	36	0	2	10	4	135	14	1,596	24	15	90	30	46	2,946
Housing, water, electricity, gas and other fuels	238	1	3	23	2	295	1,657	407	9	212	4	7	41	19	426	214	6,142	155	47	416	173	246	10,737
Health and education	133	2	7	20	4	278	1,667	613	6	203	4	9	31	13	283	223	12,223	186	39	474	373	204	16,995
Health	52	1	2	10	1	157	735	212	2	82	2	3	17	6	170	72	6,816	98	21	268	180	99	9,008
Education	81	1	5	10	3	121	932	401	4	121	2	5	14	7	113	150	5,407	88	17	206	193	105	7,987
Transportation and communication	67	2	4	11	4	170	2,108	825	6	298	2	7	16	6	152	255	5,048	176	96	362	274	148	10,037
Transportation	60	1	3	11	3	125	1,884	645	5	186	1	5	11	5	111	205	3,584	138	91	285	235	140	7,736
Recreation and culture	23	0	2	4	1	194	109	210	1	92	1	2	4	5	87	32	2,143	109	53	233	96	49	3,449
Restaurants and hotels	33	0	1	7	0	167	234	441	8	144	1	1	14	3	58	74	1,773	97	17	196	171	49	3,490
Other consumption expenditure items	134	1	2	12	8	501	2,557	757	16	265	2	9	21	14	274	355	8,632	232	78	582	392	151	14,995
Individual Consumption Expenditure by Government	28	1	6	8	2	102	677	275	3	148	3	5	13	4	110	133	8,967	96	28	336	283	86	11,312
Collective Consumption Expenditure by Government	99	2	19	6	5	160	1,467	444	16	150	3	7	78	18	173	142	6,076	181	30	295	286	115	9,772
Gross Fixed Capital Formation	633	10	39	19	7	576	5,649	2,545	44	619	16	22	152	62	365	611	40,556	696	179	918	805	415	54,938
Machinery and equipment	185	3	13	8	5	161	1,706	418	12	182	6	8	65	13	127	224	7,479	206	92	359	468	97	11,836
Construction	444	7	23	10	2	360	2,909	1,912	19	358	9	10	74	37	156	300	28,311	271	78	329	273	295	36,188
Change in Inventories and Net Acquisitions of Valuables	3	-0	-2	1	0	11	968	33	0	8	0	6	7	27	39	3	1,693	52	70	-11	-12	49	2,947
Balance of Exports and Imports	-144	-4	13	-0	-1	29	-573	80	-3	170	1	2	-38	-66	-250	-241	1,643	665	-49	571	491	49	2,344
Individual Consumption Expenditure by Households and NPISH	1,429	10	19	139	28	1,785	11,706	4,536	71	1,357	15	48	281	149	2,022	1,796	35,703	947	422	2,372	1,694	1,030	67,560
Government Final Consumption Expenditure	127	3	25	15	7	261	2,144	719	20	298	6	11	91	22	283	275	15,042	277	58	630	569	201	21,085
Actual Individual Consumption by Households[a]	1,457	11	25	147	30	1,887	12,382	4,811	75	1,505	18	52	293	153	2,131	1,929	44,670	1,043	451	2,707	1,977	1,116	78,873
All goods	1,103	8	9	98	20	641	6,609	2,804	54	791	8	29	219	117	1,311	1,193	19,324	294	228	1,126	1,002	762	37,749
Non-durables	950	5	6	86	16	322	5,191	2,043	45	606	6	23	201	104	1,083	1,075	12,567	132	161	635	765	551	26,572
Semi-durables	103	1	2	4	1	160	931	346	3	74	1	4	12	6	173	53	3,230	52	62	214	91	74	5,599
Durables	51	1	2	8	3	158	487	416	6	111	1	2	6	6	55	66	3,527	110	5	276	146	136	5,579
Services	301	3	8	34	7	1,061	5,168	1,638	22	625	8	17	62	30	701	602	16,379	644	212	1,217	657	371	29,767

0 = magnitude is less than half of unit employed; AP = Asia and the Pacific; BAN = Bangladesh; BHU = Bhutan; BRU = Brunei Darussalam; CAM = Cambodia; FIJ = Fiji; HKG = Hong Kong, China; IND = India; INO = Indonesia; LAO = Lao People's Democratic Republic; MAL = Malaysia; MLD = Maldives; MON = Mongolia; MYA = Myanmar; NEP = Nepal; NPISH=nonprofit institutions serving households; PAK = Pakistan; PHI = Philippines; PRC = People's Republic of China; SIN = Singapore; SRI = Sri Lanka; TAP = Taipei,China; THA = Thailand; VIE = Viet Nam.

a Includes individual consumption expenditure by households, nonprofit institutions serving households, and government.

Source: Asian Development Bank estimates.

Table A4.9: Economy Shares of Nominal Expenditure to Asia and the Pacific, 2017
(%)

Expenditure Category	BAN	BHU	BRU	CAM	FIJ	HKG	IND	INO	LAO	MAL	MLD	MON	MYA	NEP	PAK	PHI	PRC	SIN	SRI	TAP	THA	VIE	AP
Gross Domestic Product	1.38	0.01	0.06	0.12	0.03	1.79	13.36	5.32	0.09	1.65	0.03	0.06	0.33	0.13	1.65	1.64	63.57	1.77	0.46	3.01	2.38	1.17	100.00
Actual Individual Consumption by Households[a]	1.85	0.01	0.03	0.19	0.04	2.39	15.70	6.10	0.09	1.91	0.02	0.07	0.37	0.19	2.70	2.45	56.64	1.32	0.57	3.43	2.51	1.42	100.00
Food and non-alcoholic beverages	4.72	0.02	0.02	0.41	0.06	1.22	20.90	8.91	0.20	1.97	0.02	0.09	0.99	0.57	4.36	4.81	42.36	0.40	0.78	2.17	2.97	2.04	100.00
Food	4.90	0.02	0.02	0.41	0.06	1.20	21.47	8.29	0.17	1.98	0.01	0.09	1.01	0.59	4.32	4.60	42.84	0.37	0.80	2.11	2.69	2.04	100.00
Bread and cereals	9.61	0.03	0.02	0.58	0.05	0.54	21.59	9.64	0.21	1.23	0.01	0.06	0.98	0.92	4.66	7.64	33.39	0.29	1.11	2.22	2.53	2.68	100.00
Meat and fish	3.41	0.01	0.03	0.46	0.04	2.20	7.40	8.98	0.26	2.25	0.02	0.11	1.19	0.35	1.65	5.59	57.32	0.49	0.40	2.39	2.37	3.07	100.00
Fruits and vegetables	2.81	0.03	0.01	0.26	0.07	0.74	26.54	5.96	0.12	1.96	0.02	0.03	1.05	0.49	2.86	2.27	45.80	0.34	0.51	2.68	4.21	1.26	100.00
Other food and non-alcoholic beverages	3.72	0.03	0.02	0.36	0.07	1.21	28.26	10.59	0.20	2.27	0.02	0.15	0.78	0.57	7.76	3.95	32.82	0.46	1.10	1.55	2.88	1.22	100.00
Clothing and footwear	2.34	0.02	0.02	0.07	0.04	2.43	22.53	4.28	0.04	1.14	0.01	0.08	0.30	0.12	4.50	0.55	55.21	0.75	0.45	2.77	0.85	1.50	100.00
Clothing	2.63	0.02	0.02	0.05	0.04	2.02	22.58	4.63	0.04	1.24	0.01	0.07	0.33	0.13	4.57	0.47	54.18	0.80	0.51	3.04	1.02	1.58	100.00
Housing, water, electricity, gas and other fuels	2.21	0.01	0.03	0.21	0.02	2.74	15.44	3.79	0.08	1.97	0.04	0.07	0.38	0.18	3.97	1.99	57.21	1.44	0.44	3.87	1.61	2.30	100.00
Health and education	0.78	0.01	0.04	0.12	0.03	1.64	9.81	3.61	0.04	1.20	0.02	0.05	0.18	0.08	1.66	1.31	71.92	1.10	0.23	2.79	2.20	1.20	100.00
Health	0.58	0.01	0.02	0.11	0.01	1.75	8.16	2.35	0.03	0.91	0.02	0.04	0.18	0.07	1.88	0.80	75.67	1.09	0.24	2.98	2.00	1.10	100.00
Education	1.02	0.01	0.06	0.12	0.04	1.51	11.66	5.03	0.05	1.52	0.02	0.07	0.18	0.08	1.41	1.88	67.70	1.11	0.22	2.58	2.42	1.32	100.00
Transportation and communication	0.67	0.02	0.04	0.11	0.04	1.69	21.00	8.22	0.06	2.97	0.02	0.07	0.16	0.06	1.51	2.54	50.29	1.76	0.96	3.60	2.73	1.48	100.00
Transportation	0.78	0.02	0.04	0.14	0.04	1.62	24.36	8.34	0.06	2.41	0.01	0.06	0.14	0.06	1.43	2.65	46.33	1.78	1.18	3.69	3.04	1.81	100.00
Recreation and culture	0.67	0.01	0.05	0.12	0.01	5.63	3.15	6.08	0.04	2.68	0.02	0.06	0.11	0.15	2.52	0.94	62.13	3.16	1.53	6.75	2.77	1.42	100.00
Restaurants and hotels	0.96	0.01	0.03	0.20	0.01	4.78	6.70	12.63	0.22	4.13	0.04	0.04	0.41	0.08	1.66	2.12	50.81	2.77	0.48	5.62	4.91	1.41	100.00
Other consumption expenditure items	0.89	0.01	0.02	0.08	0.06	3.34	17.06	5.05	0.11	1.76	0.02	0.06	0.14	0.09	1.83	2.37	57.56	1.55	0.52	3.88	2.61	1.01	100.00
Individual Consumption Expenditure by Government	0.24	0.01	0.05	0.07	0.02	0.90	5.98	2.43	0.03	1.31	0.02	0.04	0.11	0.04	0.97	1.18	79.26	0.85	0.25	2.97	2.50	0.76	100.00
Collective Consumption Expenditure by Government	1.01	0.02	0.20	0.07	0.05	1.64	15.01	4.54	0.17	1.54	0.03	0.07	0.80	0.19	1.77	1.45	62.17	1.86	0.30	3.01	2.93	1.18	100.00
Gross Fixed Capital Formation	1.15	0.02	0.07	0.03	0.01	1.05	10.28	4.63	0.08	1.13	0.03	0.04	0.28	0.11	0.66	1.11	73.82	1.27	0.33	1.67	1.47	0.75	100.00
Machinery and equipment	1.57	0.03	0.11	0.07	0.04	1.36	14.41	3.53	0.10	1.54	0.05	0.06	0.55	0.11	1.07	1.89	63.18	1.74	0.78	3.03	3.95	0.82	100.00
Construction	1.23	0.02	0.06	0.03	0.01	1.00	8.04	5.28	0.05	0.99	0.03	0.03	0.20	0.10	0.43	0.83	78.23	0.75	0.22	0.91	0.75	0.82	100.00
Change in Inventories and Net Acquisitions of Valuables	0.11	-0.00	-0.06	0.03	0.02	0.37	32.84	1.11	0.00	0.27	0.02	0.20	0.22	0.92	1.33	0.10	57.45	1.77	2.39	-0.36	-0.39	1.66	100.00
Balance of Exports and Imports	-6.16	-0.17	0.56	-0.01	-0.06	1.23	-24.46	3.43	-0.15	7.26	0.03	0.09	-1.61	-2.81	-10.68	-10.27	70.11	28.36	-2.09	24.37	20.94	2.09	100.00
Individual Consumption Expenditure by Households and NPISH	2.12	0.02	0.03	0.21	0.04	2.64	17.33	6.71	0.11	2.01	0.02	0.07	0.42	0.22	2.99	2.66	52.85	1.40	0.63	3.51	2.51	1.52	100.00
Government Final Consumption Expenditure	0.60	0.02	0.12	0.07	0.03	1.24	10.17	3.41	0.09	1.42	0.03	0.05	0.43	0.10	1.34	1.30	71.34	1.31	0.27	2.99	2.70	0.95	100.00
Actual Individual Consumption by Households[a]	1.85	0.01	0.03	0.19	0.04	2.39	15.70	6.10	0.09	1.91	0.02	0.07	0.37	0.19	2.70	2.45	56.64	1.32	0.57	3.43	2.51	1.42	100.00
All goods	2.92	0.02	0.03	0.26	0.05	1.70	17.51	7.43	0.14	2.10	0.02	0.08	0.58	0.31	3.47	3.16	51.19	0.78	0.60	2.98	2.66	2.02	100.00
Non-durables	3.57	0.02	0.02	0.32	0.06	1.21	19.53	7.69	0.17	2.28	0.02	0.09	0.76	0.39	4.07	4.05	47.29	0.49	0.61	2.39	2.88	2.07	100.00
Semi-durables	1.84	0.02	0.03	0.08	0.03	2.87	16.63	6.18	0.05	1.33	0.01	0.07	0.22	0.11	3.10	0.94	57.70	0.93	1.10	3.83	1.62	1.32	100.00
Durables	0.91	0.02	0.04	0.14	0.05	2.84	8.73	7.45	0.11	1.99	0.02	0.04	0.10	0.11	0.99	1.18	63.22	1.97	0.09	4.95	2.62	2.45	100.00
Services	1.01	0.01	0.03	0.11	0.02	3.57	17.36	5.50	0.07	2.10	0.03	0.06	0.21	0.10	2.35	2.02	55.03	2.16	0.71	4.09	2.21	1.25	100.00

0.00 = magnitude of less than half of the unit employed; AP = Asia and the Pacific; BAN = Bangladesh; BHU = Bhutan; BRU = Brunei Darussalam; CAM = Cambodia; FIJ = Fiji; HKG = Hong Kong, China; IND = India; INO = Indonesia; LAO = Lao People's Democratic Republic; MAL = Malaysia; MLD = Maldives; MON = Mongolia; MYA = Myanmar; NEP = Nepal; NPISH=nonprofit institutions serving households; PAK = Pakistan; PHI = Philippines; PRC = People's Republic of China; SIN = Singapore; SRI = Sri Lanka; TAP = Taipei,China; THA = Thailand; VIE = Viet Nam.

a Includes individual consumption expenditure by households, nonprofit institutions serving households, and government.

Source: Asian Development Bank estimates.

Table A4.10: Per Capita Nominal Expenditure, 2017
(Hong Kong dollars)

Expenditure Category	BAN	BHU	BRU	CAM	FIJ	HKG	IND	INO	LAO	MAL	MLD	MON	MYA	NEP	PAK	PHI	PRC	SIN	SRI	TAP	THA	VIE	AP
Gross Domestic Product	12,654	27,094	220,065	10,904	47,572	360,247	15,194	30,217	19,026	76,589	77,137	28,278	9,268	6,754	12,349	23,295	68,262	469,907	31,748	190,165	52,444	18,506	39,326
Actual Individual Consumption by Households[a]	9,004	15,752	58,920	9,276	34,687	255,310	9,458	18,371	10,808	47,013	36,053	16,664	5,517	5,319	10,704	18,383	32,220	185,763	21,011	114,917	29,226	11,845	20,835
Food and non-alcoholic beverages	4,582	5,337	7,582	4,095	10,485	25,959	2,508	5,346	4,540	9,654	5,343	4,672	2,934	3,109	3,438	7,201	4,801	11,264	5,718	14,504	6,896	3,397	4,150
Food	4,563	4,904	6,813	3,923	9,842	24,354	2,470	4,770	3,793	9,294	4,569	4,223	2,855	3,064	3,271	6,603	4,654	10,024	5,617	13,516	5,997	3,267	3,979
Bread and cereals	2,036	1,366	1,531	1,256	2,034	2,525	565	1,261	1,049	1,315	837	685	633	1,089	801	2,496	825	1,764	1,768	3,229	1,282	974	905
Meat and fish	877	585	2,441	1,212	2,077	12,392	235	1,426	1,588	2,925	1,361	1,483	932	508	344	2,218	1,719	3,599	769	4,224	1,455	1,354	1,098
Fruits and vegetables	618	1,308	1,227	589	2,947	3,557	720	809	601	2,174	1,141	293	702	610	510	767	1,174	2,147	840	4,038	2,209	476	939
Other food and non-alcoholic beverages	1,051	2,077	2,383	1,038	3,428	7,484	987	1,850	1,303	3,240	2,005	2,211	668	901	1,783	1,719	1,083	3,754	2,341	3,013	1,950	593	1,208
Clothing and footwear	538	1,187	1,908	173	1,521	12,229	640	607	223	1,329	1,068	900	213	156	840	195	1,481	4,975	780	4,366	465	590	982
Clothing	479	853	1,583	89	1,262	8,043	508	521	178	1,139	782	701	183	132	676	132	1,151	4,190	706	3,802	445	493	778
Housing, water, electricity, gas and other fuels	1,469	1,857	6,723	1,437	2,420	39,868	1,266	1,553	1,285	6,611	8,814	2,268	763	656	2,140	2,041	4,431	27,532	2,214	17,647	2,555	2,615	2,836
Health and education	823	2,166	15,377	1,261	4,913	37,648	1,273	2,342	902	6,350	7,610	2,703	583	451	1,419	2,122	8,816	33,228	1,799	20,129	5,518	2,167	4,489
Health	322	1,233	3,950	642	1,357	21,294	562	809	346	2,570	4,104	1,024	313	216	852	688	4,916	17,488	987	11,382	2,661	1,052	2,379
Education	501	933	11,427	619	3,556	16,354	712	1,533	556	3,780	3,506	1,679	270	235	567	1,434	3,900	15,740	812	8,747	2,857	1,115	2,110
Transportation and communication	417	2,530	10,170	704	4,690	22,991	1,610	3,150	860	9,296	4,335	2,145	301	225	763	2,428	3,641	31,420	4,470	15,345	4,056	1,572	2,651
Transportation	374	2,061	7,907	682	3,260	16,963	1,439	2,465	662	5,815	2,232	1,576	209	160	557	1,953	2,585	24,531	4,259	12,115	3,473	1,488	2,044
Recreation and culture	143	449	3,727	251	585	26,263	83	801	186	2,887	1,373	627	68	177	437	310	1,546	19,451	2,459	9,888	1,414	519	911
Restaurants and hotels	206	337	2,740	439	413	22,555	179	1,683	1,123	4,502	2,538	399	268	94	291	705	1,279	17,256	779	8,322	2,533	522	922
Other consumption expenditure items	825	1,889	5,621	783	9,659	67,796	1,953	2,890	2,376	8,264	4,972	2,702	386	468	1,376	3,381	6,226	41,283	3,625	24,717	5,789	1,606	3,961
Individual Consumption Expenditure by Government	171	1,455	13,851	513	2,581	13,756	517	1,051	471	4,634	5,310	1,527	239	139	551	1,268	6,468	17,062	1,313	14,244	4,184	913	2,988
Collective Consumption Expenditure by Government	612	2,998	44,416	404	5,595	21,618	1,120	1,695	2,361	4,685	6,515	2,074	1,477	628	869	1,351	4,382	32,322	1,382	12,503	4,230	1,222	2,581
Gross Fixed Capital Formation	3,909	13,903	90,377	1,178	8,460	77,924	4,315	9,720	6,355	19,329	32,266	6,968	2,861	2,149	1,835	5,826	29,253	124,067	8,349	38,947	11,906	4,401	14,512
Machinery and equipment	1,145	4,085	30,187	536	5,285	21,838	1,303	1,595	1,793	5,683	11,982	2,397	1,215	455	638	2,131	5,394	36,788	4,290	15,244	6,912	1,026	3,127
Construction	2,743	9,305	54,172	628	2,590	48,761	2,222	7,302	2,814	11,173	19,290	3,028	1,390	1,284	784	2,857	20,421	48,255	3,642	13,974	4,030	3,131	9,559
Change in Inventories and Net Acquisitions of Valuables	20	-15	-4,391	58	538	1,485	739	125	0	246	1,010	1,902	123	940	198	29	1,221	9,313	3,288	-447	-170	518	779
Balance of Exports and Imports	-892	-5,544	30,743	-12	-1,707	3,910	-438	307	-499	5,317	1,293	669	-709	-2,282	-1,257	-2,294	1,185	118,442	-2,282	24,246	7,253	519	619
Individual Consumption Expenditure by Households and NPISH	8,833	14,296	45,068	8,763	32,106	241,555	8,941	17,320	10,337	42,379	30,743	15,137	5,278	5,180	10,153	17,115	25,753	168,702	19,698	100,673	25,042	10,932	17,846
Government Final Consumption Expenditure	783	4,453	58,267	917	8,176	35,374	1,637	2,746	2,832	9,319	11,825	3,601	1,716	766	1,420	2,619	10,850	49,384	2,696	26,747	8,414	2,136	5,570
Actual Individual Consumption by Households[a]	9,004	15,752	58,920	9,276	34,687	255,310	9,458	18,371	10,808	47,013	36,053	16,664	5,517	5,319	10,704	18,383	32,220	185,763	21,011	114,917	29,226	11,845	20,835
All goods	6,819	10,485	22,039	6,180	22,833	86,686	5,048	10,708	7,861	24,708	15,297	9,240	4,120	4,049	6,585	11,373	13,938	52,337	10,630	47,772	14,815	8,081	9,972
Non-durables	5,870	7,557	13,344	5,430	17,719	43,557	3,965	7,800	6,512	18,915	11,286	7,340	3,789	3,622	5,438	10,246	9,064	23,433	7,507	26,959	11,313	5,847	7,019
Semi-durables	636	1,595	3,992	268	1,685	21,704	711	1,321	433	2,322	1,706	1,188	227	211	871	501	2,330	9,324	2,882	9,100	1,344	785	1,479
Durables	313	1,332	4,703	482	3,428	21,425	372	1,587	916	3,471	2,305	712	104	216	277	626	2,544	19,579	241	11,713	2,158	1,448	1,474
Services	1,859	3,811	17,947	2,114	8,039	143,607	3,947	6,255	3,166	19,526	15,446	5,518	1,157	1,030	3,520	5,742	11,814	114,745	9,900	51,662	9,710	3,940	7,863

0 = magnitude of less than half of the unit employed; AP = Asia and the Pacific; BAN = Bangladesh; BHU = Bhutan; BRU = Brunei Darussalam; CAM = Cambodia; FIJ = Fiji; HKG = Hong Kong, China; IND = India; INO = Indonesia; LAO = Lao People's Democratic Republic; MAL = Malaysia; MLD = Maldives; MON = Mongolia; MYA = Myanmar; NEP = Nepal; NPISH=nonprofit institutions serving households; PAK = Pakistan; PHI = Philippines; PRC = People's Republic of China; SIN = Singapore; SRI = Sri Lanka; TAP = Taipei,China; THA = Thailand; VIE = Viet Nam.

a Includes individual consumption expenditure by households, nonprofit institutions serving households, and government.

Source: Asian Development Bank estimates.

Table A4.11: Per Capita Nominal Expenditure Index, 2017
(Asia and the Pacific = 100)

Expenditure Category	BAN	BHU	BRU	CAM	FIJ	HKG	IND	INO	LAO	MAL	MLD	MON	MYA	NEP	PAK	PHI	PRC	SIN	SRI	TAP	THA	VIE	AP
Gross Domestic Product	32	69	560	28	121	916	39	77	48	195	196	72	24	17	31	59	174	1,195	81	484	133	47	100
Actual Individual Consumption by Households[a]	43	76	283	45	166	1,225	45	88	52	226	173	80	26	26	51	88	155	892	101	552	140	57	100
Food and non-alcoholic beverages	110	129	183	99	253	625	60	129	109	233	129	113	71	75	83	173	116	271	138	349	166	82	100
Food	115	123	171	99	247	612	62	120	95	234	115	106	72	77	82	166	117	252	141	340	151	82	100
Bread and cereals	225	151	169	139	225	279	62	139	116	145	92	76	70	120	89	276	91	195	195	357	142	108	100
Meat and fish	80	53	222	110	189	1,128	21	130	145	266	124	135	85	46	31	202	157	328	70	385	132	123	100
Fruits and vegetables	66	139	131	63	314	379	77	86	64	232	122	31	75	65	54	82	125	229	89	430	235	51	100
Other food and non-alcoholic beverages	87	172	197	86	284	620	82	153	108	268	166	183	55	75	148	142	90	311	194	249	161	49	100
Clothing and footwear	55	121	194	18	155	1,245	65	62	23	135	109	92	22	16	86	20	151	506	79	444	47	60	100
Clothing	62	110	203	11	162	1,034	65	67	23	146	101	90	24	17	87	17	148	538	91	489	57	63	100
Housing, water, electricity, gas and other fuels	52	65	237	51	85	1,406	45	55	45	233	311	80	27	23	75	72	156	971	78	622	90	92	100
Health and education	18	48	343	28	109	839	28	52	20	141	170	60	13	10	32	47	196	740	40	448	123	48	100
Health	14	52	166	27	57	895	24	34	15	108	172	43	13	9	36	29	207	735	41	478	112	44	100
Education	24	44	542	29	169	775	34	73	26	179	166	80	13	11	27	68	185	746	38	415	135	53	100
Transportation and communication	16	95	384	27	177	867	61	119	32	351	163	81	11	8	29	92	137	1,185	169	579	153	59	100
Transportation	18	101	387	33	160	830	70	121	32	285	109	77	10	8	27	96	127	1,200	208	593	170	73	100
Recreation and culture	16	49	409	28	64	2,882	9	88	20	317	151	69	8	19	48	34	170	2,135	270	1,085	155	57	100
Restaurants and hotels	22	37	297	48	45	2,446	19	183	122	488	275	43	29	10	32	76	139	1,872	84	903	275	57	100
Other consumption expenditure items	21	48	142	20	244	1,712	49	73	60	209	126	68	10	12	35	85	157	1,042	92	624	146	41	100
Individual Consumption Expenditure by Government	6	49	464	17	86	460	17	35	16	155	178	51	8	5	18	42	216	571	44	477	140	31	100
Collective Consumption Expenditure by Government	24	116	1,721	16	217	837	43	66	91	181	252	80	57	24	34	52	170	1,252	54	484	164	47	100
Gross Fixed Capital Formation	27	96	623	8	58	537	30	67	44	133	222	48	20	15	13	40	202	855	58	268	82	30	100
Machinery and equipment	37	131	965	17	169	698	42	51	57	182	383	77	39	15	20	68	173	1,177	137	488	221	33	100
Construction	29	97	567	7	27	510	23	76	29	117	202	32	15	13	8	30	214	505	38	146	42	33	100
Change in Inventories and Net Acquisitions of Valuables	3	-2	-564	7	69	191	95	16	0	32	130	244	16	121	25	4	157	1,196	422	-57	-22	67	100
Balance of Exports and Imports	-144	-895	4,966	-2	-276	632	-71	50	-81	859	209	108	-115	-369	-203	-371	191	19,132	-369	3,916	1,172	84	100
Individual Consumption Expenditure by Households and NPISH	49	80	253	49	180	1,354	50	97	58	237	172	85	30	29	57	96	144	945	110	564	140	61	100
Government Final Consumption Expenditure	14	80	1,046	16	147	635	29	49	51	167	212	65	31	14	26	47	195	887	48	480	151	38	100
Actual Individual Consumption by Households[a]	43	76	283	45	166	1,225	45	88	52	226	173	80	26	26	51	88	155	892	101	552	140	57	100
All goods	68	105	221	62	229	869	51	107	79	248	153	93	41	41	66	114	140	525	107	479	149	81	100
Non-durables	84	108	190	77	252	621	56	111	93	269	161	105	54	52	77	146	129	334	107	384	161	83	100
Semi-durables	43	108	270	18	114	1,467	48	89	29	157	115	80	15	14	59	34	158	630	195	615	91	53	100
Durables	21	90	319	33	233	1,454	25	108	62	236	156	48	7	15	19	43	173	1,329	16	795	146	98	100
Services	24	48	228	27	102	1,826	50	80	40	248	196	70	15	13	45	73	150	1,459	126	657	123	50	100

0 = magnitude of less than half of the unit employed; AP = Asia and the Pacific; BAN = Bangladesh; BHU = Bhutan; BRU = Brunei Darussalam; CAM = Cambodia; FIJ = Fiji; HKG = Hong Kong, China; IND = India; INO = Indonesia; LAO = Lao People's Democratic Republic; MAL = Malaysia; MLD = Maldives; MON = Mongolia; MYA = Myanmar; NEP = Nepal; NPISH=nonprofit institutions serving households; PAK = Pakistan; PHI = Philippines; PRC = People's Republic of China; SIN = Singapore; SRI = Sri Lanka; TAP = Taipei,China; THA = Thailand; VIE = Viet Nam.

a Includes individual consumption expenditure by households, nonprofit institutions serving households, and government.

Source: Asian Development Bank estimates.

Table A4.12: Shares of Nominal Expenditure, 2017
(%)

Expenditure Category	BAN	BHU	BRU	CAM	FIJ	HKG	IND	INO	LAO	MAL	MLD	MON	MYA	NEP	PAK	PHI	PRC	SIN	SRI	TAP	THA	VIE	AP
Gross Domestic Product	100.00	100.00	100.00	100.00	100.00	100.00	100.00	100.00	100.00	100.00	100.00	100.00	100.00	100.00	100.00	100.00	100.00	100.00	100.00	100.00	100.00	100.00	100.00
Actual Individual Consumption by Households[a]	71.16	58.14	26.77	85.07	72.91	70.87	62.25	60.80	56.81	61.38	46.74	58.93	59.53	78.76	86.68	78.91	47.20	39.53	66.18	60.43	55.73	64.01	52.98
Food and non-alcoholic beverages	36.21	19.70	3.45	37.55	22.04	7.21	16.50	17.69	23.86	12.60	6.93	16.52	31.66	46.03	27.84	30.91	7.03	2.40	18.01	7.63	13.15	18.36	10.55
Food	36.07	18.10	3.10	35.98	20.69	6.76	16.26	15.79	19.94	12.13	5.92	14.94	30.81	45.36	26.49	28.34	6.82	2.13	17.69	7.11	11.44	17.65	10.12
Bread and cereals	16.09	5.04	0.70	11.52	4.28	0.70	3.72	4.17	5.51	1.72	1.08	2.42	6.83	16.13	6.49	10.72	1.21	0.38	5.57	1.70	2.44	5.27	2.30
Meat and fish	6.93	2.16	1.11	11.11	4.37	3.44	1.55	4.72	8.35	3.82	1.76	5.25	10.05	7.53	2.79	9.52	2.52	0.77	2.42	2.22	2.77	7.32	2.79
Fruits and vegetables	4.88	4.83	0.56	5.40	6.19	0.99	4.74	2.68	3.16	2.84	1.48	1.04	7.57	9.03	4.13	3.29	1.72	0.46	2.65	2.12	4.21	2.57	2.39
Other food and non-alcoholic beverages	8.31	7.67	1.08	9.52	7.21	2.08	6.50	6.12	6.85	4.23	2.60	7.82	7.21	13.34	14.44	7.38	1.59	0.80	7.37	1.58	3.72	3.20	3.07
Clothing and footwear	4.25	4.38	0.87	1.59	3.20	3.39	4.21	2.01	1.17	1.74	1.38	3.18	2.30	2.31	6.80	0.84	2.17	1.06	2.46	2.30	0.89	3.19	2.50
Clothing	3.79	3.15	0.72	0.81	2.65	2.23	3.34	1.72	0.94	1.49	1.01	2.48	1.97	1.95	5.48	0.57	1.69	0.89	2.22	2.00	0.85	2.66	1.98
Housing, water, electricity, gas and other fuels	11.61	6.86	3.05	13.18	5.09	11.07	8.33	5.14	6.76	8.63	11.43	8.02	8.23	9.71	17.33	8.76	6.49	5.86	6.97	9.28	4.87	14.13	7.21
Health and education	6.51	7.99	6.99	11.57	10.33	10.45	8.38	7.75	4.74	8.29	9.87	9.56	6.29	6.68	11.49	9.11	12.92	7.07	5.67	10.58	10.52	11.71	11.42
Health	2.55	4.55	1.79	5.89	2.85	5.91	3.70	2.68	1.82	3.36	5.32	3.62	3.37	3.20	6.90	2.95	7.20	3.72	3.11	5.99	5.07	5.68	6.05
Education	3.96	3.44	5.19	5.68	7.47	4.54	4.68	5.07	2.92	4.94	4.54	5.94	2.91	3.48	4.59	6.15	5.71	3.35	2.56	4.60	5.45	6.03	5.37
Transportation and communication	3.29	9.34	4.62	6.46	9.86	6.38	10.60	10.43	4.52	12.14	5.62	7.59	3.25	3.33	6.18	10.42	5.33	6.69	14.08	8.07	7.73	8.49	6.74
Transportation	2.95	7.61	3.59	6.25	6.85	4.71	9.47	8.16	3.48	7.59	2.89	5.57	2.26	2.37	4.51	8.39	3.79	5.22	13.42	6.37	6.62	8.04	5.20
Recreation and culture	1.13	1.66	1.69	2.30	1.23	7.29	0.55	2.65	0.98	3.77	1.78	2.22	0.74	2.63	3.54	1.33	2.26	4.14	7.74	5.20	2.70	2.81	2.32
Restaurants and hotels	1.63	1.24	1.25	4.02	0.87	6.26	1.18	5.57	5.90	5.88	3.29	1.41	2.90	1.39	2.36	3.03	1.87	3.67	2.45	4.38	4.83	2.82	2.34
Other consumption expenditure items	6.52	6.97	2.55	7.18	20.30	18.82	12.86	9.56	12.49	10.79	6.45	9.55	4.16	6.94	11.14	14.52	9.12	8.79	11.42	13.00	11.04	8.68	10.07
Individual Consumption Expenditure by Government	1.35	5.37	6.29	4.70	5.43	3.82	3.40	3.48	2.47	6.05	6.88	5.40	2.58	2.05	4.46	5.44	9.47	3.63	4.14	7.49	7.98	4.93	7.60
Collective Consumption Expenditure by Government	4.84	11.07	20.18	3.71	11.76	6.00	7.37	5.61	12.41	6.12	8.45	7.33	15.93	9.29	7.04	5.80	6.42	6.88	4.35	6.57	8.07	6.61	6.56
Gross Fixed Capital Formation	30.90	51.31	41.07	10.80	17.78	21.63	28.40	32.17	33.40	25.24	41.83	24.64	30.87	31.81	14.86	25.01	42.85	26.40	26.30	20.48	22.70	23.78	36.90
Machinery and equipment	9.05	15.08	13.72	4.91	11.11	6.06	8.58	5.28	9.43	7.42	15.53	8.48	13.11	6.74	5.17	9.15	7.90	7.83	13.51	8.02	13.18	5.54	7.95
Construction	21.68	34.34	24.62	5.76	5.44	13.54	14.62	24.17	14.79	14.59	25.01	10.71	14.99	19.01	6.35	12.27	29.92	10.27	11.47	7.35	7.68	16.92	24.31
Change in Inventories and Net Acquisitions of Valuables	0.15	-0.05	-2.00	0.53	1.13	0.41	4.87	0.41	0.00	0.32	1.31	6.73	1.33	13.92	1.60	0.13	1.79	1.98	10.36	-0.24	-0.32	2.80	1.98
Balance of Exports and Imports	-7.05	-20.46	13.97	-0.11	-3.59	1.09	-2.88	1.01	-2.62	6.94	1.68	2.37	-7.65	-33.79	-10.18	-9.85	1.74	25.21	-7.19	12.75	13.83	2.80	1.57
Individual Consumption Expenditure by Households and NPISH	69.81	52.77	20.48	80.37	67.49	67.05	58.84	57.32	54.33	55.33	39.86	53.53	56.95	76.70	82.22	73.47	37.73	35.90	62.05	52.94	47.75	59.07	45.38
Government Final Consumption Expenditure	6.19	16.44	26.48	8.41	17.19	9.82	10.78	9.09	14.88	12.17	15.33	12.74	18.51	11.35	11.50	11.24	15.89	10.51	8.49	14.07	16.04	11.54	14.16
Actual Individual Consumption by Households[a]	71.16	58.14	26.77	85.07	72.91	70.87	62.25	60.80	56.81	61.38	46.74	58.93	59.53	78.76	86.68	78.91	47.20	39.53	66.18	60.43	55.73	64.01	52.98
All goods	53.89	38.70	10.01	56.67	48.00	24.06	33.22	35.44	41.32	32.26	19.83	32.68	44.46	59.95	53.33	48.82	20.42	11.14	33.48	25.12	28.25	43.67	25.36
Non-durables	46.39	27.89	6.06	49.79	37.25	12.09	26.09	25.81	34.23	24.70	14.63	25.96	40.89	53.63	44.04	43.98	13.28	4.99	23.65	14.18	21.57	31.60	17.85
Semi-durables	5.02	5.89	1.81	2.46	3.54	6.02	4.68	4.37	2.27	3.03	2.21	4.20	2.44	3.13	7.05	2.15	3.41	1.98	9.08	4.79	2.56	4.24	3.76
Durables	2.48	4.92	2.14	4.42	7.21	5.95	2.45	5.25	4.82	4.53	2.99	2.52	1.12	3.19	2.24	2.69	3.73	4.17	0.76	6.16	4.11	7.83	3.75
Services	14.69	14.07	8.16	19.39	16.90	39.86	25.98	20.70	16.64	25.49	20.02	19.51	12.49	15.25	28.50	24.65	17.31	24.42	31.18	27.17	18.51	21.29	19.99

0.00 = magnitude of less than half of the unit employed; AP = Asia and the Pacific; BAN = Bangladesh; BHU = Bhutan; BRU = Brunei Darussalam; CAM = Cambodia; FIJ = Fiji; HKG = Hong Kong, China; IND = India; INO = Indonesia; LAO = Lao People's Democratic Republic; MAL = Malaysia; MLD = Maldives; MON = Mongolia; MYA = Myanmar; NEP = Nepal; NPISH=nonprofit institutions serving households; PAK = Pakistan; PHI = Philippines; PRC = People's Republic of China; SIN = Singapore; SRI = Sri Lanka; TAP = Taipei,China; THA = Thailand; VIE = Viet Nam.
a Includes individual consumption expenditure by households, nonprofit institutions serving households, and government.
Source: Asian Development Bank estimates.

Appendix 5: Detailed Tables: Purchasing Power Parities and Real Expenditures, 2011 Revised

The succeeding tables present the 2011 revised key results for Asia and the Pacific for broad aggregates of gross domestic product (GDP). These include the actual individual consumption by household (AICH), individual consumption expenditure by household (ICEH) and nonprofit institutions serving households (NPISH), collective consumption expenditure by government, government final consumption expenditure (GFCE), gross fixed capital formation (GFCF), change in inventories and net acquisitions of valuables, and balance of exports and imports. These aggregates were derived using the Gini-Eltetö-Köves-Szulc (GEKS) method, so real expenditures are not additive within a particular economy. The 2011 revised results are based on revisions in the 2011 estimates of GDP, population, refinements in the methodology for estimating productivity adjustment factors, changes in some reference purchasing power parities (PPPs), and changes in International Comparison Program (ICP) classification (see Appendix 6, Table A6.2). The results presented in these tables are produced by the ICP Asia Pacific regional implementing agency, based on data supplied by all the participating economies, and in accordance with the methodology recommended by the ICP Technical Advisory Group and approved by the Asia and the Pacific Regional Advisory Board. As such, these results are not produced by participating economies as part of the economies' official statistics.

Table A5.1: Purchasing Power Parities, 2011 (Revised)
(Hong Kong, China as base)

Expenditure Category	BAN	BHU	BRU	CAM	FIJ	HKG	IND	INO	LAO	MAC	MAL	MLD	MON	MYA	NEP	PAK	PHI	PRC	SIN	SRI	TAP	THA	VIE
Gross Domestic Product	4.47	3.13	0.13	262.06	0.18	1.00	2.97	671.29	509.59	0.85	0.28	1.50	101.97	50.03	4.83	4.77	3.46	0.67	0.16	7.51	2.90	2.37	1,321.50
Actual Individual Consumption by Households[a]	4.22	2.88	0.14	248.72	0.18	1.00	2.66	655.87	508.52	0.91	0.27	1.50	93.22	46.70	4.44	4.39	3.27	0.65	0.19	7.01	2.83	2.21	1,250.82
Food and non-alcoholic beverages	5.22	3.25	0.14	311.28	0.19	1.00	2.81	834.78	704.97	1.03	0.30	1.52	119.37	61.71	5.11	5.55	3.71	0.69	0.18	9.51	3.23	2.66	1,580.74
Food	5.17	3.20	0.14	308.74	0.19	1.00	2.76	831.23	688.76	1.03	0.30	1.50	117.87	60.52	5.04	5.46	3.76	0.69	0.19	9.38	3.23	2.63	1,577.37
Bread and cereals	5.83	3.59	0.13	315.08	0.20	1.00	3.02	917.57	815.50	1.13	0.34	1.95	134.47	72.99	5.49	6.48	4.22	0.79	0.20	10.04	3.83	3.16	1,695.16
Meat and fish	5.71	2.91	0.15	322.51	0.21	1.00	2.93	757.68	663.63	1.01	0.27	1.06	92.10	56.20	5.42	5.56	3.22	0.65	0.20	8.56	3.23	2.31	1,674.44
Fruits and vegetables	3.25	2.78	0.17	275.95	0.16	1.00	2.35	765.55	543.66	1.00	0.31	2.16	188.59	47.99	3.86	3.58	4.12	0.59	0.18	8.45	2.83	2.49	1,294.51
Other food and non-alcoholic beverages	5.71	3.60	0.14	333.45	0.21	1.00	3.02	902.83	790.73	1.00	0.30	1.47	123.59	71.37	5.51	6.02	3.69	0.74	0.16	10.41	3.09	2.80	1,597.29
Clothing and footwear	6.13	3.53	0.23	280.48	0.23	1.00	2.79	1,157.91	564.60	1.33	0.43	1.68	166.51	55.57	5.07	6.33	5.33	1.03	0.21	8.42	3.17	2.68	1,460.10
Clothing	6.34	3.54	0.23	287.04	0.22	1.00	2.72	1,185.09	574.15	1.37	0.43	1.79	165.72	57.01	5.20	6.51	5.49	1.07	0.21	8.44	3.27	2.75	1,499.23
Housing, water, electricity, gas and other fuels	2.85	2.51	0.12	228.96	0.10	1.00	2.17	332.53	375.99	0.75	0.18	2.08	90.82	32.85	3.17	2.67	2.42	0.49	0.21	4.30	2.89	1.27	1,276.10
Health and education	2.22	1.69	0.10	101.21	0.13	1.00	1.35	383.44	143.60	0.69	0.19	0.92	33.25	14.41	2.07	2.13	2.09	0.50	0.17	2.95	2.03	1.43	465.65
Health	2.31	1.76	0.10	112.90	0.14	1.00	1.12	504.53	237.08	0.79	0.20	0.79	32.70	19.55	2.02	1.91	2.64	0.43	0.18	3.37	1.65	1.46	485.78
Education	2.15	1.59	0.10	90.93	0.13	1.00	1.62	300.71	92.94	0.61	0.18	1.02	32.00	10.60	2.13	2.46	1.78	0.57	0.17	2.55	2.43	1.39	445.24
Transportation and communication	5.42	3.19	0.14	347.21	0.25	1.00	3.63	843.51	711.90	0.94	0.35	1.46	114.66	79.22	8.30	6.08	4.34	0.63	0.23	9.50	2.78	2.81	2,248.00
Transportation	6.01	3.06	0.10	313.41	0.20	1.00	3.52	735.38	717.83	0.89	0.28	1.53	93.50	72.67	8.22	5.71	3.41	0.57	0.21	8.92	2.71	2.55	2,032.48
Recreation and culture	7.41	4.53	0.22	379.68	0.27	1.00	4.56	876.29	897.30	1.13	0.37	2.18	155.10	66.96	6.81	6.76	4.82	0.73	0.16	10.79	3.68	3.32	1,683.11
Restaurants and hotels	4.51	2.67	0.18	252.52	0.23	1.00	3.67	723.00	608.37	0.98	0.24	1.19	119.79	42.94	4.66	5.90	3.27	0.61	0.16	10.89	2.43	1.89	1,254.33
Other consumption expenditure items	3.99	3.29	0.19	239.95	0.20	1.00	3.19	743.39	533.39	1.00	0.32	1.28	96.29	55.28	5.00	5.19	3.22	0.75	0.22	7.17	2.97	2.64	1,133.77
Individual Consumption Expenditure by Government	2.77	1.76	0.10	118.13	0.15	1.00	2.32	358.86	149.03	0.78	0.20	0.99	34.95	21.67	3.45	3.42	2.90	0.53	0.16	2.67	2.40	1.65	594.48
Collective Consumption Expenditure by Government	3.76	1.82	0.09	201.94	0.16	1.00	2.91	516.14	271.15	0.94	0.24	1.07	62.68	36.12	5.39	3.93	3.82	0.68	0.15	4.28	2.59	2.32	865.87
Gross Fixed Capital Formation	5.19	4.11	0.15	299.20	0.18	1.00	3.58	696.19	567.80	0.92	0.30	1.64	125.97	59.38	6.09	6.41	3.68	0.70	0.15	9.85	2.99	2.56	1,562.53
Machinery and equipment	8.34	6.28	0.16	496.43	0.23	1.00	5.33	1,038.22	942.20	0.90	0.38	1.85	170.20	99.68	8.73	9.89	5.42	0.87	0.15	14.60	3.45	3.74	2,338.42
Construction	3.41	2.72	0.14	182.04	0.14	1.00	2.39	477.77	339.67	0.80	0.23	1.36	93.00	34.07	4.20	4.01	2.48	0.54	0.13	6.51	2.63	1.69	1,060.56
Change in Inventories and Net Acquisitions of Valuables	5.37	3.69	0.16	324.93	0.19	1.00	3.53	777.76	621.73	1.00	0.31	1.66	123.41	61.16	5.65	5.69	3.89	0.73	0.18	9.60	3.03	2.68	1,565.61
Balance of Exports and Imports	9.53	6.00	0.16	521.39	0.23	1.00	6.00	1,126.73	1,031.61	1.03	0.39	1.88	162.58	105.08	9.51	11.09	5.56	0.83	0.16	14.20	3.79	3.92	2,634.86
Individual Consumption Expenditure by Households and NPISH	4.38	3.02	0.15	264.43	0.18	1.00	2.71	689.25	553.23	0.91	0.28	1.56	102.82	49.30	4.56	4.51	3.32	0.65	0.19	7.61	2.86	2.26	1,333.17
Government Final Consumption Expenditure	3.34	1.79	0.09	158.14	0.16	1.00	2.65	445.73	222.35	0.87	0.22	1.03	48.14	30.84	4.52	3.67	3.40	0.61	0.15	3.49	2.51	2.01	740.37
Actual Individual Consumption by Households[a]	4.22	2.88	0.14	248.72	0.18	1.00	2.66	655.87	508.52	0.91	0.27	1.50	93.22	46.70	4.44	4.39	3.27	0.65	0.19	7.01	2.83	2.21	1,250.82
All goods	5.65	3.48	0.15	336.80	0.21	1.00	3.12	895.51	699.87	1.06	0.33	1.64	119.90	65.42	5.74	5.58	4.26	0.78	0.22	9.65	3.07	2.87	1,627.87
Non-durables	4.78	3.13	0.14	311.01	0.19	1.00	2.78	798.11	649.44	1.00	0.29	1.43	109.96	58.99	4.90	4.89	3.88	0.70	0.21	8.66	2.97	2.63	1,401.57
Semi-durables	6.66	3.89	0.22	314.28	0.24	1.00	3.28	1,053.88	604.65	1.28	0.42	1.88	166.01	58.91	5.68	6.71	5.25	1.07	0.21	9.62	3.23	3.02	1,636.72
Durables	10.79	4.53	0.16	440.93	0.30	1.00	4.93	1,182.97	915.44	1.13	0.45	2.48	118.54	101.75	12.03	8.80	4.69	0.85	0.26	15.42	3.24	3.62	2,830.74
Services	3.15	2.77	0.16	199.62	0.15	1.00	2.40	511.87	421.05	0.82	0.24	1.58	92.34	32.77	3.45	3.60	2.48	0.56	0.18	5.94	2.77	1.71	1,129.23

BAN = Bangladesh; BHU = Bhutan; BRU = Brunei Darussalam; CAM = Cambodia; FIJ = Fiji; HKG = Hong Kong, China; IND = India; INO = Indonesia; LAO = Lao People's Democratic Republic; MAC = Macau, China; MAL = Malaysia; MLD = Maldives; MON = Mongolia; MYA = Myanmar; NEP = Nepal; NPISH=nonprofit institutions serving households; PAK = Pakistan; PHI = Philippines; PRC = People's Republic of China; SIN = Singapore; SRI = Sri Lanka; TAP = Taipei,China; THA = Thailand; VIE = Viet Nam.

a Includes individual consumption expenditure by households, nonprofit institutions serving households, and government.

Source: Asian Development Bank estimates.

Table A5.2: Price Level Indexes, 2011 (Revised)
(Hong Kong, China = 100)

Expenditure Category	BAN	BHU	BRU	CAM	FIJ	HKG	IND	INO	LAO	MAC	MAL	MLD	MON	MYA	NEP	PAK	PHI	PRC	SIN	SRI	TAP	THA	VIE
Gross Domestic Product	47	52	83	50	79	100	50	60	49	82	71	80	63	48	51	43	62	81	100	53	76	60	50
Actual Individual Consumption by Households[a]	44	48	89	48	77	100	44	58	49	88	70	80	57	44	47	40	59	79	118	49	75	56	47
Food and non-alcoholic beverages	55	54	89	60	83	100	47	74	68	100	77	81	73	59	54	50	67	83	113	67	85	68	60
Food	54	53	89	59	82	100	46	74	67	100	76	80	73	58	53	49	68	83	116	66	85	67	60
Bread and cereals	61	60	80	60	88	100	50	81	79	110	86	104	83	69	58	58	76	95	127	71	101	81	64
Meat and fish	60	49	91	62	89	100	49	67	64	98	69	56	57	53	57	50	58	79	122	60	85	59	64
Fruits and vegetables	34	46	104	53	68	100	39	68	53	97	80	115	116	46	41	32	74	71	108	59	75	64	49
Other food and non-alcoholic beverages	60	60	85	64	92	100	50	80	77	97	77	78	76	68	58	54	66	89	100	73	82	72	61
Clothing and footwear	64	59	145	54	98	100	46	103	55	129	109	89	102	53	53	57	96	124	133	59	84	68	55
Clothing	67	59	143	55	97	100	45	105	56	133	109	95	102	54	55	59	99	129	129	59	86	70	57
Housing, water, electricity, gas and other fuels	30	42	73	44	42	100	36	30	36	73	47	111	56	31	33	24	44	59	131	30	76	32	48
Health and education	23	28	64	19	58	100	23	34	14	67	48	49	20	14	22	19	38	60	108	21	54	36	18
Health	24	29	64	22	60	100	19	45	23	76	50	42	20	19	21	17	47	52	109	24	44	37	18
Education	23	27	60	17	55	100	27	27	9	59	46	55	20	10	22	22	32	69	104	18	64	35	17
Transportation and communication	57	53	87	67	108	100	61	75	69	91	89	78	71	75	87	55	78	76	143	67	74	72	85
Transportation	63	51	62	60	87	100	59	65	70	86	71	82	58	69	86	51	61	69	127	63	72	65	77
Recreation and culture	78	76	138	73	117	100	76	78	87	109	93	116	95	64	72	61	87	88	101	76	97	85	64
Restaurants and hotels	47	45	112	48	98	100	61	64	59	96	62	63	74	41	49	53	59	73	98	77	64	48	48
Other consumption expenditure items	42	55	116	46	88	100	53	66	52	97	80	68	59	53	53	47	58	90	138	50	78	67	43
Individual Consumption Expenditure by Government	29	29	61	23	66	100	39	32	14	76	51	53	21	21	36	31	52	63	102	19	63	42	23
Collective Consumption Expenditure by Government	39	30	54	39	72	100	49	46	26	91	60	57	39	34	57	35	69	81	92	30	68	59	33
Gross Fixed Capital Formation	54	69	96	57	77	100	60	62	55	89	76	88	77	57	64	58	66	84	90	69	79	65	59
Machinery and equipment	88	105	101	95	99	100	89	92	91	88	96	99	105	95	92	89	97	104	96	103	91	95	89
Construction	36	45	84	35	62	100	40	42	33	78	59	73	57	32	44	36	45	65	83	46	69	43	40
Change in Inventories and Net Acquisitions of Valuables	56	62	99	62	84	100	59	69	60	97	79	89	76	58	59	51	70	88	111	68	80	69	59
Balance of Exports and Imports	100	100	100	100	100	100	100	100	100	100	100	100	100	100	100	100	100	100	100	100	100	100	100
Individual Consumption Expenditure by Households and NPISH	46	50	91	51	78	100	45	61	54	89	71	83	63	47	48	41	60	79	120	54	75	58	51
Government Final Consumption Expenditure	35	30	55	30	69	100	44	40	22	84	56	55	30	29	48	33	61	73	94	25	66	51	28
Actual Individual Consumption by Households[a]	44	48	89	48	77	100	44	58	49	88	70	80	57	44	47	40	59	79	118	49	75	56	47
All goods	59	58	96	65	93	100	52	79	68	103	84	87	74	62	60	50	76	94	134	68	81	73	62
Non-durables	50	52	87	60	83	100	46	71	63	97	74	76	68	56	52	44	70	85	128	61	78	67	53
Semi-durables	70	65	136	60	104	100	55	94	59	124	106	100	102	56	60	60	94	129	129	68	85	77	62
Durables	113	76	100	85	131	100	82	105	89	110	114	132	73	97	127	79	84	102	162	109	85	92	107
Services	33	46	100	38	66	100	40	45	41	80	62	84	57	31	36	32	45	67	109	42	73	44	43

BAN = Bangladesh; BHU = Bhutan; BRU = Brunei Darussalam; CAM = Cambodia; FIJ = Fiji; HKG = Hong Kong, China; IND = India; INO = Indonesia; LAO = Lao People's Democratic Republic; MAC = Macau, China; MAL = Malaysia; MLD = Maldives; MON = Mongolia; MYA = Myanmar; NEP = Nepal; NPISH=nonprofit institutions serving households; PAK = Pakistan; PHI = Philippines; PRC = People's Republic of China; SIN = Singapore; SRI = Sri Lanka; TAP = Taipei,China; THA = Thailand; VIE = Viet Nam.
a Includes individual consumption expenditure by households, nonprofit institutions serving households, and government.
Source: Asian Development Bank estimates.

Table A5.3: Price Level Indexes, 2011 (Revised)

(Asia and the Pacific = 100)

Expenditure Category	BAN	BHU	BRU	CAM	FIJ	HKG	IND	INO	LAO	MAC	MAL	MLD	MON	MYA	NEP	PAK	PHI	PRC	SIN	SRI	TAP	THA	VIE
Gross Domestic Product	67	75	120	72	113	144	71	86	71	118	102	115	90	68	73	62	89	116	144	76	110	87	72
Actual Individual Consumption by Households[a]	70	76	140	75	121	157	70	91	77	139	110	126	90	70	73	62	92	123	186	77	117	89	75
Food and non-alcoholic beverages	83	83	135	91	126	152	71	113	104	152	117	123	112	89	82	76	101	126	172	102	130	103	91
Food	83	82	136	91	125	154	71	113	103	154	118	123	111	88	81	76	104	127	178	101	131	103	92
Bread and cereals	85	83	111	84	122	139	70	113	110	152	120	145	115	97	80	81	105	132	176	98	141	112	89
Meat and fish	86	69	130	88	127	143	70	96	92	139	99	80	81	76	82	72	83	113	175	86	122	84	91
Fruits and vegetables	62	84	188	95	122	180	71	122	95	175	144	207	209	82	73	58	133	128	195	107	135	114	89
Other food and non-alcoholic beverages	91	91	130	97	139	152	76	122	116	147	116	119	115	103	88	82	101	135	153	111	124	109	92
Clothing and footwear	73	67	165	61	112	114	53	117	62	147	124	102	117	60	61	65	109	141	151	68	95	78	63
Clothing	75	66	161	62	108	112	51	118	62	149	122	107	114	61	61	66	111	144	145	67	97	79	64
Housing, water, electricity, gas and other fuels	64	89	156	93	90	212	77	63	77	155	99	235	119	66	71	51	93	126	278	64	162	69	103
Health and education	51	62	140	43	128	221	50	75	31	149	107	108	45	30	48	42	83	133	238	46	118	80	39
Health	56	68	150	50	140	233	44	104	54	178	117	98	47	43	49	40	110	122	254	55	101	87	43
Education	50	58	131	38	120	220	59	59	20	130	102	120	43	22	49	49	70	151	229	40	141	78	37
Transportation and communication	79	74	121	92	150	139	84	104	96	127	123	108	98	105	121	76	108	105	198	93	102	100	118
Transportation	96	78	95	92	133	152	89	99	106	131	108	124	88	105	132	78	93	104	194	96	109	99	117
Recreation and culture	89	86	157	83	133	114	87	89	99	125	106	133	109	73	82	70	99	101	115	87	111	97	73
Restaurants and hotels	70	65	165	71	145	147	90	94	87	140	91	93	108	60	72	78	86	108	145	113	94	71	70
Other consumption expenditure items	57	75	159	63	120	137	73	90	71	133	110	93	81	72	72	64	79	124	188	69	107	92	59
Individual Consumption Expenditure by Government	52	52	108	40	117	178	69	57	26	135	91	94	38	37	65	55	93	113	181	34	113	75	40
Collective Consumption Expenditure by Government	61	47	84	60	110	154	75	71	41	140	93	88	59	53	87	55	106	126	141	47	105	91	51
Gross Fixed Capital Formation	71	89	124	74	100	130	77	80	71	116	98	114	100	73	83	75	86	109	117	90	102	85	77
Machinery and equipment	88	105	101	95	99	100	89	92	91	88	96	99	105	95	92	89	98	104	96	103	91	96	89
Construction	62	79	146	61	107	173	69	73	57	134	102	126	99	56	76	63	77	113	144	79	120	75	70
Change in Inventories and Net Acquisitions of Valuables	76	83	133	84	113	134	79	93	81	130	105	119	102	78	80	69	94	119	149	91	107	92	80
Balance of Exports and Imports	100	100	100	100	100	100	100	100	100	100	100	100	100	100	100	100	100	100	100	100	100	100	100
Individual Consumption Expenditure by Households and NPISH	72	79	143	80	123	157	71	96	84	139	112	130	99	74	75	64	94	124	188	84	118	90	79
Government Final Consumption Expenditure	57	49	90	49	112	163	72	64	35	137	92	89	48	48	77	54	100	119	154	40	108	84	46
Actual Individual Consumption by Households[a]	70	76	140	75	121	157	70	91	77	139	110	126	90	70	73	62	92	123	186	77	117	89	75
All goods	78	76	126	85	122	132	69	105	89	135	111	115	97	82	80	66	101	124	176	90	107	97	81
Non-durables	76	79	132	90	126	151	70	107	95	147	112	116	102	85	78	67	106	128	194	92	119	102	81
Semi-durables	72	67	141	62	107	103	56	97	61	128	109	103	105	58	62	62	98	133	134	70	88	80	64
Durables	114	76	100	85	131	101	83	106	89	111	115	133	73	97	127	80	85	103	163	109	86	93	108
Services	61	85	184	70	120	183	73	83	75	147	113	154	104	57	66	59	82	123	200	77	134	80	79

BAN = Bangladesh; BHU = Bhutan; BRU = Brunei Darussalam; CAM = Cambodia; FIJ = Fiji; HKG = Hong Kong, China; IND = India; INO = Indonesia; LAO = Lao People's Democratic Republic; MAC = Macau, China; MAL = Malaysia; MLD = Maldives; MON = Mongolia; MYA = Myanmar; NEP = Nepal; NPISH=nonprofit institutions serving households; PAK = Pakistan; PHI = Philippines; PRC = People's Republic of China; SIN = Singapore; SRI = Sri Lanka; TAP = Taipei,China; THA = Thailand; VIE = Viet Nam.

a Includes individual consumption expenditure by households, nonprofit institutions serving households, and government.

Source: Asian Development Bank estimates.

Table A5.4: Real Expenditure, 2011 (Revised)
(Billion Hong Kong dollars)

Expenditure Category	BAN	BHU	BRU	CAM	FIJ	HKG	IND	INO	LAO	MAC	MAL	MLD	MON	MYA	NEP	PAK	PHI	PRC	SIN	SRI	TAP	THA	VIE	AP
Gross Domestic Product	2,203	27	173	199	40	1,934	28,688	11,667	140	347	3,254	27	129	877	299	4,017	2,807	72,641	2,171	961	4,943	4,776	2,104	144,425
Actual Individual Consumption by Households[a]	1,762	15	28	176	31	1,289	18,921	7,022	88	77	1,811	10	81	577	259	3,705	2,301	32,179	734	775	3,139	3,169	1,409	79,559
Food and non-alcoholic beverages	723	4	3	63	10	137	5,177	1,677	24	5	314	2	18	250	127	1,295	823	5,744	49	167	316	663	336	17,927
Food	727	4	3	61	9	132	5,166	1,551	21	5	302	2	17	249	127	1,263	750	5,604	43	166	295	589	325	17,410
Bread and cereals	287	1	1	19	2	12	1,162	421	5	1	38	0	2	56	48	249	245	1,061	7	53	57	108	90	3,927
Meat and fish	126	0	1	18	2	74	394	457	10	2	113	1	7	83	20	117	302	1,953	15	24	93	167	127	4,106
Fruits and vegetables	157	1	0	10	3	16	1,633	261	4	1	59	0	1	75	28	263	79	1,666	8	20	102	213	58	4,663
Other food and non-alcoholic beverages	151	1	1	15	3	35	1,994	517	5	1	109	1	8	43	30	661	194	1,148	18	65	68	180	57	5,308
Clothing and footwear	73	1	1	3	1	60	1,082	152	2	3	31	0	2	17	6	119	19	1,410	17	33	110	81	56	3,278
Clothing	63	1	0	1	1	41	892	130	1	2	27	0	2	14	5	95	13	1,124	14	31	93	75	46	2,671
Housing, water, electricity, gas and other fuels	451	3	4	28	5	210	3,596	1,234	13	13	403	2	12	122	41	1,172	371	5,914	106	115	498	449	313	15,075
Health and education	305	5	11	60	6	183	4,340	1,523	19	14	398	3	33	135	52	847	347	10,502	129	167	803	853	619	21,356
Health	118	3	3	27	2	98	2,100	434	6	6	146	2	10	58	24	534	80	7,249	59	81	509	393	280	12,220
Education	189	2	8	33	4	85	2,172	1,214	15	8	259	1	24	76	28	319	291	3,709	72	87	326	465	342	9,732
Transportation and communication	64	2	5	10	3	117	2,289	946	8	8	272	1	13	17	6	216	229	3,090	101	103	451	396	87	8,431
Transportation	52	1	5	10	2	90	2,051	802	7	6	221	0	14	13	4	183	226	2,155	82	104	349	380	89	6,846
Recreation and culture	7	1	1	3	0	145	120	230	1	6	86	0	1	5	7	27	27	1,560	112	49	206	93	46	2,733
Restaurants and hotels	37	0	1	8	0	125	307	533	8	12	182	0	1	28	5	28	81	1,758	81	16	230	288	63	3,794
Other consumption expenditure items	171	1	2	15	6	311	2,928	877	17	9	310	2	9	31	24	334	422	4,376	134	130	633	481	200	11,422
Individual Consumption Expenditure by Government	51	4	10	21	3	65	1,188	739	8	10	297	2	21	19	14	171	138	7,953	71	108	455	538	209	12,096
Collective Consumption Expenditure by Government	95	6	38	10	4	103	2,305	861	19	14	260	6	14	134	17	345	142	4,524	140	77	416	421	190	10,140
Gross Fixed Capital Formation	529	14	46	20	8	455	7,882	3,522	41	40	678	8	51	231	51	389	495	31,892	608	193	1,120	1,166	529	49,968
Machinery and equipment	73	4	15	5	4	200	1,604	445	4	8	195	2	21	64	8	75	106	7,141	183	72	400	511	90	11,228
Construction	604	12	31	16	3	214	6,784	3,751	33	35	423	7	23	162	41	297	366	25,892	342	122	489	554	532	40,733
Change in Inventories and Net Acquisitions of Valuables	14	-0	-2	1	1	12	1,338	175	2	4	33	0	10	1	42	54	43	1,787	28	53	12	42	90	3,739
Balance of Exports and Imports	-80	-4	57	-0	-2	74	-788	172	-2	166	361	2	-18	-16	-36	-114	-63	1,515	599	-67	254	59	-44	2,026
Individual Consumption Expenditure by Households and NPISH	1,665	12	20	157	28	1,224	17,575	6,298	79	68	1,557	9	66	538	242	3,473	2,146	25,675	664	676	2,729	2,708	1,229	68,836
Government Final Consumption Expenditure	150	10	49	28	7	169	3,577	1,592	28	24	547	8	34	171	31	528	277	11,941	212	177	865	927	390	21,739
Actual Individual Consumption by Households[a]	1,762	15	28	176	31	1,289	18,921	7,022	88	77	1,811	10	81	577	259	3,705	2,301	32,179	734	775	3,139	3,169	1,409	79,559
All goods	997	7	9	87	16	468	8,835	3,080	45	19	763	4	33	319	146	2,063	1,126	13,913	194	292	1,236	1,328	704	35,685
Non-durables	1,012	6	6	83	14	231	7,986	2,442	38	10	656	4	29	329	153	2,056	1,117	9,996	96	250	715	1,073	611	28,914
Semi-durables	79	1	1	4	1	108	1,067	317	3	4	57	0	3	17	7	143	43	1,924	37	57	230	143	68	4,314
Durables	24	0	2	5	1	128	387	401	5	4	84	0	3	5	4	56	50	2,108	56	6	287	154	63	3,835
Services	486	4	7	49	9	701	8,411	2,934	31	40	886	4	29	173	71	1,142	946	10,639	489	398	1,413	1,279	531	30,673

0 = magnitude is less than half of unit employed; AP = Asia and the Pacific; BAN = Bangladesh; BHU = Bhutan; BRU = Brunei Darussalam; CAM = Cambodia; FIJ = Fiji; HKG = Hong Kong, China; IND = India; INO = Indonesia; LAO = Lao People's Democratic Republic; MAC = Macau, China; MAL = Malaysia; MLD = Maldives; MON = Mongolia; MYA = Myanmar; NEP = Nepal; NPISH=nonprofit institutions serving households; PAK = Pakistan; PHI = Philippines; PRC = People's Republic of China; SIN = Singapore; SRI = Sri Lanka; TAP = Taipei,China; THA = Thailand; VIE = Viet Nam.

Note: Each real aggregate value is derived by using a purchasing power parity that is specific to that aggregate, so real aggregates may not sum up to the total of their real components for an economy.

a Includes individual consumption expenditure by households, nonprofit institutions serving households, and government.

Source: Asian Development Bank estimates.

Table A5.5: Economy Shares of Real Expenditure to Asia and the Pacific, 2011 (Revised)
(%)

Expenditure Category	BAN	BHU	BRU	CAM	FIJ	HKG	IND	INO	LAO	MAC	MAL	MLD	MON	MYA	NEP	PAK	PHI	PRC	SIN	SRI	TAP	THA	VIE	AP
Gross Domestic Product	1.53	0.02	0.12	0.14	0.03	1.34	19.86	8.08	0.10	0.24	2.25	0.02	0.09	0.61	0.21	2.78	1.94	50.30	1.50	0.67	3.42	3.31	1.46	100.00
Actual Individual Consumption by Households[a]	2.21	0.02	0.03	0.22	0.04	1.62	23.78	8.83	0.11	0.10	2.28	0.01	0.10	0.73	0.33	4.66	2.89	40.45	0.92	0.97	3.94	3.98	1.77	100.00
Food and non-alcoholic beverages	4.03	0.02	0.02	0.35	0.06	0.77	28.88	9.35	0.13	0.03	1.75	0.01	0.10	1.40	0.71	7.22	4.59	32.04	0.27	0.93	1.76	3.70	1.87	100.00
Food	4.17	0.02	0.02	0.35	0.05	0.76	29.67	8.91	0.12	0.03	1.73	0.01	0.10	1.43	0.73	7.26	4.31	32.19	0.24	0.95	1.70	3.38	1.87	100.00
Bread and cereals	7.32	0.02	0.02	0.49	0.05	0.31	29.59	10.72	0.12	0.02	0.97	0.01	0.04	1.43	1.23	6.34	6.25	27.01	0.17	1.36	1.46	2.76	2.30	100.00
Meat and fish	3.07	0.01	0.03	0.44	0.05	1.81	9.59	11.12	0.23	0.05	2.74	0.02	0.18	2.02	0.47	2.84	7.36	47.57	0.37	0.57	2.27	4.08	3.08	100.00
Fruits and vegetables	3.37	0.02	0.01	0.22	0.07	0.35	35.03	5.61	0.09	0.02	1.27	0.01	0.03	1.61	0.61	5.63	1.69	35.73	0.18	0.44	2.19	4.58	1.24	100.00
Other food and non-alcoholic beverages	2.85	0.02	0.02	0.28	0.05	0.65	37.57	9.75	0.10	0.02	2.05	0.01	0.16	0.81	0.57	12.46	3.66	21.63	0.35	1.22	1.28	3.40	1.07	100.00
Clothing and footwear	2.22	0.03	0.02	0.09	0.03	1.83	33.02	4.63	0.05	0.09	0.94	0.01	0.06	0.52	0.17	3.64	0.58	43.00	0.53	1.00	3.35	2.48	1.70	100.00
Clothing	2.36	0.02	0.02	0.06	0.03	1.52	33.40	4.86	0.05	0.08	1.01	0.01	0.07	0.53	0.17	3.58	0.48	42.09	0.53	1.15	3.47	2.82	1.72	100.00
Housing, water, electricity, gas and other fuels	2.99	0.02	0.03	0.19	0.03	1.39	23.85	8.18	0.09	0.09	2.68	0.01	0.08	0.81	0.27	7.77	2.46	39.23	0.70	0.77	3.30	2.98	2.08	100.00
Health and education	1.43	0.02	0.05	0.28	0.03	0.86	20.32	7.13	0.09	0.07	1.87	0.01	0.15	0.63	0.24	3.97	1.63	49.18	0.61	0.78	3.76	3.99	2.90	100.00
Health	0.96	0.02	0.02	0.22	0.01	0.80	17.18	3.55	0.05	0.05	1.20	0.01	0.08	0.47	0.19	4.37	0.65	59.32	0.48	0.66	4.16	3.22	2.29	100.00
Education	1.95	0.02	0.09	0.34	0.04	0.88	22.32	12.47	0.16	0.08	2.66	0.01	0.24	0.79	0.29	3.27	2.99	38.11	0.74	0.90	3.35	4.78	3.52	100.00
Transportation and communication	0.76	0.02	0.06	0.11	0.03	1.39	27.15	11.22	0.10	0.09	3.22	0.02	0.16	0.20	0.07	2.56	2.72	36.65	1.19	1.22	5.35	4.69	1.03	100.00
Transportation	0.76	0.02	0.08	0.15	0.03	1.32	29.96	11.71	0.10	0.09	3.23	0.01	0.20	0.19	0.06	2.67	3.30	31.47	1.19	1.51	5.10	5.55	1.30	100.00
Recreation and culture	0.27	0.02	0.04	0.12	0.02	5.32	4.40	8.40	0.03	0.21	3.14	0.01	0.05	0.17	0.24	0.97	0.99	57.07	4.11	1.81	7.54	3.39	1.68	100.00
Restaurants and hotels	0.99	0.00	0.03	0.22	0.01	3.30	8.10	14.04	0.20	0.32	4.79	0.01	0.03	0.73	0.13	0.74	2.13	46.34	2.14	0.43	6.06	7.59	1.67	100.00
Other consumption expenditure items	1.49	0.01	0.02	0.13	0.05	2.72	25.64	7.68	0.15	0.08	2.72	0.01	0.08	0.27	0.21	2.93	3.70	38.31	1.17	1.13	5.54	4.21	1.75	100.00
Individual Consumption Expenditure by Government	0.42	0.03	0.09	0.17	0.02	0.54	9.82	6.11	0.07	0.09	2.45	0.01	0.17	0.16	0.11	1.41	1.14	65.75	0.59	0.90	3.76	4.45	1.73	100.00
Collective Consumption Expenditure by Government	0.94	0.06	0.38	0.09	0.04	1.02	22.73	8.49	0.18	0.13	2.56	0.06	0.14	1.32	0.17	3.40	1.40	44.62	1.38	0.76	4.10	4.15	1.87	100.00
Gross Fixed Capital Formation	1.06	0.03	0.09	0.04	0.02	0.91	15.77	7.05	0.08	0.08	1.36	0.02	0.10	0.46	0.10	0.78	0.99	63.83	1.22	0.39	2.24	2.33	1.06	100.00
Machinery and equipment	0.65	0.03	0.13	0.05	0.03	1.78	14.29	3.96	0.03	0.07	1.74	0.02	0.18	0.57	0.07	0.66	0.94	63.60	1.63	0.65	3.56	4.55	0.80	100.00
Construction	1.48	0.03	0.08	0.04	0.01	0.53	16.65	9.21	0.08	0.09	1.04	0.02	0.06	0.40	0.10	0.73	0.90	63.57	0.84	0.30	1.20	1.36	1.31	100.00
Change in Inventories and Net Acquisitions of Valuables	0.37	-0.00	-0.06	0.02	0.03	0.31	35.80	4.68	0.04	0.11	0.87	0.00	0.28	0.02	1.13	1.44	1.15	47.79	0.75	1.43	0.32	1.12	2.40	100.00
Balance of Exports and Imports	-3.93	-0.20	2.81	-0.01	-0.09	3.68	-38.91	8.49	-0.11	8.18	17.83	0.12	-0.88	-0.77	-1.80	-5.61	-3.13	74.79	29.54	-3.31	12.55	2.90	-2.15	100.00
Individual Consumption Expenditure by Households and NPISH	2.42	0.02	0.03	0.23	0.04	1.78	25.53	9.15	0.11	0.10	2.26	0.01	0.10	0.78	0.35	5.05	3.12	37.30	0.97	0.98	3.96	3.93	1.79	100.00
Government Final Consumption Expenditure	0.69	0.04	0.22	0.13	0.03	0.78	16.45	7.32	0.13	0.11	2.51	0.04	0.15	0.78	0.14	2.43	1.27	54.93	0.98	0.81	3.98	4.26	1.79	100.00
Actual Individual Consumption by Households[a]	2.21	0.02	0.03	0.22	0.04	1.62	23.78	8.83	0.11	0.10	2.28	0.01	0.10	0.73	0.33	4.66	2.89	40.45	0.92	0.97	3.94	3.98	1.77	100.00
All goods	2.79	-0.00	0.03	0.24	0.04	1.31	24.76	8.63	0.13	0.05	2.14	0.01	0.09	0.89	0.41	5.78	3.15	38.99	0.54	0.82	3.46	3.72	1.97	100.00
Non-durables	3.50	0.02	0.02	0.29	0.05	0.80	27.62	8.45	0.13	0.03	2.27	0.01	0.10	1.14	0.53	7.11	3.86	34.57	0.33	0.87	2.47	3.71	2.11	100.00
Semi-durables	1.84	0.02	0.03	0.09	0.03	2.51	24.74	7.35	0.07	0.09	1.31	0.01	0.06	0.39	0.17	3.32	0.99	44.59	0.85	1.33	5.33	3.31	1.57	100.00
Durables	0.63	0.01	0.05	0.14	0.03	3.35	10.09	10.47	0.14	0.11	2.18	0.01	0.08	0.12	0.10	1.47	1.29	54.98	1.45	0.16	7.47	4.02	1.65	100.00
Services	1.58	0.01	0.02	0.16	0.03	2.29	27.42	9.57	0.10	0.13	2.89	0.01	0.09	0.56	0.23	3.72	3.08	34.69	1.60	1.30	4.61	4.17	1.73	100.00

0.00 = magnitude of less than half of the unit employed; AP = Asia and the Pacific; BAN = Bangladesh; BHU = Bhutan; BRU = Brunei Darussalam; CAM = Cambodia; FIJ = Fiji; HKG = Hong Kong, China; IND = India; INO = Indonesia; LAO = Lao People's Democratic Republic; MAC = Macau, China; MAL = Malaysia; MLD = Maldives; MON = Mongolia; MYA = Myanmar; NEP = Nepal; NPISH=nonprofit institutions serving households; PAK = Pakistan; PHI = Philippines; PRC = People's Republic of China; SIN = Singapore; SRI = Sri Lanka; TAP = Taipei,China; THA = Thailand; VIE = Viet Nam.

Note: Each real aggregate value is derived by using a purchasing power parity that is specific to that aggregate, so real aggregates may not sum up to the total of their real components for an economy.

a Includes individual consumption expenditure by households, nonprofit institutions serving households, and government.

Source: Asian Development Bank estimates.

Table A5.6: Per Capita Real Expenditures, 2011 (Revised)
(Hong Kong dollars)

Expenditure Category	BAN	BHU	BRU	CAM	FIJ	HKG	IND	INO	LAO	MAC	MAL	MLD	MON	MYA	NEP	PAK	PHI	PRC	SIN	SRI	TAP	THA	VIE	AP
Gross Domestic Product	14,715	39,896	439,565	13,888	47,339	273,549	23,589	48,211	22,951	627,887	111,962	66,359	46,365	17,669	11,270	22,680	29,803	54,043	418,895	47,607	213,157	72,134	23,874	40,517
Actual Individual Consumption by Households[a]	11,770	21,456	70,526	12,331	35,883	182,347	15,558	29,019	14,394	139,419	62,327	24,814	28,936	11,616	9,773	20,922	24,430	23,940	141,677	38,396	135,339	47,858	15,995	22,320
Food and non-alcoholic beverages	4,831	5,525	8,884	4,394	11,562	19,439	4,257	6,929	3,855	8,963	10,819	5,385	6,504	5,044	4,786	7,311	8,735	4,273	9,397	8,263	13,639	10,019	3,811	5,029
Food	4,855	5,345	7,974	4,244	10,997	18,647	4,248	6,409	3,408	8,530	10,394	4,731	6,042	5,022	4,787	7,133	7,966	4,169	8,205	8,201	12,735	8,890	3,690	4,884
Bread and cereals	1,920	1,326	1,991	1,331	2,134	1,711	955	1,740	760	1,312	1,307	962	609	1,133	1,823	1,406	2,605	789	1,316	2,649	2,471	1,637	1,025	1,102
Meat and fish	843	701	2,790	1,255	2,390	10,484	324	1,888	1,566	3,893	3,878	2,015	2,648	1,673	736	659	3,209	1,453	2,969	1,164	4,026	2,528	1,437	1,152
Fruits and vegetables	1,049	1,641	1,221	713	3,852	2,330	1,343	1,080	674	1,936	2,044	618	439	1,515	1,074	1,484	837	1,239	1,635	1,009	4,411	3,223	654	1,308
Other food and non-alcoholic beverages	1,012	1,836	2,900	1,040	3,225	4,913	1,640	2,138	876	1,887	3,744	1,933	2,976	866	1,146	3,733	2,065	854	3,555	3,219	2,937	2,723	646	1,489
Clothing and footwear	487	1,275	1,367	206	1,271	8,474	890	628	265	5,282	1,064	542	749	343	211	674	201	1,049	3,338	1,616	4,732	1,230	633	920
Clothing	420	863	1,147	103	1,061	5,730	733	537	208	3,935	927	404	666	286	171	539	135	836	2,742	1,518	3,993	1,135	521	749
Housing, water, electricity, gas and other fuels	3,010	4,299	9,602	1,983	6,111	29,727	2,957	5,099	2,178	23,684	13,878	4,962	4,417	2,466	1,536	6,617	3,941	4,400	20,359	5,715	21,456	6,787	3,553	4,229
Health and education	2,040	7,539	27,230	4,187	6,816	25,924	3,568	6,292	3,159	25,147	13,706	7,005	11,834	2,716	1,966	4,783	3,689	7,814	24,970	8,293	34,645	12,881	7,028	5,991
Health	786	4,033	6,981	1,914	1,925	13,867	1,726	1,792	941	11,021	5,041	3,732	3,664	1,168	889	3,016	849	5,393	11,303	3,988	21,943	5,941	3,178	3,428
Education	1,265	3,555	21,547	2,285	5,115	12,057	1,786	5,016	2,479	14,356	8,908	3,424	8,553	1,540	1,074	1,799	3,086	2,760	13,985	4,322	14,052	7,029	3,883	2,730
Transportation and communication	429	2,292	12,097	678	3,185	16,518	1,882	3,908	1,320	13,907	9,347	3,296	4,824	339	225	1,219	2,434	2,299	19,411	5,078	19,451	5,975	986	2,365
Transportation	347	1,905	13,169	727	2,662	12,769	1,687	3,314	1,089	11,188	7,609	1,126	5,001	257	156	1,031	2,396	1,603	15,773	5,136	15,051	5,739	1,008	1,921
Recreation and culture	48	838	2,840	221	512	20,567	99	949	143	10,411	2,949	375	497	92	252	150	288	1,160	21,666	2,448	8,890	1,399	523	767
Restaurants and hotels	250	263	2,534	580	359	17,703	253	2,201	1,236	21,979	6,250	677	364	558	181	159	857	1,308	15,690	807	9,922	4,351	720	1,064
Other consumption expenditure items	1,140	1,222	5,097	1,056	6,796	43,994	2,408	3,624	2,736	15,879	10,680	3,924	3,125	632	922	1,888	4,482	3,256	25,840	6,415	27,284	7,268	2,264	3,204
Individual Consumption Expenditure by Government	340	5,635	26,252	1,449	3,352	9,203	977	3,053	1,326	18,957	10,204	4,420	7,527	382	516	966	1,462	5,917	13,760	5,365	19,635	8,125	2,377	3,393
Collective Consumption Expenditure by Government	636	8,315	97,009	668	5,252	14,627	1,895	3,557	3,045	24,643	8,945	15,845	5,047	2,705	635	1,948	1,509	3,366	26,967	3,795	17,920	6,357	2,154	2,845
Gross Fixed Capital Formation	3,535	20,649	117,023	1,410	8,823	64,383	6,481	14,554	6,652	72,324	23,331	20,320	18,170	4,647	1,911	2,199	5,255	23,727	117,279	9,542	48,307	17,610	6,007	14,018
Machinery and equipment	487	5,182	36,917	361	4,324	28,218	1,319	1,839	614	14,330	6,715	6,017	7,444	1,282	290	421	1,122	5,312	35,363	3,586	17,244	7,716	1,025	3,150
Construction	4,032	18,128	79,510	1,153	3,377	30,292	5,578	15,499	5,439	63,182	14,564	16,355	8,198	3,258	1,544	1,678	3,886	19,263	65,905	6,024	21,107	8,363	6,041	11,427
Change in Inventories and Net Acquisitions of Valuables	93	-92	-5,478	60	1,190	1,660	1,100	722	253	7,210	1,124	304	3,731	15	1,596	304	457	1,329	5,402	2,644	511	634	1,019	1,049
Balance of Exports and Imports	-531	-6,106	144,701	-8	-2,034	10,532	-648	711	-372	299,974	12,428	6,131	-6,367	-315	-1,374	-642	-674	1,127	115,480	-3,320	10,966	887	-495	568
Individual Consumption Expenditure by Households and NPISH	11,122	17,216	51,391	10,951	32,651	173,144	14,452	26,024	12,874	122,664	53,569	21,101	23,675	10,835	9,122	19,610	22,781	19,101	128,182	33,458	117,693	40,892	13,947	19,311
Government Final Consumption Expenditure	1,000	14,038	124,044	1,936	8,651	23,830	2,941	6,577	4,601	43,569	18,810	20,751	12,036	3,436	1,151	2,983	2,937	8,884	40,966	8,763	37,301	14,002	4,427	6,099
Actual Individual Consumption by Households[a]	11,770	21,456	70,526	12,331	35,883	182,347	15,558	29,019	14,394	139,419	62,327	24,814	28,936	11,616	9,773	20,922	24,430	23,940	141,677	38,396	135,339	47,858	15,995	22,320
All goods	6,657	10,481	23,960	6,108	18,597	66,211	7,265	12,727	7,292	33,954	26,262	10,443	11,970	6,421	5,498	11,650	11,952	10,351	37,496	14,446	53,311	20,054	7,994	10,011
Non-durables	6,757	8,888	15,922	5,809	16,868	32,719	6,566	10,091	6,191	18,089	22,589	9,573	10,482	6,621	5,775	11,610	11,859	7,437	18,535	12,397	30,814	16,203	6,933	8,111
Semi-durables	530	1,401	3,040	285	1,317	15,328	878	1,311	508	7,026	1,952	765	961	343	270	808	452	1,431	7,052	2,845	9,915	2,155	768	1,210
Durables	161	699	4,894	365	1,437	18,164	318	1,659	848	7,831	2,882	792	1,039	91	142	318	527	1,569	10,711	307	12,359	2,329	720	1,076
Services	3,245	5,606	18,645	3,415	10,958	99,132	6,916	12,126	5,030	71,970	30,487	9,989	10,231	3,482	2,688	6,450	10,044	7,915	94,394	19,696	60,930	19,322	6,030	8,605

AP = Asia and the Pacific; BAN = Bangladesh; BHU = Bhutan; BRU = Brunei Darussalam; CAM = Cambodia; FIJ = Fiji; HKG = Hong Kong, China; IND = India; INO = Indonesia; LAO = Lao People's Democratic Republic; MAC = Macau, China; MAL = Malaysia; MLD = Maldives; MON = Mongolia; MYA = Myanmar; NEP = Nepal; NPISH=nonprofit institutions serving households; PAK = Pakistan; PHI = Philippines; PRC = People's Republic of China; SIN = Singapore; SRI = Sri Lanka; TAP = Taipei,China; THA = Thailand; VIE = Viet Nam.

Note: Each real aggregate value is derived by using a purchasing power parity that is specific to that aggregate, so real aggregates may not sum up to the total of their real components for an economy.

a Includes individual consumption expenditure by households, nonprofit institutions serving households, and government.

Source: Asian Development Bank estimates.

Table A5.7: Per Capita Real Expenditure Index, 2011 (Revised)
(Asia and the Pacific = 100)

Expenditure Category	BAN	BHU	BRU	CAM	FIJ	HKG	IND	INO	LAO	MAC	MAL	MLD	MON	MYA	NEP	PAK	PHI	PRC	SIN	SRI	TAP	THA	VIE	AP
Gross Domestic Product	36	98	1,085	34	117	675	58	119	57	1,550	276	164	114	44	28	56	74	133	1,034	117	526	178	59	100
Actual Individual Consumption by Households[a]	53	96	316	55	161	817	70	130	64	625	279	111	130	52	44	94	109	107	635	172	606	214	72	100
Food and non-alcoholic beverages	96	110	177	87	230	387	85	138	77	178	215	107	129	100	95	145	174	85	187	164	271	199	76	100
Food	99	109	163	87	225	382	87	131	70	175	213	97	124	103	98	146	163	85	168	168	261	182	76	100
Bread and cereals	174	120	181	121	194	155	87	158	69	119	119	87	55	103	165	128	237	72	119	240	224	149	93	100
Meat and fish	73	61	242	109	207	910	28	164	136	338	337	175	230	145	64	57	279	126	258	101	350	219	125	100
Fruits and vegetables	80	125	93	55	294	178	103	83	51	148	156	47	116	116	82	113	64	95	125	77	337	246	50	100
Other food and non-alcoholic beverages	68	123	195	70	217	330	110	144	59	127	251	130	200	58	77	251	139	57	239	216	197	183	43	100
Clothing and footwear	53	139	149	22	138	922	97	68	29	574	116	59	81	37	23	73	22	114	363	176	515	134	69	100
Clothing	56	115	153	14	142	765	98	72	28	525	124	54	89	38	23	72	18	112	366	203	533	152	70	100
Housing, water, electricity, gas and other fuels	71	102	227	47	144	703	70	121	51	560	328	117	104	58	36	156	93	104	481	135	507	160	84	100
Health and education	34	126	454	70	114	433	60	105	53	420	229	117	198	45	33	80	62	130	417	138	578	215	117	100
Health	23	118	204	56	56	405	50	52	27	321	147	109	107	34	26	88	25	157	330	116	640	173	93	100
Education	46	130	789	84	187	442	65	184	91	526	326	125	313	56	39	66	113	101	512	158	515	257	142	100
Transportation and communication	18	97	511	29	135	698	80	165	56	588	395	139	204	14	9	52	103	97	821	215	822	253	42	100
Transportation	18	99	686	38	139	665	88	173	57	583	396	59	260	13	8	54	125	83	821	267	784	299	53	100
Recreation and culture	6	109	370	29	67	2,682	13	124	19	1,358	385	49	65	12	33	20	38	151	2,825	319	1,159	182	68	100
Restaurants and hotels	23	25	238	55	34	1,663	24	207	116	2,065	587	64	34	52	17	15	81	123	1,474	76	932	409	68	100
Other consumption expenditure items	36	38	159	33	212	1,373	75	113	85	496	333	122	98	20	29	59	140	102	806	200	851	227	71	100
Individual Consumption Expenditure by Government	10	166	774	43	99	271	29	90	39	559	301	130	222	11	15	28	43	174	405	158	579	239	70	100
Collective Consumption Expenditure by Government	22	292	3,410	23	185	514	67	125	107	866	314	557	177	95	22	68	53	118	948	133	630	223	76	100
Gross Fixed Capital Formation	25	147	835	10	63	459	46	104	47	516	166	145	130	33	14	16	37	169	837	68	345	126	43	100
Machinery and equipment	15	164	1,172	11	137	896	42	58	19	455	213	191	236	41	9	13	36	169	1,123	114	547	245	33	100
Construction	35	159	696	10	30	265	49	136	48	553	127	143	72	29	14	15	34	169	577	53	185	73	53	100
Change in Inventories and Net Acquisitions of Valuables	9	-9	-522	6	113	158	105	69	24	687	107	29	356	1	152	29	44	127	515	252	49	60	97	100
Balance of Exports and Imports	-93	-1,074	25,456	-1	-358	1,853	-114	125	-65	52,771	2,186	1,079	-1,120	-55	-242	-113	-118	198	20,315	-584	1,929	156	-87	100
Individual Consumption Expenditure by Households and NPISH	58	89	266	57	169	897	75	135	67	635	277	109	123	56	47	102	118	99	664	173	609	212	72	100
Government Final Consumption Expenditure	16	230	2,034	32	142	391	48	108	75	714	308	340	197	56	19	49	48	146	672	144	612	230	73	100
Actual Individual Consumption by Households[a]	53	96	316	55	161	817	70	130	64	625	279	111	130	52	44	94	109	107	635	172	606	214	72	100
All goods	66	105	239	61	186	661	73	127	73	339	262	104	120	64	55	116	119	103	375	144	533	200	80	100
Non-durables	83	110	196	72	208	403	81	124	76	223	278	118	129	82	71	143	146	92	229	153	380	200	85	100
Semi-durables	44	116	251	24	109	1,266	73	108	42	580	161	63	79	28	22	67	37	118	583	235	819	178	63	100
Durables	15	65	455	34	134	1,688	30	154	79	728	268	74	97	8	13	30	49	146	996	29	1,149	216	67	100
Services	38	65	217	40	127	1,152	80	141	58	836	354	116	119	40	31	75	117	92	1,097	229	708	225	70	100

AP = Asia and the Pacific; BAN = Bangladesh; BHU = Bhutan; BRU = Brunei Darussalam; CAM = Cambodia; FIJ = Fiji; HKG = Hong Kong, China; IND = India; INO = Indonesia; LAO = Lao People's Democratic Republic; MAC = Macau, China; MAL = Malaysia; MLD = Maldives; MON = Mongolia; MYA = Myanmar; NEP = Nepal; NPISH=nonprofit institutions serving households; PAK = Pakistan; PHI = Philippines; PRC = People's Republic of China; SIN = Singapore; SRI = Sri Lanka; TAP = Taipei,China; THA = Thailand; VIE = Viet Nam.

Note: Each real aggregate value is derived by using a purchasing power parity that is specific to that aggregate, so real aggregates may not sum up to the total of their real components for an economy.

a Includes individual consumption expenditure by households, nonprofit institutions serving households, and government.

Source: Asian Development Bank estimates.

Table A5.8: Nominal Expenditure, 2011 (Revised)

(Billion Hong Kong dollars)

Expenditure Category	BAN	BHU	BRU	CAM	FIJ	HKG	IND	INO	LAO	MAC	MAL	MLD	MON	MYA	NEP	PAK	PHI	PRC	SIN	SRI	TAP	THA	VIE	AP
Gross Domestic Product	1,035	14	144	100	32	1,934	14,220	6,951	69	286	2,319	22	81	418	152	1,727	1,745	58,945	2,175	508	3,780	2,886	1,055	100,598
Actual Individual Consumption by Households[a]	780	7	25	84	24	1,289	8,393	4,088	43	68	1,264	8	46	256	121	1,466	1,354	25,294	868	383	2,348	1,789	669	50,667
Food and non-alcoholic beverages	396	2	3	38	8	137	2,423	1,242	16	5	242	2	13	147	68	648	549	4,753	55	112	270	450	201	11,781
Food	394	2	3	36	8	132	2,376	1,144	14	5	231	2	12	144	67	622	507	4,633	49	109	252	395	195	11,332
Bread and cereals	176	1	1	12	2	12	586	343	4	1	33	0	1	39	28	145	186	1,006	9	38	58	87	58	2,825
Meat and fish	76	0	1	11	2	74	192	307	6	2	78	0	4	44	11	59	175	1,537	19	14	80	99	80	2,872
Fruits and vegetables	54	1	1	5	2	16	641	178	2	1	48	0	1	34	12	85	58	1,187	9	12	77	136	28	2,588
Other food and non-alcoholic beverages	91	1	1	10	3	35	1,004	415	4	1	83	1	6	29	18	359	129	1,023	19	48	56	129	35	3,496
Clothing and footwear	47	1	1	2	1	60	503	156	1	4	34	0	2	9	3	68	18	1,748	23	19	92	56	31	2,878
Clothing	42	0	1	1	1	41	404	137	1	3	29	0	2	8	2	56	13	1,448	18	18	80	53	26	2,383
Housing, water, electricity, gas and other fuels	135	1	3	12	2	210	1,304	364	5	10	188	2	7	38	14	282	162	3,506	138	35	380	146	152	7,095
Health and education	71	1	7	12	3	183	979	518	3	9	193	1	7	19	11	163	131	6,339	139	35	431	311	109	9,676
Health	29	1	2	6	1	98	393	194	1	5	74	1	2	11	5	92	38	3,794	64	19	222	146	52	5,249
Education	43	1	5	6	2	85	585	324	1	5	120	1	5	8	6	71	93	2,545	75	16	209	165	58	4,427
Transportation and communication	37	1	4	6	3	117	1,388	708	6	7	241	1	9	13	5	118	179	2,337	144	69	332	284	74	6,082
Transportation	33	1	3	6	2	90	1,203	523	5	5	157	0	8	9	4	94	138	1,478	104	65	250	248	69	4,495
Recreation and culture	6	0	2	2	1	145	92	179	1	6	80	0	1	3	5	16	23	1,374	114	38	200	79	29	2,396
Restaurants and hotels	18	0	1	4	0	125	188	342	4	12	112	0	1	11	2	15	47	1,288	80	12	148	139	30	2,581
Other consumption expenditure items	72	0	2	7	5	311	1,558	579	9	8	249	1	5	17	13	156	244	3,949	184	65	496	324	86	8,340
Individual Consumption Expenditure by Government	15	1	6	5	2	65	460	235	1	8	151	1	5	4	5	53	72	5,042	73	20	288	227	47	6,785
Collective Consumption Expenditure by Government	38	2	21	4	3	103	1,119	394	5	12	157	4	5	46	10	122	97	3,686	128	23	284	249	62	6,575
Gross Fixed Capital Formation	288	10	44	12	6	455	4,709	2,176	22	36	512	7	39	130	32	225	327	26,872	549	134	884	761	314	38,545
Machinery and equipment	64	4	15	5	4	200	1,428	410	3	7	187	2	22	60	7	66	103	7,453	176	74	364	488	80	11,222
Construction	216	6	26	6	2	214	2,707	1,590	11	27	249	5	13	52	18	108	163	16,957	284	56	340	239	214	23,504
Change in Inventories and Net Acquisitions of Valuables	8	-0	-2	1	1	12	787	121	1	4	26	0	8	0	25	28	30	1,578	31	36	9	29	53	2,785
Balance of Exports and Imports	-80	-4	57	-0	-2	74	-788	172	-2	166	361	2	-18	-16	-36	-114	-63	1,515	599	-67	254	59	-44	2,026
Individual Consumption Expenditure by Households and NPISH	765	6	18	79	22	1,224	7,933	3,852	42	60	1,113	7	42	252	116	1,414	1,282	20,252	795	362	2,060	1,562	622	43,882
Government Final Consumption Expenditure	52	3	27	8	5	169	1,579	630	6	20	308	5	10	50	15	175	169	8,728	201	43	573	476	110	13,360
Actual Individual Consumption by Households[a]	780	7	25	84	24	1,289	8,393	4,088	43	68	1,264	8	46	256	121	1,466	1,354	25,294	868	383	2,348	1,789	669	50,667
All goods	591	4	9	56	15	468	4,604	2,448	30	19	641	4	25	199	88	1,037	861	13,121	260	198	1,001	973	435	27,087
Non-durables	508	3	5	50	12	231	3,702	1,730	24	10	485	3	20	185	79	906	779	8,483	123	153	560	721	325	19,096
Semi-durables	55	1	2	2	1	108	583	297	2	5	60	0	3	10	4	87	40	2,483	47	39	196	110	42	4,177
Durables	27	0	2	4	2	128	318	421	5	5	96	0	2	4	5	45	42	2,155	90	7	245	142	68	3,814
Services	160	2	7	19	6	701	3,371	1,333	13	32	545	3	16	54	26	370	421	7,131	534	166	1,032	560	228	16,732

0 = magnitude is less than half of unit employed; AP = Asia and the Pacific; BAN = Bangladesh; BHU = Bhutan; BRU = Brunei Darussalam; CAM = Cambodia; FIJ = Fiji; HKG = Hong Kong, China; IND = India; INO = Indonesia; LAO = Lao People's Democratic Republic; MAC = Macau, China; MAL = Malaysia; MLD = Maldives; MON = Mongolia; MYA = Myanmar; NEP = Nepal; NPISH=nonprofit institutions serving households; PAK = Pakistan; PHI = Philippines; PRC = People's Republic of China; SIN = Singapore; SRI = Sri Lanka; TAP = Taipei,China; THA = Thailand; VIE = Viet Nam.

Note: Bureau of Statistics of the People's Republic of China does not recognize these results as official statistics.

a Includes individual consumption expenditure by households, nonprofit institutions serving households, and government.

Source: Asian Development Bank estimates.

Table A5.9: Economy Shares of Nominal Expenditure to Asia and the Pacific, 2011 (Revised)

(%)

Expenditure Category	BAN	BHU	BRU	CAM	FIJ	HKG	IND	INO	LAO	MAC	MAL	MLD	MON	MYA	NEP	PAK	PHI	PRC	SIN	SRI	TAP	THA	VIE	AP
Gross Domestic Product	1.03	0.01	0.14	0.10	0.03	1.92	14.14	6.91	0.07	0.28	2.31	0.02	0.08	0.42	0.15	1.72	1.73	58.59	2.16	0.51	3.76	2.87	1.05	100.00
Actual Individual Consumption by Households[a]	1.54	0.01	0.05	0.17	0.05	2.55	16.57	8.07	0.09	0.13	2.49	0.02	0.09	0.51	0.24	2.89	2.67	49.92	1.71	0.75	4.64	3.53	1.32	100.00
Food and non-alcoholic beverages	3.36	0.02	0.03	0.32	0.07	1.17	20.57	10.55	0.14	0.04	2.05	0.02	0.11	1.25	0.58	5.50	4.66	40.35	0.47	0.95	2.29	3.82	1.71	100.00
Food	3.48	0.02	0.02	0.32	0.07	1.16	20.97	10.10	0.12	0.04	2.04	0.01	0.11	1.27	0.59	5.49	4.47	40.89	0.44	0.97	2.22	3.48	1.72	100.00
Bread and cereals	6.23	0.02	0.02	0.41	0.06	0.43	20.73	12.14	0.13	0.03	1.16	0.01	0.05	1.38	0.99	5.15	6.59	35.62	0.31	1.34	2.05	3.09	2.06	100.00
Meat and fish	2.63	0.01	0.03	0.39	0.06	2.58	6.69	10.69	0.21	0.07	2.71	0.02	0.15	1.55	0.39	2.04	6.09	53.53	0.65	0.49	2.78	3.43	2.80	100.00
Fruits and vegetables	2.07	0.02	0.02	0.21	0.09	0.64	24.78	6.86	0.08	0.04	1.84	0.01	0.05	1.33	0.45	3.28	2.26	45.86	0.36	0.47	2.96	5.24	1.09	100.00
Other food and non-alcoholic beverages	2.60	0.02	0.03	0.27	0.07	0.99	28.71	11.86	0.12	0.03	2.39	0.02	0.18	0.84	0.50	10.27	3.69	29.25	0.53	1.36	1.59	3.69	0.99	100.00
Clothing and footwear	1.63	0.02	0.03	0.06	0.04	2.08	17.49	5.42	0.03	0.13	1.17	0.01	0.07	0.31	0.10	2.37	0.63	60.74	0.80	0.67	3.19	1.94	1.07	100.00
Clothing	1.76	0.01	0.03	0.03	0.04	1.70	16.97	5.73	0.03	0.12	1.23	0.01	0.08	0.32	0.10	2.35	0.53	60.75	0.77	0.76	3.35	2.21	1.10	100.00
Housing, water, electricity, gas and other fuels	1.90	0.02	0.04	0.18	0.03	2.96	18.38	5.13	0.07	0.13	2.65	0.03	0.10	0.54	0.19	3.97	2.28	49.41	1.95	0.49	5.35	2.06	2.14	100.00
Health and education	0.74	0.01	0.07	0.12	0.03	1.89	10.11	5.36	0.03	0.10	2.00	0.01	0.07	0.19	0.12	1.68	1.35	65.51	1.44	0.36	4.45	3.21	1.13	100.00
Health	0.54	0.02	0.03	0.11	0.02	1.87	7.49	3.70	0.03	0.09	1.40	0.01	0.04	0.21	0.10	1.76	0.72	72.29	1.22	0.36	4.22	2.79	0.98	100.00
Education	0.96	0.01	0.11	0.13	0.05	1.93	13.22	7.32	0.03	0.11	2.70	0.02	0.11	0.17	0.14	1.59	2.10	57.48	1.70	0.35	4.73	3.72	1.31	100.00
Transportation and communication	0.60	0.01	0.07	0.11	0.05	1.92	22.81	11.64	0.09	0.12	3.97	0.02	0.16	0.21	0.09	1.95	2.94	38.42	2.37	1.13	5.45	4.67	1.22	100.00
Transportation	0.73	0.01	0.07	0.14	0.04	2.01	26.76	11.64	0.10	0.12	3.50	0.01	0.18	0.20	0.08	2.09	3.08	32.88	2.31	1.45	5.56	5.51	1.52	100.00
Recreation and culture	0.24	0.02	0.06	0.10	0.02	6.07	3.82	7.46	0.03	0.26	3.34	0.01	0.06	0.12	0.20	0.68	0.98	57.37	4.74	1.57	8.37	3.28	1.23	100.00
Restaurants and hotels	0.69	0.00	0.04	0.16	0.01	4.85	7.29	13.24	0.17	0.45	4.34	0.01	0.03	0.44	0.09	0.58	1.84	49.89	3.10	0.48	5.73	5.40	1.17	100.00
Other consumption expenditure items	0.86	0.01	0.03	0.08	0.06	3.73	18.68	6.94	0.10	0.10	2.98	0.01	0.06	0.20	0.15	1.88	2.93	47.35	2.21	0.78	5.94	3.88	1.03	100.00
Individual Consumption Expenditure by Government	0.22	0.02	0.09	0.07	0.03	0.96	6.77	3.47	0.02	0.12	2.23	0.01	0.07	0.06	0.07	0.78	1.06	74.30	1.07	0.30	4.25	3.35	0.70	100.00
Collective Consumption Expenditure by Government	0.57	0.03	0.32	0.06	0.05	1.57	17.02	6.00	0.07	0.19	2.38	0.06	0.08	0.70	0.15	1.86	1.48	56.06	1.95	0.35	4.32	3.79	0.95	100.00
Gross Fixed Capital Formation	0.75	0.02	0.11	0.03	0.02	1.18	12.22	5.65	0.06	0.09	1.33	0.02	0.10	0.34	0.08	0.58	0.85	69.72	1.42	0.35	2.29	1.98	0.81	100.00
Machinery and equipment	0.57	0.03	0.13	0.04	0.03	1.78	12.72	3.65	0.03	0.06	1.66	0.02	0.19	0.54	0.06	0.59	0.92	66.42	1.57	0.66	3.25	4.35	0.71	100.00
Construction	0.92	0.02	0.11	0.02	0.01	0.91	11.52	6.77	0.05	0.12	1.06	0.02	0.06	0.22	0.08	0.46	0.69	72.15	1.21	0.24	1.45	1.02	0.91	100.00
Change in Inventories and Net Acquisitions of Valuables	0.28	-0.00	-0.08	0.02	0.03	0.42	28.27	4.33	0.03	0.14	0.92	0.00	0.28	0.02	0.90	0.99	1.08	56.65	1.11	1.30	0.34	1.03	1.92	100.00
Balance of Exports and Imports	-3.93	-0.20	2.81	-0.01	-0.09	3.68	-38.91	8.49	-0.11	8.18	17.83	0.12	-0.88	-0.77	-1.80	-5.61	-3.13	74.79	29.54	-3.31	12.55	2.90	-2.15	100.00
Individual Consumption Expenditure by Households and NPISH	1.74	0.01	0.04	0.18	0.05	2.79	18.08	8.78	0.10	0.14	2.54	0.02	0.10	0.58	0.26	3.22	2.92	46.15	1.81	0.83	4.69	3.56	1.42	100.00
Government Final Consumption Expenditure	0.39	0.02	0.20	0.06	0.04	1.26	11.82	4.71	0.05	0.15	2.30	0.03	0.07	0.37	0.11	1.31	1.27	65.33	1.50	0.33	4.29	3.56	0.82	100.00
Actual Individual Consumption by Households[a]	1.54	0.01	0.05	0.17	0.05	2.55	16.57	8.07	0.09	0.13	2.49	0.02	0.09	0.51	0.24	2.89	2.67	49.92	1.71	0.75	4.64	3.53	1.32	100.00
All goods	2.18	0.02	0.03	0.21	0.05	1.73	17.00	9.04	0.11	0.07	2.37	0.01	0.09	0.73	0.32	3.83	3.18	48.44	0.96	0.73	3.70	3.59	1.61	100.00
Non-durables	2.66	0.02	0.03	0.26	0.06	1.21	19.39	9.06	0.12	0.05	2.54	0.02	0.10	0.97	0.41	4.74	4.08	44.42	0.64	0.80	2.93	3.77	1.70	100.00
Semi-durables	1.33	0.01	0.04	0.06	0.03	2.59	13.97	7.10	0.04	0.12	1.44	0.01	0.07	0.23	0.10	2.07	0.96	59.43	1.13	0.93	4.69	2.64	1.01	100.00
Durables	0.72	0.01	0.05	0.12	0.04	3.37	8.34	11.05	0.12	0.12	2.51	0.01	0.06	0.12	0.13	1.17	1.10	56.50	2.36	0.18	6.42	3.73	1.79	100.00
Services	0.96	0.01	0.04	0.11	0.04	4.19	20.15	7.97	0.08	0.19	3.26	0.02	0.10	0.32	0.15	2.21	2.52	42.62	3.19	0.99	6.17	3.35	1.36	100.00

0.00 = magnitude of less than half of the unit employed; AP = Asia and the Pacific; BAN = Bangladesh; BHU = Bhutan; BRU = Brunei Darussalam; CAM = Cambodia; FIJ = Fiji; HKG = Hong Kong, China; IND = India; INO = Indonesia; LAO = Lao People's Democratic Republic; MAC = Macau, China; MAL = Malaysia; MLD = Maldives; MON = Mongolia; MYA = Myanmar; NEP = Nepal; NPISH=nonprofit institutions serving households; PAK = Pakistan; PHI = Philippines; PRC = People's Republic of China; SIN = Singapore; SRI = Sri Lanka; TAP = Taipei,China; THA = Thailand; VIE = Viet Nam.

a Includes individual consumption expenditure by households, nonprofit institutions serving households, and government.

Source: Asian Development Bank estimates.

Table A5.10: Per Capita Nominal Expenditure, 2011 (Revised)
(Hong Kong dollars)

Expenditure Category	BAN	BHU	BRU	CAM	FIJ	HKG	IND	INO	LAO	MAC	MAL	MLD	MON	MYA	NEP	PAK	PHI	PRC	SIN	SRI	TAP	THA	VIE	AP
Gross Domestic Product	6,911	20,851	366,586	6,980	37,256	273,549	11,692	28,724	11,337	517,164	79,804	53,144	29,081	8,413	5,720	9,754	18,525	43,854	419,491	25,167	163,021	43,593	11,974	28,222
Actual Individual Consumption by Households[a]	5,212	10,321	62,743	5,882	27,709	182,347	6,901	16,892	7,095	123,254	43,482	19,887	16,591	5,162	4,561	8,279	14,372	18,818	167,452	18,940	101,271	27,014	7,593	14,214
Food and non-alcoholic beverages	2,645	2,998	7,878	2,623	9,568	19,439	1,992	5,134	2,635	8,951	8,316	4,361	4,775	2,962	2,572	3,658	5,826	3,536	10,638	5,535	11,636	6,803	2,286	3,305
Food	2,634	2,851	7,080	2,513	8,966	18,647	1,954	4,728	2,276	8,530	7,949	3,782	4,381	2,892	2,538	3,514	5,380	3,447	9,520	5,416	10,871	5,960	2,209	3,179
Bread and cereals	1,176	794	1,591	805	1,869	1,711	482	1,417	601	1,439	1,130	1,000	504	787	1,051	821	1,977	749	1,669	1,873	2,499	1,320	660	792
Meat and fish	505	340	2,537	776	2,131	10,484	158	1,269	1,007	3,798	2,680	1,135	1,500	895	420	330	1,858	1,144	3,624	702	3,439	1,488	913	806
Fruits and vegetables	358	761	1,275	377	2,610	2,330	527	734	355	1,886	1,637	710	509	692	436	479	620	883	1,774	600	3,302	2,047	321	726
Other food and non-alcoholic beverages	607	1,103	2,476	665	2,958	4,913	825	1,713	671	1,829	2,869	1,516	2,262	588	665	2,027	1,371	761	3,571	2,360	2,396	1,948	392	981
Clothing and footwear	313	752	1,982	111	1,249	8,474	414	645	145	6,831	1,155	484	767	181	113	385	193	1,301	4,431	958	3,964	842	351	807
Clothing	280	510	1,645	57	1,027	5,730	333	564	116	5,219	1,012	385	679	155	94	317	133	1,077	3,541	902	3,445	797	297	668
Housing, water, electricity, gas and other fuels	900	1,802	7,036	871	2,577	29,727	1,072	1,505	794	17,302	6,462	5,491	2,468	771	512	1,591	1,717	2,608	26,645	1,730	16,380	2,203	1,721	1,990
Health and education	475	2,128	17,315	813	3,946	25,924	805	2,141	440	16,927	6,647	3,439	2,420	373	429	919	1,388	4,716	26,896	1,724	18,587	4,698	1,242	2,715
Health	190	1,185	4,490	414	1,158	13,867	323	803	216	8,405	2,531	1,570	737	217	188	521	402	2,823	12,352	947	9,554	2,210	586	1,472
Education	285	942	12,824	398	2,788	12,057	481	1,339	223	8,522	4,116	1,869	1,683	155	240	398	985	1,893	14,544	777	9,033	2,488	656	1,242
Transportation and communication	244	1,221	10,568	451	3,440	16,518	1,141	2,926	911	12,724	8,298	2,573	3,402	256	196	668	1,900	1,738	27,768	3,397	14,306	4,289	841	1,706
Transportation	219	973	8,217	437	2,326	12,769	989	2,163	758	9,614	5,410	918	2,876	178	135	531	1,470	1,100	20,073	3,226	10,771	3,741	778	1,261
Recreation and culture	38	634	3,915	161	598	20,567	75	738	124	11,394	2,750	435	474	59	180	91	249	1,023	21,900	1,860	8,643	1,187	334	672
Restaurants and hotels	118	117	2,847	281	354	17,703	155	1,413	729	20,995	3,859	428	268	228	89	84	503	958	15,429	619	6,378	2,104	343	724
Other consumption expenditure items	478	671	5,930	486	5,979	43,994	1,281	2,391	1,415	15,364	8,565	2,674	1,851	333	485	883	2,596	2,938	35,531	3,239	21,378	4,889	974	2,340
Individual Consumption Expenditure by Government	99	1,654	15,892	328	2,202	9,203	378	973	191	14,367	5,202	2,338	1,618	79	188	298	762	3,751	14,010	1,009	12,438	3,428	536	1,904
Collective Consumption Expenditure by Government	251	2,530	52,761	259	3,755	14,627	920	1,629	800	22,442	5,389	9,039	1,946	930	360	690	1,035	2,742	24,699	1,144	12,251	3,761	708	1,844
Gross Fixed Capital Formation	1,926	14,163	111,812	809	6,821	64,383	3,872	8,993	3,661	64,523	17,622	17,819	14,079	2,626	1,225	1,270	3,471	19,992	105,876	6,615	38,123	11,497	3,562	10,813
Machinery and equipment	426	5,429	37,346	343	4,261	28,218	1,174	1,695	560	12,547	6,422	5,945	7,793	1,216	267	375	1,094	5,545	33,908	3,687	15,714	7,365	910	3,148
Construction	1,443	8,227	67,019	403	2,088	30,292	2,226	6,572	1,791	49,026	8,581	11,874	4,689	1,056	681	607	1,730	12,615	54,837	2,761	14,659	3,607	2,432	6,594
Change in Inventories and Net Acquisitions of Valuables	53	-57	-5,432	37	1,005	1,660	647	499	152	6,971	883	269	2,832	9	948	156	320	1,174	5,985	1,786	409	434	606	781
Balance of Exports and Imports	-531	-6,106	144,701	-8	-2,034	10,532	-648	711	-372	299,974	12,428	6,131	-6,367	-315	-1,374	-642	-674	1,127	115,480	-3,320	10,966	887	-495	568
Individual Consumption Expenditure by Households and NPISH	5,113	8,666	46,851	5,554	25,507	173,144	6,523	15,920	6,904	108,886	38,280	17,548	14,973	5,084	4,373	7,982	13,610	15,067	153,442	17,931	88,833	23,586	7,057	12,311
Government Final Consumption Expenditure	350	4,184	68,653	587	5,957	23,830	1,298	2,602	992	36,809	10,590	11,377	3,564	1,008	548	988	1,797	6,493	38,708	2,153	24,690	7,189	1,244	3,748
Actual Individual Consumption by Households[a]	5,212	10,321	62,743	5,882	27,709	182,347	6,901	16,892	7,095	123,254	43,482	19,887	16,591	5,162	4,561	8,279	14,372	18,818	167,452	18,940	101,271	27,014	7,593	14,214
All goods	3,947	6,076	22,903	3,946	17,277	66,211	3,785	10,115	4,947	34,917	22,067	9,136	8,827	3,998	3,318	5,856	9,139	9,762	50,232	9,814	43,166	14,695	4,939	7,599
Non-durables	3,394	4,640	13,866	3,465	14,028	32,719	3,044	7,148	3,897	17,564	16,703	7,321	7,089	3,717	2,977	5,115	8,268	6,311	23,756	7,554	24,150	10,882	3,688	5,357
Semi-durables	371	908	4,148	172	1,370	15,328	480	1,226	298	8,731	2,068	766	981	192	161	489	427	1,847	9,126	1,927	8,453	1,663	477	1,172
Durables	182	528	4,889	309	1,879	18,164	262	1,741	752	8,622	3,296	1,049	758	88	180	252	445	1,603	17,350	334	10,562	2,150	774	1,070
Services	1,072	2,590	18,667	1,307	7,192	99,132	2,772	5,509	2,053	57,597	18,752	8,412	5,811	1,086	974	2,091	4,470	5,305	103,096	8,238	44,522	8,458	2,584	4,694

AP = Asia and the Pacific; BAN = Bangladesh; BHU = Bhutan; BRU = Brunei Darussalam; CAM = Cambodia; FIJ = Fiji; HKG = Hong Kong, China; IND = India; INO = Indonesia; LAO = Lao People's Democratic Republic; MAC = Macau, China; MAL = Malaysia; MLD = Maldives; MON = Mongolia; MYA = Myanmar; NEP = Nepal; NPISH=nonprofit institutions serving households; PAK = Pakistan; PHI = Philippines; PRC = People's Republic of China; SIN = Singapore; SRI = Sri Lanka; TAP = Taipei,China; THA = Thailand; VIE = Viet Nam.

a Includes individual consumption expenditure by households, nonprofit institutions serving households, and government.

Source: Asian Development Bank estimates.

Table 5.11: Per Capita Nominal Expenditure Index, 2011 (Revised)
(Asia and the Pacific = 100)

Expenditure Category	BAN	BHU	BRU	CAM	FIJ	HKG	IND	INO	LAO	MAC	MAL	MLD	MON	MYA	NEP	PAK	PHI	PRC	SIN	SRI	TAP	THA	VIE	AP
Gross Domestic Product	24	74	1,299	25	132	969	41	102	40	1,832	283	188	103	30	20	35	66	155	1,486	89	578	154	42	100
Actual Individual Consumption by Households[a]	37	73	441	41	195	1,283	49	119	50	867	306	140	117	36	32	58	101	132	1,178	133	712	190	53	100
Food and non-alcoholic beverages	80	91	238	79	289	588	60	155	80	271	252	132	144	90	78	111	176	107	322	167	352	206	69	100
Food	83	90	223	79	282	587	61	149	72	268	250	119	138	91	80	111	169	108	299	170	342	187	69	100
Bread and cereals	148	100	201	102	236	216	61	179	76	182	143	126	64	99	133	104	250	94	211	236	315	167	69	100
Meat and fish	63	42	315	96	264	1,301	20	158	125	471	333	141	186	111	52	41	231	142	450	87	427	185	83	100
Fruits and vegetables	49	105	176	52	360	321	73	101	49	260	225	98	70	95	60	66	85	122	244	83	455	282	44	100
Other food and non-alcoholic beverages	62	112	252	68	302	501	84	175	68	186	293	155	231	60	68	207	140	78	364	241	244	199	40	100
Clothing and footwear	39	93	245	14	155	1,050	51	80	18	846	143	60	95	22	14	48	24	161	549	119	491	104	43	100
Clothing	42	76	246	9	154	857	50	84	17	781	151	58	102	23	14	47	20	161	530	135	515	119	44	100
Housing, water, electricity, gas and other fuels	45	91	354	44	129	1,494	54	76	40	869	325	276	124	39	26	80	86	131	1,339	87	823	111	86	100
Health and education	18	78	638	30	145	955	30	79	16	624	245	127	89	14	16	34	51	174	991	64	685	173	46	100
Health	13	80	305	28	79	942	22	55	15	571	172	107	50	15	13	35	27	192	839	64	649	150	40	100
Education	23	76	1,033	32	224	971	39	108	18	686	331	151	136	12	19	32	79	152	1,171	63	727	200	53	100
Transportation and communication	14	72	619	26	202	968	67	171	53	746	486	151	199	15	11	39	111	102	1,627	199	838	251	49	100
Transportation	17	77	652	35	184	1,012	78	171	60	762	429	73	228	14	11	42	117	87	1,592	256	854	297	62	100
Recreation and culture	6	94	582	24	89	3,060	11	110	18	1,695	409	65	71	9	27	14	37	152	3,258	277	1,286	177	50	100
Restaurants and hotels	16	16	393	39	49	2,445	21	195	101	2,899	533	59	37	32	12	12	69	132	2,131	85	881	291	47	100
Other consumption expenditure items	20	29	253	21	256	1,880	55	102	60	657	366	114	79	14	21	38	111	126	1,519	138	914	209	42	100
Individual Consumption Expenditure by Government	5	87	835	17	116	483	20	51	10	755	273	123	85	4	10	16	40	197	736	53	653	180	28	100
Collective Consumption Expenditure by Government	14	137	2,861	14	204	793	50	88	43	1,217	292	490	105	50	20	37	56	149	1,339	62	664	204	38	100
Gross Fixed Capital Formation	18	131	1,034	7	63	595	36	83	34	597	163	165	130	24	11	12	32	185	979	61	353	106	33	100
Machinery and equipment	14	172	1,186	11	135	896	37	54	18	399	204	189	248	39	8	12	35	176	1,077	117	499	234	29	100
Construction	22	125	1,016	6	32	459	34	100	27	744	130	180	71	16	10	9	26	191	832	42	222	55	37	100
Change in Inventories and Net Acquisitions of Valuables	7	-7	-695	5	129	212	83	64	19	892	113	34	362	1	121	20	41	150	766	229	52	56	78	100
Balance of Exports and Imports	-93	-1,074	25,456	-1	-358	1,853	-114	125	-65	52,771	2,186	1,079	-1,120	-55	-242	-113	-118	198	20,315	-584	1,929	156	-87	100
Individual Consumption Expenditure by Households and NPISH	42	70	381	45	207	1,406	53	129	56	884	311	143	122	41	36	65	111	122	1,246	146	722	192	57	100
Government Final Consumption Expenditure	9	112	1,832	16	159	636	35	69	26	982	283	304	95	27	15	26	48	173	1,033	57	659	192	33	100
Actual Individual Consumption by Households[a]	37	73	441	41	195	1,283	49	119	50	867	306	140	117	36	32	58	101	132	1,178	133	712	190	53	100
All goods	52	80	301	52	227	871	50	133	65	459	290	120	116	53	44	77	120	128	661	129	568	193	65	100
Non-durables	63	87	259	65	262	611	57	133	73	328	312	137	132	69	56	95	154	118	443	141	451	203	69	100
Semi-durables	32	78	354	15	117	1,308	41	105	25	745	177	84	84	16	14	42	36	158	779	164	721	142	41	100
Durables	17	49	457	29	176	1,698	24	163	70	806	308	98	71	8	17	24	42	150	1,621	31	987	201	72	100
Services	23	55	398	28	153	2,112	59	117	44	1,227	399	179	124	23	21	45	95	113	2,196	175	948	180	55	100

AP = Asia and the Pacific; BAN = Bangladesh; BHU = Bhutan; BRU = Brunei Darussalam; CAM = Cambodia; FIJ = Fiji; HKG = Hong Kong, China; IND = India; INO = Indonesia; LAO = Lao People's Democratic Republic; MAC = Macau, China; MAL = Malaysia; MLD = Maldives; MON = Mongolia; MYA = Myanmar; NEP = Nepal; NPISH=nonprofit institutions serving households; PAK = Pakistan; PHI = Philippines; PRC = People's Republic of China; SIN = Singapore; SRI = Sri Lanka; TAP = Taipei,China; THA = Thailand; VIE = Viet Nam.
a Includes individual consumption expenditure by households, nonprofit institutions serving households, and government.
Source: Asian Development Bank estimates.

Table A5.12: Shares of Nominal Expenditure, 2011 (Revised)

(%)

Expenditure Category	BAN	BHU	BRU	CAM	FIJ	HKG	IND	INO	LAO	MAC	MAL	MLD	MON	MYA	NEP	PAK	PHI	PRC	SIN	SRI	TAP	THA	VIE	AP
Gross Domestic Product	100.00	100.00	100.00	100.00	100.00	100.00	100.00	100.00	100.00	100.00	100.00	100.00	100.00	100.00	100.00	100.00	100.00	100.00	100.00	100.00	100.00	100.00	100.00	100.00
Actual Individual Consumption by Households[a]	75.42	49.50	17.12	84.27	74.37	66.66	59.02	58.81	62.58	23.83	54.49	37.42	57.05	61.36	79.74	84.88	77.58	42.91	39.92	75.26	62.12	61.97	63.41	50.37
Food and non-alcoholic beverages	38.27	14.38	2.15	37.58	25.68	7.11	17.04	17.87	23.24	1.73	10.42	8.21	16.42	35.21	44.98	37.50	31.45	8.06	2.54	21.99	7.14	15.61	19.09	11.71
Food	38.12	13.67	1.93	36.01	24.06	6.82	16.71	16.46	20.07	1.65	9.96	7.12	15.06	34.38	44.37	36.02	29.04	7.86	2.27	21.52	6.67	13.67	18.45	11.26
Bread and cereals	17.01	3.81	0.43	11.53	5.02	0.63	4.12	4.93	5.30	0.28	1.42	1.88	1.73	9.36	18.38	8.42	10.67	1.71	0.40	7.44	1.53	3.03	5.51	2.81
Meat and fish	7.30	1.63	0.69	11.12	5.72	3.83	1.35	4.42	8.89	0.73	3.36	2.13	5.16	10.64	7.34	3.39	10.03	2.61	0.86	2.79	2.11	3.41	7.63	2.86
Fruits and vegetables	5.18	3.65	0.35	5.41	7.01	0.85	4.51	2.56	3.13	0.36	2.05	1.34	1.75	8.22	7.63	4.91	3.35	2.01	0.42	2.38	2.03	4.70	2.68	2.57
Other food and non-alcoholic beverages	8.78	5.29	0.68	9.53	7.94	1.80	7.06	5.96	5.92	0.35	3.60	2.85	7.78	6.99	11.62	20.78	7.40	1.73	0.85	9.38	1.47	4.47	3.27	3.48
Clothing and footwear	4.53	3.61	0.54	1.59	3.35	3.10	3.54	2.25	1.28	1.32	1.45	0.91	2.64	2.15	1.97	3.94	1.04	2.97	1.06	3.81	2.43	1.93	2.93	2.86
Clothing	4.05	2.44	0.45	0.81	2.76	2.09	2.84	1.96	1.02	1.01	1.27	0.72	2.33	1.85	1.64	3.25	0.72	2.46	0.84	3.59	2.11	1.83	2.48	2.37
Housing, water, electricity, gas and other fuels	13.02	8.64	1.92	12.47	6.92	10.87	9.17	5.24	7.00	3.35	8.10	10.33	8.49	9.17	8.96	16.31	9.27	5.95	6.35	6.87	10.05	5.05	14.37	7.05
Health and education	6.88	10.20	4.72	11.64	10.59	9.48	6.88	7.46	3.88	3.27	8.33	6.47	8.32	4.43	7.50	9.42	7.49	10.75	6.41	6.85	11.40	10.78	10.37	9.62
Health	2.76	5.68	1.22	5.94	3.11	5.07	2.77	2.79	1.91	1.63	3.17	2.95	2.53	2.58	3.29	5.34	2.17	6.44	2.94	3.76	5.86	5.07	4.89	5.22
Education	4.12	4.52	3.50	5.71	7.48	4.41	4.12	4.66	1.97	1.65	5.16	3.52	5.79	1.85	4.20	4.08	5.32	4.32	3.47	3.09	5.54	5.71	5.48	4.40
Transportation and communication	3.53	5.85	2.88	6.47	9.23	6.04	9.76	10.19	8.03	2.46	10.40	4.84	11.70	3.04	3.42	6.85	10.26	3.96	6.62	13.50	8.78	9.84	7.02	6.05
Transportation	3.17	4.66	2.24	6.26	6.24	4.67	8.46	7.53	6.68	1.86	6.78	1.73	9.89	2.12	2.36	5.44	7.94	2.51	4.79	12.82	6.61	8.58	6.50	4.47
Recreation and culture	0.55	3.04	1.07	2.31	1.60	7.52	0.64	2.57	1.10	2.20	3.45	0.82	1.63	0.70	3.15	0.94	1.35	2.33	5.22	7.39	5.30	2.72	2.79	2.38
Restaurants and hotels	1.71	0.56	0.78	4.03	0.95	6.47	1.32	4.92	6.43	4.06	4.84	0.81	0.92	2.71	1.55	0.87	2.72	2.18	3.68	2.46	3.91	4.83	2.86	2.57
Other consumption expenditure items	6.92	3.22	1.62	6.96	16.05	16.08	10.95	8.32	12.48	2.97	10.73	5.03	6.37	3.96	8.48	9.05	14.01	6.70	8.47	12.87	13.11	11.22	8.14	8.29
Individual Consumption Expenditure by Government	1.43	7.93	4.34	4.70	5.91	3.36	3.23	3.39	1.69	2.78	6.52	4.40	5.56	0.94	3.28	3.05	4.11	8.55	3.34	4.01	7.63	7.86	4.48	6.75
Collective Consumption Expenditure by Government	3.64	12.13	14.39	3.71	10.08	5.35	7.87	5.67	7.06	4.34	6.75	17.01	6.69	11.05	6.30	7.08	5.59	6.25	5.89	4.55	7.52	8.63	5.91	6.54
Gross Fixed Capital Formation	27.87	67.92	30.50	11.59	18.31	23.54	33.11	31.31	32.29	12.48	22.08	33.53	48.41	31.22	21.41	13.02	18.74	45.59	25.24	26.29	23.39	26.37	29.75	38.32
Machinery and equipment	6.16	26.04	10.19	4.92	11.44	10.32	10.04	5.90	4.94	2.43	8.05	11.19	26.80	14.46	4.66	3.85	5.91	12.64	8.08	14.65	9.64	16.90	7.60	11.16
Construction	20.89	39.46	18.28	5.77	5.61	11.07	19.04	22.88	15.80	9.48	10.75	22.34	16.12	12.56	11.91	6.22	9.34	28.77	13.07	10.97	8.99	8.27	20.31	23.36
Change in Inventories and Net Acquisitions of Valuables	0.76	-0.27	-1.48	0.53	2.70	0.61	5.54	1.74	1.34	1.35	1.11	0.51	9.74	0.11	16.57	1.60	1.73	2.68	1.43	7.10	0.25	1.00	5.06	2.77
Balance of Exports and Imports	-7.69	-29.28	39.47	-0.11	-5.46	3.85	-5.54	2.47	-3.28	58.00	15.57	11.54	-21.89	-3.74	-24.02	-6.58	-3.64	2.57	27.53	-13.19	6.73	2.03	-4.13	2.01
Individual Consumption Expenditure by Households and NPISH	73.99	41.56	12.78	79.57	68.46	63.30	55.79	55.42	60.90	21.05	47.97	33.02	51.49	60.43	76.46	81.83	73.47	34.36	36.58	71.25	54.49	54.10	58.94	43.62
Government Final Consumption Expenditure	5.07	20.07	18.73	8.41	15.99	8.71	11.10	9.06	8.75	7.12	13.27	21.41	12.26	11.99	9.58	10.13	9.70	14.81	9.23	8.56	15.15	16.49	10.39	13.28
Actual Individual Consumption by Households[a]	75.42	49.50	17.12	84.27	74.37	66.66	59.02	58.81	62.58	23.83	54.49	37.42	57.05	61.36	79.74	84.88	77.58	42.91	39.92	75.26	62.12	61.97	63.41	50.37
All goods	57.11	29.14	6.25	56.53	46.37	24.20	32.38	35.22	43.64	6.75	27.65	17.19	30.35	47.52	58.02	60.04	49.34	22.26	11.97	39.00	26.48	33.71	41.25	26.93
Non-durables	49.11	22.25	3.78	49.64	37.65	11.96	26.04	24.89	34.38	3.40	20.93	13.78	24.38	44.18	52.04	52.44	44.63	14.39	5.66	30.01	14.81	24.96	30.80	18.98
Semi-durables	5.36	4.36	1.13	2.46	3.68	5.60	4.10	4.27	2.63	1.69	2.59	1.44	3.37	2.29	2.82	5.01	2.30	4.21	2.18	7.66	5.19	3.82	3.98	4.15
Durables	2.64	2.53	1.33	4.43	5.04	6.64	2.24	6.06	6.64	1.67	4.13	1.97	2.61	1.05	3.15	2.58	2.40	3.66	4.14	1.33	6.48	4.93	6.46	3.79
Services	15.51	12.42	5.09	18.73	19.30	36.24	23.71	19.18	18.11	11.14	23.50	15.83	19.98	12.91	17.03	21.44	24.13	12.10	24.58	32.73	27.31	19.40	21.58	16.63

AP = Asia and the Pacific; BAN = Bangladesh; BHU = Bhutan; BRU = Brunei Darussalam; CAM = Cambodia; FIJ = Fiji; HKG = Hong Kong, China; IND = India; INO = Indonesia; LAO = Lao People's Democratic Republic; MAC = Macau, China; MAL = Malaysia; MLD = Maldives; MON = Mongolia; MYA = Myanmar; NEP = Nepal; NPISH=nonprofit institutions serving households; PAK = Pakistan; PHI = Philippines; PRC = People's Republic of China; SIN = Singapore; SRI = Sri Lanka; TAP = Taipei,China; THA = Thailand; VIE = Viet Nam.

a Includes individual consumption expenditure by households, nonprofit institutions serving households, and government.

Source: Asian Development Bank estimates.

Appendix 6: 2017 International Comparison Program: Structure of Gross Domestic Product and Changes in the ICP Classification

Table A6: Structure of Gross Domestic Product, Asia and the Pacific, 2017

Category	Components	Number of Basic Headings	Number of Products	Share in GDP (%)
Gross Domestic Product	A, B, C, D, E	155	1,175	100.0
A. Actual final consumption by households	A1, A2	136	901	53.0
A1. Individual consumption expenditure by households (ICEH) and nonprofit institutions serving households (NPISH)	A1.a–A1.h	115	887	45.4
A1.a. Food and non-alcoholic beverages		29	251	10.6
A1.b. Clothing and footwear		5	82	2.5
A1.c. Housing, water, electricity, gas and other fuels		9	17	7.2
A1.d. Health and education[a]		10	181	5.2
A1.e. Transportation and communication		16	106	6.7
A1.f. Recreation and culture		14	60	2.0
A1.g. Restaurants and hotels		2	21	2.3
A1.h. Other consumption expenditure items		30	169	8.9
A2. Individual consumption expenditure by government		21	14	7.6
B. Collective consumption expenditure by government		5	20	6.6
C. Gross fixed capital formation		10	254	36.9
D. Changes in inventories and net acquisitions of valuables		2	b	2.0
E. Balance of exports and imports		2	b	1.6

GDP = gross domestic product, ICP = International Comparison Program.
Notes: Share in region's GDP is based on exchange rate converted GDP estimates of 22 participating economies. The components may not add up to total due to rounding.
a Includes split items for pharmaceutical products.
b Reference purchasing power parities, listed in Appendix 7, were used.
Source: Asian Development Bank estimates.

Figure A6.1: Changes in Classification from 2011 to 2017 International Comparison Program

2011 ICP Classification			2017 ICP Revised Classification		
Code	Headings	Level	Code	Headings	Level
110117	Vegetables	Class	1101170	Vegetables	Class
1101171	Fresh or chilled vegetables other than potatoes	Basic Heading	1101171	Fresh or chilled vegetables, other than potatoes and other tuber vegetables	Basic Heading
1101172	Fresh or chilled potatoes	Basic Heading	1101172	Fresh or chilled potatoes and other tuber vegetables	Basic Heading
110400	HOUSING, WATER, ELECTRICITY, GAS, AND OTHER FUELS	Category	1104000	HOUSING, WATER, ELECTRICITY, GAS AND OTHER FUELS	Category
110410	ACTUAL AND IMPUTED RENTALS FOR HOUSING	Group	1104100	ACTUAL RENTALS FOR HOUSING	Group
110411	Actual and imputed rentals for housing	Class	1104110	Actual rentals for housing	Class
1104111	Actual and imputed rentals for housing	Basic Heading	1104111	Actual rentals for housing	Basic Heading
			1104200	IMPUTED RENTALS FOR HOUSING	Group
			1104210	Imputed rentals for housing	Class
			1104211	Imputed rentals for housing	Basic Heading
111300	BALANCE OF EXPENDITURES OF RESIDENTS ABROAD AND EXPENDITURES OF NON-RESIDENTS IN THE ECONOMIC TERRITORY	Category	1113000	NET PURCHASES ABROAD	Category
111310	BALANCE OF EXPENDITURES OF RESIDENTS ABROAD AND EXPENDITURES OF NON-RESIDENTS IN THE ECONOMIC TERRITORY	Group	1113100	NET PURCHASES ABROAD	Group
111311	Balance of expenditures of residents abroad and expenditures of non-residents in the economic territory	Class	1113110	Net purchases abroad	Class
1113111	Final consumption expenditure of resident households in the rest of the world	Basic Heading	1113111	Net purchases abroad	Basic Heading
1113112	Final consumption expenditure of non-resident households in the economic territory	Basic Heading			
120000	INDIVIDUAL CONSUMPTION EXPENDITURE BY NPISHs	Main Aggregate	1200000	INDIVIDUAL CONSUMPTION EXPENDITURE BY NPISHs	Main Aggregate
120100	INDIVIDUAL CONSUMPTION EXPENDITURE BY NPISHs	Category	1201000	HOUSING	Category
120110	INDIVIDUAL CONSUMPTION EXPENDITURE BY NPISHs	Group	1201100	HOUSING	Group
120111	Individual consumption expenditure by NPISHs	Class	1201110	Housing	Class
1201111	Individual consumption expenditure by NPISHs	Basic Heading	1201111	Housing	Basic Heading
			1202000	HEALTH	Category
			1202100	HEALTH	Group
			1202110	Health	Class
			1202111	Health	Basic Heading
			1203000	RECREATION AND CULTURE	Category
			1203100	RECREATION AND CULTURE	Group
			1203110	Recreation and culture	Class
			1203111	Recreation and culture	Basic Heading
			1204000	EDUCATION	Category
			1204100	EDUCATION	Group
			1204110	Education	Class
			1204111	Education	Basic Heading
			1205000	SOCIAL PROTECTION AND OTHER SERVICES	Category
			1205100	SOCIAL PROTECTION AND OTHER SERVICES	Group
			1205110	Social protection and other services	Class
			1205111	Social protection and other services	Basic Heading
			1500000	GROSS CAPITAL FORMATION	Main Aggregate
150000	GROSS FIXED CAPITAL FORMATION	Main Aggregate	1501000	GROSS FIXED CAPITAL FORMATION	Category
150100	MACHINERY AND EQUIPMENT	Category	1501100	MACHINERY AND EQUIPMENT	Group
150110	METAL PRODUCTS AND EQUIPMENT	Group	1501110	Metal products and equipment	Class
150111	Fabricated metal products, except machinery and equipment	Class			
1501111	Fabricated metal products, except machinery and equipment	Basic Heading	1501111	Fabricated metal products, except machinery and equipment - *formerly 1501111*	Basic Heading
150112	General purpose machinery	Class	1501112	Electrical and optical equipment – *formerly 1501141*	Basic Heading
1501121	General purpose machinery	Basic Heading	1501115	General purpose machinery - *formerly 1501121*	Basic Heading
150113	Special purpose machinery	Class	1501116	Special purpose machinery - *formerly 1501131*	Basic Heading
1501131	Special purpose machinery	Basic Heading			
150114	Electrical and optical equipment	Class			
1501141	Electrical and optical equipment	Basic Heading			
150115	Other manufactured goods n.e.c.	Class			
1501151	Other manufactured goods n.e.c.	Basic Heading			
150120	TRANSPORT EQUIPMENT	Group			
150121	Road transport equipment	Class	1501120	Transport equipment	Class
1501211	Motor vehicles, trailers and semi-trailers	Basic Heading	1501121	Road transport equipment – *formerly 1501211 and 1501212*	Basic Heading
1501212	Other road transport	Basic Heading			
150122	Other transport equipment	Class			
1501221	Other transport equipment	Basic Heading	1501122	Other transport equipment – *formerly 1501221*	Basic Heading
150300	OTHER PRODUCTS	Category			
150310	OTHER PRODUCTS	Group	1501300	OTHER PRODUCTS	Group
150311	Other products	Class	1501310	Other products	Class
1503111	Other products	Basic Heading	1501311	Other products – *formerly 1501151 and 1503111*	Basic Heading

ICP = International Comparison Program, n.e.c. = not elsewhere classified; NPISH = nonprofit institutions serving households.

Source: World Bank. 2016b. *International Comparison Program: Classification of Final Expenditure on GDP.* Washington, DC. http://pubdocs.worldbank.org/en/708531575560035925/pdf/ICP-Classification-description-2019-1205.pdf.

Figure A6.2: Changes in the Descriptions in the Headings of International Comparison Program Classification from 2011 to 2017

2011 ICP Classification			2017 ICP Revised Classification		
Code	Headings	Level	Code	Headings	Level
1101115	Pasta products	Basic Heading	1101115	Pasta products and couscous	Basic Heading
1101143	Cheese	Basic Heading	1101143	Cheese and curd	Basic Heading
110200	ALCOHOL BEVERAGES, TOBACCO AND NARCOTICS	Category	1102000	ALCOHOLIC BEVERAGES, TOBACCO AND NARCOTICS	Category
110210	ALCOHOL BEVERAGES	Group	1102100	ALCOHOLIC BEVERAGES	Group
110500	FURNISHING, HOUSEHOLD EQUIPMENT AND ROUTINE MAINTENANCE OF THE HOUSE	Category	1105000	FURNISHINGS, HOUSEHOLD EQUIPMENT AND ROUTINE HOUSEHOLD MAINTENANCE	Category
111230	PERSONAL EFFECTS	Group	1112300	PERSONAL EFFECTS N.E.C.	Group
111260	FINANCIAL SERVICES	Group	1112600	FINANCIAL SERVICES N.E.C.	Group
111262	Other financial services	Class	1112620	Other financial services n.e.c.	Class
1112621	Other financial services	Basic Heading	1112621	Other financial services n.e.c.	Basic Heading
111270	OTHER SERVICES	Group	1112700	OTHER SERVICES N.E.C.	Group
111271	Other services n.e.c.	Class	1112710	Other services n.e.c.	Class
1112711	Other services n.e.c.	Basic Heading	1112711	Other services n.e.c.	Basic Heading
111300	BALANCE OF EXPENDITURES OF RESIDENTS ABROAD AND EXPENDITURES OF NON-RESIDENTS IN THE ECONOMIC TERRITORY	Category	1113000	NET PURCHASES ABROAD	Category
111310	BALANCE OF EXPENDITURES OF RESIDENTS ABROAD AND EXPENDITURES OF NON-RESIDENTS IN THE ECONOMIC TERRITORY	Group	1113100	NET PURCHASES ABROAD	Group
111311	Balance of expenditures of residents abroad and expenditures of non-residents in the economic territory	Class	1113110	Net purchases abroad	Class

n.e.c. = not elsewhere classified.
Note: The red-highlighted text reflects the changes in the ICP classification.
Source: World Bank. 2016b. *International Comparison Program: Classification of Final Expenditure on GDP*. Washington, DC. http://pubdocs.worldbank.org/en/708531575560035925/pdf/ICP-Classification-description-2019-1205.pdf.

Appendix 7: List of Reference Purchasing Power Parities

	2011 International Comparison Program			2017 International Comparison Program[a]	
Code	Description	Reference	Code	Description	Reference
1102311	Narcotics	Tobacco	1102311	Narcotics	Tobacco
1104111	Actual and imputed rentals for housing	Volume relatives of individual consumption expenditures by households	1104A	Actual and imputed rentals for housing	Volume relatives of individual consumption expenditures by households
1104421	Miscellaneous services relating to the dwelling	Maintenance and repair of dwelling water supply	1104421	Miscellaneous services relating to the dwelling	Maintenance and repair of dwelling water supply
1105131	Repair of furniture, furnishings and floor coverings	Maintenance and repair of dwelling	1105131	Repair of furniture, furnishings and floor coverings	Maintenance and repair of dwelling
1105331	Repair of household appliances	Maintenance and repair of dwelling	1105331	Repair of household appliances	Maintenance and repair of dwelling
1105511	Major tools and equipment	Major household appliances whether electric or not small electric household appliances small tools and miscellaneous accessories	1105511	Major tools and equipment	Not a reference BH in 2017 ICP
1105622	Household services	Maintenance and repair of dwelling	1105622	Household services	Not a reference BH in 2017 ICP
1106311	Hospital services	Medical services dental services paramedical services	1106311	Hospital services	Medical services dental services paramedical services
1107121	Motor cycles	Motor cars	1107121	Motor cycles	Not a reference BH in 2017 ICP
1107141	Animal drawn vehicles	Bicycles	1107141	Animal drawn vehicles	Bicycles
1107341	Passenger transport by sea and inland waterway	Passenger transport by railway passenger transport by road passenger transport by air	1107341	Passenger transport by sea and inland waterway	Not a reference BH in 2017 ICP
1107351	Combined passenger transport	Fuels and lubricants for personal transport equipment maintenance and repair of personal transport equipment other services in respect of personal transport equipment passenger transport by railway passenger transport by road passenger transport by air	1107351	Combined passenger transport	Fuels and lubricants for personal transport equipment maintenance and repair of personal transport equipment other services in respect of personal transport equipment passenger transport by railway passenger transport by road passenger transport by air passenger transport by sea and inland waterway
1107361	Other purchased transport services	Fuels and lubricants for personal transport equipment maintenance and repair of personal transport equipment other services in respect of personal transport equipment passenger transport by railway passenger transport by road passenger transport by air	1107361	Other purchased transport services	Not a reference BH in 2017 ICP
1109211	Major durables for outdoor and indoor recreation	Bicycles audio-visual, photographic and information processing equipment recording media	1109211	Major durables for outdoor and indoor recreation	Bicycles audio-visual, photographic and information processing equipment recording media repair of audio-visual, photographic and information processing equipment
1109231	Maintenance and repair of other major durables for recreation and culture	PPPs for maintenance and repair of the dwelling; and audio-visual, photographic and information processing equipment	1109231	Maintenance and repair of other major durables for recreation and culture	Maintenance and repair of personal transport equipment repair of audio-visual, photographic and information processing equipment
1109331	Gardens and pets	PPPs for ICEH on the domestic market (excluding reference PPPs basic headings)	1109331	Gardens and pets	Not a reference BH in 2017 ICP
1109351	Veterinary and other services for pets	Weighted PPPs for ICEH on the domestic market (excluding reference PPPs basic headings)	1109351	Veterinary and other services for pets	Not a reference BH in 2017 ICP
1109431	Games of chance	PPP for recreational and sporting services	1109431	Games of chance	Recreational and sporting services
1112211	Prostitution	PPP for individual consumption expenditure by households (110000), excluding health and education BHs and BHs with reference PPPs	1112211	Prostitution	PPP for individual consumption expenditure by households (110000), excluding health and education BHs and BHs with reference PPPs
1112411	Social protection	Compensation of employees from health and education services	1112411	Social protection	Compensation of employees from health and education services
1112511	Insurance	PPP for individual consumption expenditure by households (110000), excluding health and education BHs and BHs with reference PPPs	1112511	Insurance	PPP for individual consumption expenditure by households (110000), excluding health and education BHs and BHs with reference PPPs
1112611	Financial intermediation services indirectly measured (FISIM)	PPP for individual consumption expenditure by households (110000), excluding health and education BHs and BHs with reference PPPs	1112611	Financial intermediation services indirectly measured (FISIM)	PPP for individual consumption expenditure by households (110000), excluding health and education BHs and BHs with reference PPPs
1112621	Other financial services, n.e.c.	PPP for individual consumption expenditure by households (110000), excluding health and education BHs and BHs with reference PPPs	1112621	Other financial services n.e.c.	PPP for individual consumption expenditure by households (110000), excluding health and education BHs and BHs with reference PPPs
1112711	Other services n.e.c.	PPPs for ICEH on the domestic market (excluding health and education basic headings and reference PPPs basic headings)	1112711	Other services n.e.c.	PPP for individual consumption expenditure by households (110000), excluding health and education BHs and BHs with reference PPPs
1113111	Net purchases abroad	Exchange rates	1113111	Net purchases abroad	Exchange rates

continued on next page

Appendix 7: List of Reference Purchasing Power Parities   *continued*

2011 International Comparison Program			2017 International Comparison Program[a]		
Code	Description	Reference	Code	Description	Reference
1201111	Housing NPISH	Actual and imputed rentals for housing	1201111	Housing NPISH	Actual and imputed rentals for housing
1202111	Health - NPISH	Compensation of employees from production of health services	1202111	Health - NPISH	Compensation of employees from production of health services
1203111	Recreation and culture NPISH	Cultural services Recreational and sporting services	1203111	Recreation and culture NPISH	Cultural services Recreational and sporting services
1204111	Education - NPISH	Compensation of employees from production of education services	1204111	Education - NPISH	Compensation of employees from production of education services
1205111	Social protection and other services - NPISH	Compensation of employees from production of health and education services	1205111	Social protection and other services - NPISH	Compensation of employees from production of health and education services
1301111	Housing	Actual and imputed rents	1301111	Housing	Actual and imputed rents
1302111	Pharmaceutical products	Pharmaceutical products (HHC)	1302111	Pharmaceutical products	Pharmaceutical products (HHC)
1302112	Other medical products	Other medical products (HHC)	1302112	Other medical products	Other medical products (HHC)
1302113	Therapeutic appliances and equipment	Therapeutic appliances and equipment (HHC)	1302113	Therapeutic appliances and equipment	Therapeutic appliances and equipment (HHC)
1302121	Outpatient medical services	Medical services (HHC)	1302121	Out-patient medical services	Medical services (HHC)
1302122	Outpatient dental services	Dental services (HHC)	1302122	Out-patient dental services	Dental services (HHC)
1302123	Outpatient paramedical services	Paramedical services (HHC)	1302123	Out-patient paramedical services	Paramedical services (HHC)
1302124	Hospital services	Hospital services (HHC)	1302124	Hospital services	Hospital services (HHC)
1302221	Intermediate consumption	PPP for individual consumption expenditure by households (110000), excluding BHs with reference PPPs	1302221	Intermediate consumption	PPP for individual consumption expenditure by households (110000), excluding BHs with reference PPPs
1302231	Gross operating surplus	PPP for gross fixed capital formation (150000), excluding BHs with reference PPPs	1302231	Gross operating surplus	PPP for gross fixed capital formation (150000), excluding BHs with reference PPPs
1302241	Net taxes on production	Compensation of employees from production of health services	1302241	Net taxes on production	Compensation of employees from Production of Health services
1302251	Receipts from sales: health services	Compensation of employees from production of health services	1302251	Receipts from sales	Compensation of employees from production of health services
1303111	Recreation and culture	Cultural services Recreational and sporting services	1303111	Recreation and culture	Cultural services Recreational and sporting services
1304111	Education benefits and reimbursements	Education (1110000)	1304111	Education benefits and reimbursements	Education (1110000)
1304221	Intermediate consumption	PPP for individual consumption expenditure by households (110000), excluding BHs with reference PPPs	1304221	Intermediate consumption	PPP for individual consumption expenditure by households (110000), excluding BHs with reference PPPs
1304231	Gross operating surplus	PPP for gross fixed capital formation (150000), excluding BHs with reference PPPs	1304231	Gross operating surplus	PPP for gross fixed capital formation (150000), excluding BHs with reference PPPs
1304241	Net taxes on production	Compensation of employees from production of education services	1304241	Net taxes on production	Compensation of employees from production of education services
1304251	Receipt from sales: education	Compensation of employees from production of education services	1304251	Receipt from sales	Compensation of employees from production of education services
1305111	Social protection	Compensation of employees from production of health and education services	1305111	Social protection	Compensation of employees from production of health and education services
1401121	Intermediate consumption	PPP for individual consumption expenditure by households (110000), excluding BHs with reference PPPs	1401121	Intermediate consumption	PPP for individual consumption expenditure by households (110000), excluding BHs with reference PPPs
1401131	Gross operating surplus	PPP for gross fixed capital formation (150000), excluding BHs with reference PPPs	1401131	Gross operating surplus	PPP for gross fixed capital formation (150000), excluding BHs with reference PPPs
1401141	Net taxes on production	Compensation of employees from production of collective services	1401141	Net taxes on production	Compensation of employees from production of collective services
1401151	Receipts from sales: collective services	Compensation of employees from production of collective services	1401151	Receipts from sales	Compensation of employees from production of collective services
1501122	Other transport equipment	Road transport equipment	1501122	Other transport equipment	Road transport equipment
1501311	Other products	Electrical and optical equipment General purpose machinery Special purpose machinery Road transport equipment	1501311	Other products	Electrical and optical equipment General purpose machinery Special purpose machinery Road transport equipment
1502111	Change in inventories	Referenced to BHs classified as containing predominantly goods, excluding BHs with reference PPPs	1502111	Change in inventories	Referenced to BHs classified as containing predominantly goods, excluding BHs with reference PPPs
1503111	Acquisitions less disposals of valuables	Exchange rates	1503111	Acquisitions less disposals of valuables	Exchange rates
1601111	Exports of goods and services	Exchange rates	1601111	Exports of goods and services	Exchange rates
1601112	Imports of goods and services	Exchange rates	1601112	Imports of goods and services	Exchange rates

BH = basic heading, HHC = household consumption, ICEH = individual consumption expenditure by households, PPP = purchasing power parity.

a Based on the references used in the 2011 ICP and recommendations from the ICP Global Office.

Source: Based on ICP Inter-Agency Coordination Group meeting (23 - 25 October 2019) and recommendations from the 2017 ICP Technical Advisory Group.

Appendix Table 8: Scope and Coverage of Main Gross Domestic Product Aggregates—2011 and 2017 Cycles

Aggregate	2011	2017
Individual consumption expenditure by households	Collected price for 923 items in the Asia and Pacific list. The 2011 ICP list was taken from the 2005 and 2009 product lists which were updated for obsolescence and supplemented with poverty-specific items. Collected monthly and quarterly prices for most items but collected more frequently for some products (e.g., weekly for fruits and vegetables). Collected bi-annual or annually prices of less volatile items, such as utilities. Nationwide price collection	Collected 887 items in the Asia Pacific list. The 2017 ICP list was prepared based on the 2011 ICP list, with some obsolete items dropped and new items added using the information gathered from the 2016 PPP Update exercise and the global core list. Collected monthly, quarterly, semi-annual and annual prices depending on the volatility of the item, with some economies even collected weekly prices for fruits and vegetables and fresh meat products. Nationwide price collection
Government final consumption expenditure	Collected average compensation for 44 government posts; 38 items included in the PPP computation as approved by the 2011 ICP in Asia and the Pacific Regional Advisory Board.	Collected annual average compensation for 35 occupations in the government, mainly coming from the ICP Global Office, with one additional occupation priced only in Asia and the Pacific.
Gross fixed capital formation in construction	Collected prices for 46 global input items relevant to the Asia and Pacific region, and used relevance indicators. Used reference PPPs from aggregate machinery and equipment for PPPs for rental of equipment.	Collected annual average prices for 58 construction inputs, equipment and labor; regional relevance indicators and resource mixes coming from inputs from economies.
Gross fixed capital formation in machinery and equipment	Collected prices for 177 global items relevant to the Asia and Pacific region.	Collected annual average prices for 196 machinery and equipment including other products.
Change in inventories and net acquisitions of valuables	Referenced from PPPs for durable and non-durable goods, and gross fixed capital formation (excluding reference PPPs basic headings).	Referenced from PPPs for consumer goods and investment goods (excluding reference PPP basic headings.

ICP = International Comparison Program, PPP = purchasing power parity.
Source: 2017 and 2011 ICP for Asia and the Pacific.

Glossary

Term	Definition
Actual individual consumption by households (AICH)	Total value of household final consumption expenditure, including expenditures by nonprofit institutions serving households (NPISHs) and by government on services provided to households.
Additivity	The concept that the real expenditures for higher-level aggregates can be obtained simply by adding the real expenditures of the sub-aggregates of which they are composed. *Real expenditures obtained using the Gini-Èltetö-Köves-Szulc (GEKS)-based purchasing power parities (PPPs) are not additive, so the sum of the real expenditures for the components of gross domestic product (GDP) does not equal the real expenditure on GDP.*
Base economy invariance, Invariant	The property whereby the relativities between the PPPs, price level indexes (PLIs), and volume indexes of economies are not affected by either the choice of currency as numeraire or the choice of reference economy.
Basic heading	In principle, a group of similar well-defined goods or services for which a sample of products can be selected that are both representative of their type and of the purchases made in economies. In practice, a basic heading is defined as the smallest aggregate for which expenditure data are available.
Benchmark	A standard, or point of reference, against which an estimate can be compared, assessed, measured, or judged. PPPs are computed using price data from a full list of household and non-household products and weights derived from the expenditures on GDP for a specified reference year. In the International Comparison Program (ICP), this reference year is often referred to as the "benchmark year" or simply as the "benchmark."
Big Mac index	An index developed and used by *The Economist* to illustrate the use of PPPs. It is based on the price of a McDonald's Big Mac hamburger compared across economies.
Binary comparison	A price or volume comparison between two economies that draws on data only for those two economies. Also referred to as a "bilateral comparison."
Change in inventories	Changes in (i) stocks of outputs that are still held by the units that produced them prior to their being further processed, sold, delivered to other units, or used in other ways; and (ii) stocks of products acquired from other units that are intended to be used for intermediate consumption or for resale without further processing. They are measured by the value of the entries into inventories less the value of withdrawals and the value of any recurrent losses of goods held in inventories.
Characteristicity	The property that requires transitive multilateral comparisons between members of a group of economies to retain the essential features of the intransitive binary comparisons that existed between them before transitivity. A transitive multilateral comparison between a pair of economies is influenced by the price and quantity data of all other economies. Characteristicity requires that the impact of these influences be kept to a minimum when they are introduced into the intransitive binary comparison. In other words, the multilateral PPP between two economies should deviate as little as possible from their binary PPP.
Classification of Individual Consumption According to Purpose	A classification used to identify the objectives of both individual consumption expenditure and actual individual consumption.

continued on next page

Glossary

Term	Definition
Collective consumption expenditure by government	A service provided by general government simultaneously to all members of the community or to all members of a particular section of the community, such as all households living in a particular region.
Comparability	A requirement for economies to price products that are identical or, if not identical, equivalent. Pricing comparable products ensures that differences in prices between economies for a product reflect actual price differences and are not influenced by differences in quality. Two, or more, products are said to be comparable either if their physical and economic characteristics are identical, or if they are sufficiently similar that consumers are indifferent between them.
Comparison-resistant	A term first used to describe nonmarket services that are difficult to compare across economies because (i) they have no economically significant prices with which to value outputs; (ii) their units of output cannot be otherwise defined and measured, or the institutional arrangements for their provision and the conditions of payment differ from economy to economy; and (iii) their quality varies between economies but the differences cannot be identified and quantified. Increasingly, the term is being used to describe capital goods and many market services whose complexity, variation, and economy specificity make it difficult for them to be priced comparably across economies.
Compensation of employees	The total remuneration, in cash or in kind, payable by enterprises to employees in return for work done by the employees during the accounting period.
Consumer price index (CPI)	An index of price changes within an economy across time.
Dwellings	Buildings that are used entirely or primarily as residences, including any associated structures, such as garages, and all permanent fixtures customarily installed in residences. Movable structures, such as caravans, used as principal residences of households are included.
Expenditures	The values of the amounts that buyers pay, or agree to pay, to sellers in exchange for goods or services that sellers provide to them or to other institutional units designated by the buyers.
Final consumption	Goods and services used up by individual households or the community to satisfy their individual or collective needs or wants.
Fixity	The principle that the PPPs between economies in a region (and therefore the volume relativities based on the PPPs) do not change when the results from that region are combined with those from another region (or regions).
Gini-Èltetö-Köves-Szulc (GEKS) method	A procedure that enables binary PPPs, which are nontransitive when more than two economies are involved in the comparison, to be transformed into transitive PPPs, so that comparisons made between any pair of economies are mutually consistent. The GEKS method produces transitive PPPs that are as close as possible to the nontransitive PPPs originally calculated in the binary comparisons. In practice, the GEKS method is relevant only to the second part of this process (i.e., making the PPPs transitive). Real expenditures obtained using GEKS-based PPPs are not additive, so the sum of the real expenditures for the components of GDP does not equal the real expenditure on GDP.

continued on next page

Glossary

Term	Definition
government final consumption expenditure (GFCE)	Final consumption expenditure by government consisting of expenditure, including imputed expenditure, incurred by general government on both individual consumption goods and services and on collective consumption services.
Gross capital formation (GCF)	Measures the total value of gross fixed capital formation, changes in inventories, and acquisitions less disposals of valuables for a unit or sector.
Gross domestic product—expenditure based	Total final expenditures at purchasers' prices (including the free-on-board value of exports of goods and services), less the free-on-board value of imports of goods and services.
Gross fixed capital formation (GFCF)	Measures the total value of a producer's acquisitions, less disposals, of fixed assets during the accounting period. It includes certain additions to the value of non-produced assets (such as subsoil assets or major improvements in the quantity, quality, or productivity of land) realized by the productive activity of institutional units.
Household products	Refer to the consumption of households for the following components: • Food and non-alcoholic beverages • Alcoholic beverages, tobacco and narcotics • Clothing and footwear • Housing, water, electricity, gas, and other fuels • Furnishings, household equipment, and routine maintenance of the house • Health • Transport • Communication • Recreation and culture • Education • Restaurant and hotels • Miscellaneous goods and services (personal grooming, personal care, personal effects, financial services, and other services).
Individual consumption expenditure by households (ICEH)	Final consumption expenditure by households, consisting of the expenditure, including imputed expenditure, incurred by resident households on individual consumption goods and services, including those sold at prices that are not economically significant; also includes the individual consumption expenditure by NPISHs, in the context of the 2017 ICP in Asia and the Pacific.
Local currency unit (LCU)	The monetary unit in which economic values are expressed in an economy. Also known as the national currency unit.
Lorenz curve	Developed by Max Lorenz in 1905, it is a graphical representation of the distribution of income or wealth. The horizontal axis of the graph represents the percentiles of population, while the vertical axis represents the cumulative income or wealth.
Multilateral comparison	A simultaneous price or volume comparison of more than two economies that produces consistent relations among all pairs of economies—that is, one that satisfies the transitivity requirement.

continued on next page

Glossary

Term	Definition
National annual average price	A price that has been averaged over all localities of an economy to account for regional variations in prices and over the days, weeks, months, or quarters of the reference year to allow for seasonal variations in prices, as well as general inflation and changes in price structures.
Net purchases abroad	Purchases by residential households in the rest of the world (as tourists, travelling businessmen and government officials, crews, border and seasonal workers, diplomatic and military personal stationed abroad), less purchases by non-residential households in the economic territory of the country (as tourists, travelling businessmen, and government officials, crews, border and seasonal workers, diplomatic and military personal stationed abroad). An institutional unit is resident in an economy when it has a center of economic interest in the economic territory.
Nonprofit institutions serving households (NPISH)	Nonprofit institutions that are not predominantly financed and controlled by government and that provide goods or services to households free or at prices that are not economically significant.
Price	The value of one unit of a particular good or service.
Price level index (PLI)	The ratio of a PPP to the corresponding exchange rate. It shows how the price levels of an economy compare with each other. It is expressed as an index on a base of 100. A PLI greater than 100 means that when the national average prices are converted at exchange rates, the resulting prices tend to be higher on average than prices in the base economy. At the level of GDP, PLIs provide a measure of the differences in the general price levels of economies. PLIs are also referred to as "comparative price levels."
Purchasing power parity (PPP)	A relative price that measures the number of units of economy B's currency that are needed in economy B to purchase the same quantity and quality of an individual good or service, which one unit of economy A's currency can purchase in economy A.
Real expenditure	Measures obtained by using PPPs to convert final expenditures on product groups, major aggregates, and GDP of different economies into a common currency, by valuing them at a uniform price level. Expenditures so converted reflect only volume differences between economies. They are the spatial equivalent of a time series of GDP for a single economy expressed at constant prices. They provide a measure of the relative magnitudes of the product groups or aggregates being compared. At the level of GDP, they are used to compare the sizes of economies. They may be presented either in terms of a particular currency or as an index number.
Reference PPPs	Used for basic headings which are based on prices collected for other basic headings.
Relative price levels	The ratios of PPPs for components of GDP to the overall PPP for GDP for an economy. They indicate whether the price level for a given basic heading or aggregate is higher or lower relative to the general price level in the economy.

continued on next page

Glossary

Term	Definition
Resident	An institutional unit is resident in an economy when it has a center of economic interest in the economic territory.
Rest of the world	The rest of the world consists of all nonresident institutional units that enter into transactions with resident units, or that have other economic links with resident units.
Structured product descriptions	Generic descriptions that list the characteristics relevant to a particular narrow cluster of products.
System of National Accounts	Consists of a coherent, consistent, and integrated set of macroeconomic accounts, balance sheets, and tables based on a set of internationally agreed concepts, definitions, classifications, and accounting rules (United Nations 2009).
Transitivity	The property whereby the direct PPP between any two economies (or regions) yields the same result as an indirect comparison via a third economy (or region). It is sometimes referred to as "circularity."
Volume	See "Real expenditure."

References

Asian Development Bank. 2014. *Purchasing Power Parities and Real Expenditures*. Manila: Asian Development Bank.

Asian Development Bank. 2019. *Corporate Results Framework, 2019-2024: Policy Paper*. Manila: Asian Development Bank.

Asian Development Bank. Key Indicators Database. https://kidb.adb.org/kidb/ (accessed 16 March 2020).

Diewert, W. E. 2013. "Methods of Aggregation above the Basic Heading Level within Regions." In *Measuring the Real Size of the World Economy*, edited by World Bank. Washington, DC: World Bank.

Feenstra, Robert C., R. Inklaar, and M. P. Timmer. 2015. "The Next Generation of the Penn World Table," *American Economic Review* 105 no.10: 3150–3182. www.ggdc.net/pwt.

Gilbert, M. and associates. 1958. *Comparative National Products and Price Levels: A Study of Western Europe and the United States*. Paris: Organisation for European Economic Co-operation.

Gilbert, M. and I. Kravis. 1954. *An International Comparison of National Products and Purchasing Power of Currencies: A Study of the United States, the United Kingdom, France, Germany, and Italy*. Paris: Organisation for European Economic Co-operation.

Hamadeh, N. and H. Shanab. 2016. "Uses of Purchasing Power Parities to Better Inform Policy Making and Poverty Measurement." Paper presented at the Conference of the International Association for Official Statistics, Abu Dhabi, December 6–8.

Inklaar, R.C. 2019. "Productivity Adjustment in ICP." Paper presented at the 4th Technical Advisory Group Meeting, International Comparison Program, World Bank, Washington, DC.

Inklaar, R.C. and D.S. Prasada Rao. 2017. "Cross-Country Income Levels over Time: Did the Developing World Suddenly Become Much Richer?" *American Economic Journal: Macroeconomics* 9, no. 1 (January): 265–290.

Inklaar, R.C. and M. P. Timmer. 2013a. "Productivity Adjustment for Government Services PPPs: Alternative and Proposal for ICP 2011." Paper presented to the 9th Technical Advisory Group Meeting, Washington, DC, September 25–27.

Inklaar, R. C. and M. P. Timmer. 2013b. "Using Expenditure PPPs for Sectoral Output and Productivity Comparisons." In *Measuring the Real Size of the World Economy*, edited by World Bank, 617–644. Washington, DC: World Bank.

International Monetary Fund. International Financial Statistics. http://data.imf.org/ (accessed 17 September 2019).

McCarthy, P. 2013. "Extrapolating PPPs and Comparing ICP Benchmark Results." In *Measuring the Real Size of the World Economy*, edited by World Bank. Washington, DC: World Bank.

Rao, D.S. Prasada. 2013. "The Framework of the International Comparison Program." In *Measuring the Real Size of the World Economy*, edited by World Bank. Washington, DC: World Bank.

Silver, M. 2013. "PPP Estimates: Applications by the International Monetary Fund." In *Measuring the Real Size of the World Economy*, edited by World Bank, 603–616. Washington, DC: World Bank.

Stiglitz, Joseph E., A. Sen, and J. Fitoussi. 2009. *Report by the Commission on the Measurement of Economic Performance and Social Progress*. Paris: Government of France.

United Nations. 2009. *System of National Accounts 2008*. New York: United Nations. https://unstats.un.org/unsd/nationalaccount/docs/SNA2008.pdf.

Ward, M. 2009. "Purchasing Power Parities and their Policy Relevance." In *Purchasing Power Parities of Currencies: Recent Advances In Methods And Applications, edited by D.S. Prasada Rao, 301–*

333. Cheltenham, UK: Edward Elgar Publishing Company.

World Bank. 2013. *Measuring the Real Size of the World Economy: The Framework, Methodology, and Results of the International Comparison Program—ICP.* Washington, DC: World Bank.

World Bank. 2015. *Purchasing Power Parities and the Real Size of World Economics: A Comprehensive Report of the 2011 International Comparison Program.* Washington, DC: World Bank.

World Bank. 2016a. *International Comparison Program: Governance Framework.* Washington, DC: World Bank. http://pubdocs.worldbank.org/en/255521487200449880/ICP-GB01-Doc-Governance-Framework-Final.pdf.

World Bank. 2016b. *International Comparison Program: Classification of Final Expenditure on GDP.* Washington, DC: World Bank. http://pubdocs.worldbank.org/en/708531575560035925/pdf/ICP-Classification-description-2019-1205.pdf.

World Bank. World Development Indicators. https://databank.worldbank.org/source/world-development-indicators (accessed 18 and 27 March 2020).